THE YEAR IN C-SPAN ARCHIVES RESEARCH
Volume 4

OTHER BOOKS IN THE YEAR IN C-SPAN ARCHIVES RESEARCH SERIES

The C-SPAN Archives: An Interdisciplinary Resource for Discovery, Learning, and Engagement

Exploring the C-SPAN Archives: Advancing the Research Agenda

Advances in Research Using the C-SPAN Archives

"Robert Browning's annual C-SPAN research series has become a veritable scholarly institution. This year marks the 30th anniversary of the C-SPAN Video Library, and this volume's incredible array of research projects drawn from it demonstrates its importance for our understanding of public life. In the chapters collected here, scholars analyze everything from congressional debates over mental health and law enforcement to speeches from the campaign trail in 2016. In doing so, the scholarship in this volume sheds light on elite rhetoric and the claims that ground policymaking and the search for public legitimacy. As importantly, this volume sets a research agenda for the future in demonstrating the varied methodological approaches and substantive objects of interest that this invaluable archive supports. As this volume makes clear, research using the C-SPAN Archives is particularly important at a time marked by declining trust in political institutions and elected representatives."

—*Daniel Kreiss, School of Media and Journalism, University of North Carolina at Chapel Hill*

"This volume clearly demonstrates the value and versatility of the C-SPAN Video Library. From comparisons of Trump's speeches and tweets to analyses of congressional debates on law enforcement, the chapters in this volume highlight the array of methodological and theoretical approaches that can leverage the Archives to answer our most pressing research questions. In addition to answering the valuable questions posed, the studies in this volume serve as excellent models for future research by demonstrating numerous innovative research designs that can be built around the Archives' content. The volume brings together work from several disciplines to provide key insights into what we can learn from careful analyses of elite rhetoric, narrative, and debate."

—*Johanna Dunaway, Department of Communication, Texas A&M University*

THE YEAR IN C-SPAN ARCHIVES RESEARCH
Volume 4

edited by
Robert X. Browning

Purdue University Press, West Lafayette, Indiana

Copyright 2018 by Robert X. Browning. All rights reserved.
Printed in the United States of America.

Cataloging-in-Publication data available from the Library of Congress.

Paper ISBN: 978-1-55753-814-7
ePDF ISBN: 978-1-61249-533-0
ePUB ISBN: 978-1-61249-534-7

For
Timothy E. Cook
Gary King
Lyn Ragsdale

CONTENTS

FOREWORD *xi*
PREFACE *xv*
ACKNOWLEDGMENTS *xix*

CHAPTER 1
    Constructing Congressional Discourses: C-SPAN Archives and Congressional Speeches on Crises and Scandals *1*
    Alyssa A. Wildrick and Alison N. Novak

CHAPTER 2
    Exploring Congressional "Law Enforcement" Talk *21*
    Cody Blake Wilson and Joshua M. Scacco

CHAPTER 3
    Communication as an Economic Tool and Constitutive Force: Chairman Greenspan's Talk About Uncertainties in Future U.S. Conditions *45*
    Lauren Berkshire Hearit and Patrice M. Buzzanell

CHAPTER 4
    Reflections on the C-SPAN Video Library and the Study of Congress *65*
    Janet M. Martin

CHAPTER 5
    Using C-SPAN to Examine the Political Discourse of HIV/AIDS, 1985–1987 *71*
    Nancy E. Brown

CHAPTER 6
    Treatment or Gun Control? Congressional Discourse on Mental Illness and Violence *93*
    Elizabeth Wulbrecht

CHAPTER 7
    Health and Politics: Portrayal of Health and Its Narratives on C-SPAN *123*
    Chervin Lam and Somrita Ganchoudhuri

CHAPTER 8
    Portrayals of Public Policy Discourse *141*
    Zoe M. Oxley

CHAPTER 9
    Donald Trump Meets the Ubiquitous Presidency *145*
    Delaney Harness and Joshua M. Scacco

CHAPTER 10
    C-SPAN and Journalism *173*
    Michael Buozis, Shannon Rooney, and Brian Creech

CHAPTER 11
    Nobody Saw This Coming? Support for Hillary Clinton and Donald Trump Through Audience Reactions During the 2016 Presidential Debates *199*
    Austin D. Eubanks, Patrick A. Stewart, and Reagan G. Dye

CHAPTER 12
    Selecting C-SPAN Video Clips for Creative Collaborative Learning *219*
    Pavla Hlozkova

CHAPTER 13
    C-SPAN in Changing Spaces of Political Communications *229*
    Terri L. Towner

CHAPTER 14
    "Look at the Tape, Mr. Chairman": Reflections on Congress and Television *237*
    Keynote Remarks of Dr. Ray Smock

CONCLUSION *247*
CONTRIBUTORS *251*
INDEX *257*

CELEBRATING 30 YEARS OF THE C-SPAN ARCHIVES' ONLINE VIDEO RESOURCES: A FOREWORD

It is quite an honor to help introduce the fourth volume of research that utilizes the C-SPAN Archives as its primary source material. My relationship with C-SPAN began quite early in my career as an educator. In fact, I recall as a college student being one of those political junkies often glued to C-SPAN for the pageantry, power, and drama of our national civic conversation. Whether to enjoy a State of the Union Address, or perhaps my marathon-viewing of the daylong events of a presidential inauguration; to partake in the confirmation hearings of a Supreme Court nominee; to catch a daily press briefing from the White House; or just to listen in on the House and Senate floor proceedings, I found the broadcasts of our national political processes to be an essential part of my media diet, and still do. Even before I had formally taken up the study of media effects, including such notions as news framing and media bias, I understood the value of "hearing it straight from the horse's mouth," which allowed me to be a bit less dependent on media interpreters who themselves may be influenced by corporate or partisan and ideological interests. Indeed, I understood that the more unvarnished account of our daily politics could be found on C-SPAN.

Very early in my career as an assistant professor of communication at the University of Oklahoma, I had the great pleasure of attending a workshop for educators at the C-SPAN studios in Washington, DC. Later, C-SPAN founder

Brian Lamb was a keynote speaker at a conference on civic engagement hosted by OU's Political Communication Center and the National Communication Association just before the 2000 presidential election. Then several years after that, when I was teaching an undergraduate political communication course at the University of Missouri, my students enjoyed a visit to our campus by the C-SPAN bus. I know my story is not unique—that countless educators and students since C-SPAN's founding in 1979 have utilized its many resources, especially the C-SPAN Archives housed in the Purdue Research Park and available online now for the past 30 years. As a scholar of political communication, and one who studies presidential campaigns and campaign communication, including political advertising and televised presidential debates, I can think of no other resource that I have used more often in the classroom and in my own research than the programming and archival resources of C-SPAN.

The current volume of research demonstrates the creative intellectual juices that the C-SPAN Archives fosters. As in the first three volumes, the featured studies span methodological and intellectual boundaries and represent the broad topic areas that constitute C-SPAN programming. The chapters that follow analyze public policy debates, congressional speeches and proceedings, testimony provided in congressional hearings, presidential campaign communication, citizens' responses as part of the political communication process, C-SPAN resources as civics education, and C-SPAN as a resource for journalists. Both broad and focused, these essays cut a wide and successful path through the Archives' intellectual riches.

Little did I know when C-SPAN first sustained my political junkie habit, even before I had decided on a college major and a career path as a teacher and scholar of political communication, that my need for it would be a lifelong addiction. My daily C-SPAN fix, even then, was most likely influential in the selection of my life's work. As we've now entered a troubling era of "fake news" and "alternative facts" most dangerous to our democracy, we must have a resource such as C-SPAN that provides us with the primary source and official record of our national political dialogue. As we lament the lack of civics knowledge among our citizenry, especially our youngest citizens, C-SPAN provides educators and classrooms at all levels access to the greatest resources available for civics education. Truly, we are fortunate to have this national treasure, and fortunate to enjoy yet another collection of outstanding studies that have mined the vast resources of the C-SPAN Archives.

Mitchell S. McKinney
Professor of Communication
Director, Political Communication Institute
University of Missouri

PREFACE

In this fourth volume of the C-SPAN annual research series, we see some new approaches to the study of political and social phenomena. With each volume, the research has developed in terms of the range and depth of studies. We find an analysis of President Trump's tweets and speeches as well as audience reactions to the Trump and Clinton debates. There are also multiple analyses of speeches, but each takes a different approach and emphasis.

This year marks the 30th anniversary of the creation of the C-SPAN Archives' online Video Library. The goal was to assist educators in using the vast programming for teaching and research. Now, with the fourth volume in the C-SPAN annual research collection we continue to demonstrate the value of this primary source archive for academic research.

There is one chapter in this edition that focuses on teaching. Pavla Hlozkova's chapter demonstrates C-SPAN's value in an online master's MBA program. She discusses what works and does not work to illustrate concepts and lessons in this academic program. Her chapter could encourage others to consider using C-SPAN videos as examples and to select the type of videos that would work.

Other chapters are focused on research and a number rely on textual analysis in the communication tradition. Wulbrecht analyzes how mental health is framed in congressional debates. Wildrick and Novak look at the rhetorical use of crises and scandals, also in congressional debates. Law enforcement as a concept in debate is the subject of the Wilson and Scacco chapter. Lam and Ganchoudhuri examine health care policy. Uncertainty management in the testimony of the Federal Reserve chairman provides the basis for Hearit and Buzzanell's chapter.

Finally, four chapters take a different approach. Harness and Scacco take an innovative approach in looking at the relationship between President Trump's tweets in his first 30 days and his speeches during the same period. Eubanks and colleagues analyze the audience reactions to Trump and Clinton during the 2016 presidential debates. Nancy Brown, a historian, studies the history of the characterization of the AIDS/HIV phenomenon. Buozis and colleagues contribute a thoughtful essay on a new area of research for the Video Library. They examine the research possibilities for journalism, drawing upon a variety of organizations covered by C-SPAN. Each chapter in this volume is distinctive in the research methods that it employs.

All these chapters base their research on the C-SPAN Video Library content. They offer advances in the research questions asked, the research methods applied, and in the research conclusions reached. Together they advance our understanding of politics, communication, and history.

Wulbrecht examines mental illness and gun violence. She examines congressional discourse during a time period when mass shootings became prevalent. She finds that the issue is framed as treating the mentally ill or the dangerousness of this population. To further refine this study, she looks at whether there is a difference when adults, children, veterans, or mass shootings are debated. Her study consists of 254 coded cases from 2013 to 2015 to which she applied logistic regression.

In another study of congressional rhetoric, Wildrick and Novak examine the use of scandals and crises in debates. They use a longer time period, the 24 years from 1992 to 2016, and examine 631 cases. Three types of congressional discourse are analyzed. These are building support or opposition, enhancing relationships, and fostering media and public attention. They report percentages and examples of each discourse.

Another analysis of congressional rhetoric is undertaken by Wilson and Scacco. They look at law enforcement from 2013 to 2015 and in a vein similar to Wulbrecht's, they examine how the discourse changes in the midst of a changing view of law enforcement. Here the shift is from the hero orientation following 9/11 to police actions in community shootings. They use Hart's DICTION program to look at three discursive tones: narrative force, transcendence, and tradition. They give examples as well as conduct a regression analysis.

We shift to presidential rhetoric with the Lam and Ganchoudhuri health portrayal study. They study 102 videos from April 2015 to November 2016 in which health issues were discussed in the presidential campaign. They report on the frequency of specific health issues within these videos, comparing Trump's and Clinton's emphases on health.

Another executive department analysis is that of Hearit and Buzzanell, who examined 2,934 sentences of Federal Reserve chairman Alan Greenspan's congressional testimony drawn from 20 of his appearances. There were 241 total appearances in the Video Library, but they sampled from the beginning, middle, and end of his tenure. After establishing the reliability of their content analysis, they ran chi-square tests with positive and negative sentiments of how the economy would perform.

As mentioned, four other studies differed from these textual analyses. The Harness and Scacco chapter does analyze the text of President Trump's speeches, but it is the addition of his tweets in the same 30-day period that sets off this method. They collected a total of 192 tweets and 49 speech transcripts for the first 30 days of the Trump presidency. They then were able to do a network analysis of terms referenced in each of these separate collections.

In a very different type of analysis, Eubanks, Stewart, and Dye used video software to precisely measure and separate clips of speaking time by Trump and Clinton in their presidential debates. In the first debate of 2016, for example, they found that Trump had 80 speaking turns versus 43 for Clinton. There were 31 audience responses: 18 in response to Trump and 13 in response to Clinton. The largest difference was more laughter for Trump.

One chapter in this volume takes a historical approach to study the AIDS/HIV epidemic and how it was characterized by the media. This chapter by Nancy Brown emphasizes the influence of various organizations as they publicized the issue. Historians, such as Brown, are beginning to see the value of the Video Library

The chapter by Buozis and colleagues is more of a review essay. However, it takes in a relatively new area of research for the Video Library. The authors examine the research possibilities for journalistic studies looking at four journalistic organizations: the American Society of Newspaper Editors, the Society of Professional Journalists, the National Press Club, and the Freedom Forum, which represent a range of ideology, composition, managerial type, and elite type. This chapter sets the stage for the next round of empirical work in journalistic studies.

The studies in this volume represent a variety of methodological approaches. Each varies in its focus and approach. They demonstrate the value and depth of the C-SPAN Video Library for a wide variety of scholars and scholarship. All of the primary authors are graduate students who demonstrate what can be done in applying a range of disciplines and approaches to the video content of the C-SPAN Video Library.

This volume, then, is unique in displaying the approaches and methods of various authors. These chapters demonstrate the richness of the C-SPAN Video Library in that researchers from various disciplines can tackle different topics with different approaches. The result is a blueprint for others who follow in their footsteps.

ACKNOWLEDGMENTS

This is the fourth volume in the C-SPAN Research Conference proceedings. Each year we hold a conference at Purdue University that focuses on research from the C-SPAN Archives. The authors of the papers presented all use video from the online C-SPAN Video Library to advance our understanding of research in political science, communication, and history. This year's conference was unique in that each paper (and now, chapter in this volume) was authored or coauthored by a graduate student. The topics range from content analysis of speeches of members of Congress to presidential tweets.

Many people helped make this conference possible. Brian Lamb, Susan Swain, and Robert Kennedy, executives of C-SPAN, have encouraged us in this research endeavor. They facilitated funding from the C-SPAN Education Foundation that resulted in the grants to the scholars to complete their work. The C-SPAN Board of Directors, all representatives of the cable television industry that supports C-SPAN, was instrumental in the initiative to digitize the archive and has been enthusiastic about encouraging its use.

Nita Stickrod Granger skillfully managed the planning, interacting with Purdue Conferences staff, Ethan Kingery in particular. She also worked with all participants to pull off a very successful conference. The entire staff of the Archives—Kevin Ingle, Alan Cloutier, Matt Long, Josh Tamlin, Karen Adams, Martin Swoverland, Steve Strother, and Gary Daugherty—helped along the way.

At Purdue University we were assisted by Professors Rosie Clawson and Marifran Mattson, heads of the Department of Political Science and the Lamb School of Communication, respectively. Donna Wireman of Communication assisted with many campus details. Fara Stalker and Paige Pfiefer of the Liberal Arts Business Office helped with financial management for the conference.

Dr. Raymond Smock of the Robert C. Byrd Center for Congressional History and Education at Shepherd University quickly and graciously agreed to keynote the conference. His remarks are printed in this volume.

The Purdue University Press made sure that everything went smoothly, from the initial idea through publication of the book. Rebecca Corbin, Katherine Purple, and Bryan Shaffer helped throughout. Kelley Kimm provided very skillful editing to ensure that every chapter looked and read well.

As we move forward with additional conferences and research activities, I am pleased to announce that Purdue University has created the Center for C-SPAN Scholarship and Engagement in the Brian Lamb School of Communication. Connie Doebele has joined the Center as managing director, bringing 25 years of experience at C-SPAN. The Center will sponsor the future conferences, bring in speakers, and encourage research and teaching using the C-SPAN Video Library. I welcome Connie and look forward to more activities promoting the extensive holdings of the C-SPAN Video Library.

I dedicate this book to three of my graduate school colleagues, who each went on to very successful careers in political science: Timothy E. Cook, Gary King, and Lyn Ragsdale. Unfortunately, Tim Cook's career was cut way too short by his death in 2006. I miss him and the advice he would offer as a leading communication scholar on using the Archives for research. Gary King and Lyn Ragsdale are both prolific scholars who teach at Harvard and Rice Universities, respectively. They each influenced me in untold ways.

The C-SPAN Archives observed its 30th anniversary in 2017. When we started in 1987, we had a vision of how C-SPAN could be used in teaching and research. With each volume in this series, we get closer to realizing that vision. There will be future conferences and future volumes, each showing a diverse range of research in multiple disciplines. I never cease to be impressed by what scholars propose and execute for each of these volumes. It is our hope that professors and graduate students will pick up these volumes and propose new research that will appear in the future volumes. Let the research continue.

Robert X. Browning, Editor
Winter 2018

CHAPTER 1

CONSTRUCTING CONGRESSIONAL DISCOURSES: C-SPAN ARCHIVES AND CONGRESSIONAL SPEECHES ON CRISES AND SCANDALS

Alyssa A. Wildrick and Alison N. Novak

In July 2016, Speaker Paul Ryan spoke before Congress, asking his colleagues to vote against a bill designed to add consumer protections against credit card fraud. He stated, "It's in these times of crisis and scandal that we swarm to support underdeveloped and underresearched bills that act as a Band-Aid more than a solution. We need to fight against this popular urge and consider the long-term implications of rash decisions." Reactionary policy, where legislation is enacted or promoted due to its relevance and relationship to a salient public crisis or scandal, is common within Congress (Novak & Vilceanu, 2017). Ryan's speech is emblematic of many instances in which the language of crisis and scandal is used to support or oppose legislation in Congress. Previous scholarship notes the impact that this language has in ensuring public and governmental support for legislation, policy enforcement, and political positioning (Wilcox, Cameron, Ault, & Agee, 2003). However, few studies have described how the language of crisis and scandal is used to fulfill a variety of tasks, including building support for or opposition to legislation, enacting relationships within and outside the congressional community, and fostering media and public attention. Using C-SPAN videos, this study attempts to fill this void and study how the language of crisis and scandal is used throughout Congress.

BACKGROUND

Crisis and Scandal

Although there is no standard definition of crisis or scandal, previous research demonstrates that the variety of the terms used partially defines why such instances are difficult to fix or respond to. Makropoulos (2012) argues that there are several parts of a crisis, including sudden or unexpected situation(s), impact on members of the public, reputational risks for responsible parties, and an implied solution or remedy. Although the depth of crisis communication research has studied these four parts extensively, scholars note that the conceptualization of "crisis" is still rather challenging. Shank (2008) notes that applying the term crisis is often the most challenging part. For example, many organizations are hesitant to call a problem a "crisis" because of the negative connotation and frenzy of public attention this can create (Shank, 2008). Cleeren and colleagues (2013) note that often the terms crisis or scandal are not applied by those directly involved, but rather by constituents, the media, or competitors seeking to take advantage of a situation. This means that recognizing a crisis is challenging because of the many parties seeking to minimize or maximize the potential for harm that a crisis may cause.

Although many studies use the terms *scandal* and *crisis* interchangeably, the field of public relations draws important distinctions between the uses of the terms. Hansen (2012) argues that the term *scandal* is more specific regarding its implications for fault, while *crisis* may relate to indirect responsibilities or causes. For example, an economic scandal results from an individual or organization's fault, while an economic crisis results from unforeseen consequences of individual or organizational behavior (Hansen, 2012). In short, it is the invoking of responsibility and intentionality that changes between the two words. Ravenscroft and Williams (2005) add that a crisis is often the original phase of a scandal. An organization may have a crisis, but it is their response that may generate a scandal (Ravenscroft & Williams, 2005).

Quaglia (2014) notes that the choice of using the terms *crisis* and *scandal* is often a conscious discourse, in which the speaker invokes or uses each term for specific effect. In his study of government interventions in banking systems, Quaglia (2014) found that speakers referred to the larger problems as crises, but interpersonal issues (such as bank managers mismanaging funds) as scandals. This is consistent with the findings of other studies of governmental communication, where the term *scandal* is used to invoke individual responsibility and *crisis* is invoked to encourage immediate response and solutions (Grebe, 2013; Vila & Küster, 2014).

Crisis and scandal in governmental relations draw heavily on the work of the public relations industry (Kim & Sung, 2014). Studies in crisis communication suggest that the terms are often used by those in political power to garner media and public attention to an issue (Kim, Avery, & Lariscy, 2001). Fink (2013) notes that the 24/7 media climate requires politicians to frame their work and policies in a way that will encourage media attention. Framing their policies and positions in a response to a crisis or scandal is one way that this can be accomplished (Wilcox et al., 2003).

The language of crisis and scandal in governance is popular because of the ripple effect suggested by their presence (Wilcox et al., 2003). The unpredictability of a crisis or scandal, as well as the evolving implications over time, garner media support, thus encouraging politicians who seek this attention to use this framework (Fink, 2013). Therefore, public relations communication strategies are necessary and heightened during "scandals and crises" to ensure that the proper steps are taken to prevent further incidents from occurring.

Andreaseen (1994) argues that economic crises in particular garner media and public interest faster than other types. Members of Congress, particularly, invoke the crisis and scandal language when explaining why financial policies matter. Problematically, this also requires politicians to position their policy as a reaction to the crisis or scandal (Bodenheimer, 1996). Eisenbeis (2010) argues that framing policy in response to a crisis comes as a trade-off, because reactionary policy is inherently weaker for its reflection on past problems rather than being predictive of future issues. Although scholarship does not have consensus on the merits of reactionary policy (there are arguments for and against it), there is a public perception that reactionary policies should, at the very least, merit additional critique and criticism (Frey & Noys, 2007).

Crisis and Congress

The field of crisis communication has pivoted its attention to governance and the use of crisis language since 2008 (Fink, 2013). As a facet of public relations, the 24/7 coverage of government entities from sources such as C-SPAN, cable news, and local news has increased the reach of crisis as a topic within Congress and the federal government (Kim & Sung, 2014). Congressional representatives identifying and reacting to crises (business, government, or interpersonal) on a local and national level have a larger reach due to this media coverage (Kim et al., 2001). Therefore, scholars are charged with studying how crisis language appears, persists, and impacts government operations, relationships with the public, and the building of reactionary legislation.

Academically, research on how Congress uses the language of crisis and scandal is important because of its implications for media attention and the formation of reactive policies. If, as previous research suggests, crisis and scandal act as buzzwords for political news coverage, scholars should investigate the effects of such discourse on public engagement, legislation development, and political efficacy (Cigler, 2004).

Additionally, the examination of crisis and scandal holds implications for practitioners seeking ways to make congressional speech, action, or legislation more salient within public and media communities. Scholarship notes that because the use of "crisis" or "scandal" by those in political power often cements the reputation of the problem entity (e.g., Ryan's credit card security crisis), research into the use of language may provide insight into how a crisis or scandal develops (Kim & Sung, 2014).

Previous research demonstrates the importance of "scandals" and crises" in Congress, policy development, and public engagement. Romano (2005) notes that congressional speakers who construct discourses around crises are more likely to gain salient media coverage, gain support from their home districts, and incur more public support for policies proposed during the wake of a scandal or crisis. Although there is a myriad of research that reports the statistical relevance of crisis and scandal in Congress, there is limited prior work that descriptively looks at how members of Congress work together to construct discourses on the subject, the language and mechanisms of Congress's terms of reference, or the relationship between crisis and scandal within congressional interactions (Cigler, 2004; Jacobs, 2009). As a result, scholars have requested more research that blends concepts from crisis management and public relations with studies of Congress and government (Cigler, 2004; Lodge, 2011; Silva, Jenkins-Smith, & Waterman, 2007).

Congressional Speeches and Governance

Speeches from the congressional floor and other addresses to members of Congress are an opportunity to frame, influence, and position arguments for or against a policy, draw attention to an issue, or gain notoriety on a specific topic (Fodor, 2014). Thompson (2014) notes that although speeches on the congressional floor are a common way to address colleagues and the public (through television coverage), this is not the only opportunity for address. Interviews, press conferences, and town hall meetings are further instances of public address. Although these speeches rarely gain public or media attention beyond live-broadcasting systems (such as C-SPAN), they sometimes reflect the inner workings of the legislative branch and the persuasive efforts of speakers to influence public policy (Kriner & Shen, 2014). Scholars thus can use them to determine how members of Congress plan to garner support for or opposition to an issue, topic, or piece of legislation (Fodor, 2014). Further, the amount of planning and preparation that goes into these speeches reflects the official nature of communication on specific topics (Pearson & Dancey, 2011). Previous scholarship has examined congressional speeches by members and nonmembers of Congress to look for patterns of speech, terms of reference, discourses, and rhetorical strategies within a number of contexts (Rocca, 2007). This study follows in this vein of scholarship to examine two specific terms of reference, "crisis" and "scandal," to examine how they are used by members of Congress.

THE C-SPAN DATA SET AND METHODOLOGICAL APPROACH

This project uses a collection of clips from the C-SPAN Archives' online Video Library as a data set. Using the search functions of the site, the authors created a collection of 631 videos of congressional hearings, testimony, speeches, and votes using the words scandal and crisis or crises. These 631 videos were collected from December 1, 1992 (the first mention within the Video Library), to December 1, 2016. Importantly, this 24-year period will allow researchers to exhaustively identify the ways that congressional speakers construct, use, and invoke discourses of crises and scandals. This chapter adopts Ansolabehere and Jones's (2010) conceptualization that congressional interactions extend beyond members of Congress. This means a study of congressional discourses should include nonmembers who engage Congress such as expert testimonials, witnesses at congressional hearings, and appeals by members of the public. The data set thus includes both nonmembers who address Congress and all mentions of scandals and crises from members (even off the congressional floor).

Through a discursive methodology based on Gee's (2010) seven meaning-making principles, researchers can identify the ways congressional speakers use this terminology. The two authors independently watched the 631 clips, then built a set of codes focused on how the terms of reference are used. For example, precursory findings suggested that congressional leaders use the language of scandal and crises to demonstrate their awareness of and connection to current events and political issues. After examining the clips, the researchers met to determine a common set of discursive codes that could then be applied to the larger data set. Three codes were identified: building support for or opposition to legislation, enacting relationships within and outside of Congress, and fostering media and public attention. After developing these three codes, the researchers watched the 631 clips again for categorization and application. The findings below give an overview of each of the three discourses. Quotes and examples are provided to demonstrate the intricacies of each set, as well as for qualitative reliability. From the 24-year data set provided in the C-SPAN Video Library, longitudinal trends were also identified and analyzed.

FINDINGS

Discourse One: Building Support for or Opposition to Legislation

Throughout the 691 speeches, the dominant use of the term crisis was to enact a response from members of Congress as they determined whether to support or oppose a bill being presented. In total, this discourse appeared in 392 (56.7%) videos and mentions of crisis. Specifically, the term crisis was used to couch the presentation of a bill or policy that would attempt to fix or rectify the problem statement. This discourse is broken into two frameworks. First, crisis and scandal are used as motivation to support legislation; then, they are used to garner opposition. Each draws on the discourse in a unique way, providing two arguments for the audience.

Crisis as Motivation

Of the congressional speeches identified in this discourse, 211 (56.7%) used the term crisis as a way to garner support for proposed legislation. For example, in May 2016, Representative Sheila Jackson Lee (D-TX) used the terms crisis and scandal to discuss mismanagement of Veterans Affairs hospitals and the need for Congress to intervene immediately (C-SPAN, 2014). Here, Jackson Lee frames her calls for legislative support through the language of crisis and scandal. She begins by arguing, "The organizational mismanagement of veterans' hospitals in the United States is a crisis beyond all belief. Your lack of support is scandalous." Next, she implores her colleagues to "think about the long-term consequences of inaction. If you don't support this bill, then how many more veterans are not going to get the care they need? How many more are going to be ignored? How many more from your district are you willing to overlook?" Her argument, framed through the language of crisis and scandal, suggests she aims to build support and motivate House members to support her proposed bill, which would restructure the hiring process for veterans' hospital managers.

Jackson Lee's use of the motivation framework within the discourse demonstrates how members of Congress use crisis to motivate support for the bill. In these cases, a "crisis" demonstrates an urgency to a problem, one that perhaps is sudden and unexpected, but thus requires a solution. The speaker then suggests his or her bill or legislation as that solution, thus addressing the problems that have caused the crisis. Scandal is then a supportive term, one that implies individual responsibility for the problem. Thus, in order to reduce the crisis and resolve the scandal, a person should take the course of action proposed in the speech (in this case, supporting Jackson Lee's policy proposal).

Earlier examples of crisis and scandal similarly suggested this pattern and significance to the terms of reference. In March 1993, National Security Adviser to President George H. W. Bush (1989–1993) Brent Scowcroft reflected on the need for more humanitarian aid to Russia (C-SPAN, 1993). While not a member of Congress, his speech was designed to motivate congressional support for proposed policy. He concluded his speech with "they are in an unexpected crisis, they won't admit it, which is needlessly to say scandalous, but we can help by giving them more aid. It's as simple as that." Similar to Jackson Lee's use, Scrowcroft positions Russian poverty as a humanitarian crisis, again implying that a solution is necessary. Inaction, in which either the Russian government or the American government does nothing to help, is scandalous, thus members of Congress need to support Scowcroft's proposal to send more aid to the country.

Jackson Lee's and Scowcroft's speeches both imply a similar argumentative framework using the terms *crisis* and *scandal*. First, the speaker uses the term *crisis* to suggest an unforeseen problem with large consequences; next, the speaker uses the term *scandal* to imply individual responsibility; and finally, the speaker proposes legislation, policy, or actions that may solve or reduce the crisis and scandal. This rhetorical framework accompanies this discourse, especially as speakers attempt to motivate support by other members. This invokes Gee's (2010) practices meaning-making task, as the speaker uses the terms as a call to action for future behavior (voting in favor of the proposed bill).

Legislatively, this pattern appears frequently throughout the C-SPAN Archives data set, as speakers use the language to motivate members of Congress to support their proposed policies. Although outside the scope of the study, it is important to note that of the nearly 100 bills proposed using this discourse, only 22 of them were approved by Congress. While it's unclear if the speaker's arguments are responsible for this success rate, more research should investigate such a relationship.

Crisis as a Warning

Alternatively, this discourse using crisis for legislative purposes was also frequently used to warn against or garner opposition to proposed legislation. Of the 392 speeches, 181 (46.2%) used the term as a warning. Like Speaker Ryan's earlier speech on the credit card security policies, frequently members of Congress spoke out against policies that they felt were constructed too quickly in regard to a crisis.

For example, in May 2016, members of Congress such as Representative Rob Bishop (R-UT) spoke before Congress asking members not to make any "rash moves" regarding the "Puerto Rico debt crisis" (C-SPAN, 2016d). His seven-minute speech warns representatives to "think carefully" and "consider the long-term impacts of any sudden moves that claim to fix the debt problems." As one of only five speeches on Puerto Rico in 2016, Bishop's words not only signify the only instance when the debt crisis is discussed, but also the singular argument against pursuing policy changes that could impact Puerto Rico economics. His warning is indicative of many instances of crisis within congressional speeches, in that members of Congress should be careful not to pursue or support legislation that has been hastily created to fix a problem. Crisis policy is discursively constructed as "problematic" and "rash" rather than a thoughtful solution. Like Speaker Ryan, these lawmakers frame crisis policy as a Band-Aid, not a comprehensive solution to a complex problem.

Similarly, in July 2011, former Democratic governor of Virginia Tim Kaine spoke on the ongoing U.S. financial crisis and recession (C-SPAN, 2011). His four-minute speech discussed and responded to two proposed bills that capped governmental spending as a temporary solution to the crisis. He encouraged members of Congress not to vote to support the bills, citing his experiences in Virginia: "I get it, we're in a financial crisis unlike any that we've seen in our lifetime. But you can't just go and write any plan hoping to fix the problem, you've got to think it through. The people of Virginia and your home districts need you to think more carefully than that. I promise, if you vote for this reactionary policy, you'll have a scandal on your hands." Kaine linked the use of crisis and reactionary policy in his speech. Those speakers using crisis as a warning frequently discussed how proposed policies were only a reaction to the current problems, not a long-term predictive solution to future ones. Reactionary policy is then framed as the real problem, in some cases bigger than the original crisis. Kaine's warning, that scandal would follow reactionary policy, again implies individual responsibility for the crisis and the solution, thus the audience should think carefully about the long-term implications of a vote before making their decisions.

Just as speakers used an argumentative framework to support crisis policy, they also used a rather consistent argumentative framework to oppose crisis policy. First, the crisis is introduced as an unexpected and generalizable problem. Next, the speaker introduces the proposed solution as reactionary and thus only a shortsighted solution. Finally, the speaker suggests that supporting reactionary policy would produce interpersonal scandals within members' constituencies. Unlike in the motivation framework, the scandal is not in inaction, but rather in hasty action. This discourse similarly implies Gee's (2010) connections meaning-making process, as it relies upon the audience to link a type of personal scandal to supporting the proposed legislation.

These two frameworks within the first discourse suggest that each speaker can manipulate the discourse for its own purpose, in this case garnering support for or opposition to a piece of legislation. They further show that the discourse is argumentative in nature, and that crisis and scandal are terms of reference for these arguments that support or oppose a bill. However, this was not the only way that members of Congress used the terms.

Discourse Two: Enacting Relationships Within and Outside the Congressional Community

Crisis and scandal were also used to denote relationships between members of Congress, similar problems across the country (and globe), and relationships with constituents. This discourse invokes the sign-systems and knowledge meaning-making task from Gee (2010) as speakers use the terms of reference to draw attention to other issues and demonstrate a larger network of ideas and individuals involved in the public policy process.

First, speakers used crisis and scandal to show their relationship with other members of Congress and other elected officials. Frequently, this was done to invoke credibility for their arguments, such as referencing presidential leadership on a topic. In 2015, Assistant Secretary of State Anne Richard spoke before a congressional committee reminding the audience that "both Secretary Kerry and President Obama have made humanitarian aid in Syria a priority. Failure to help in this matter will only encourage the crisis to proliferate" (C-SPAN, 2015e). Here, Richard reminds Congress that it was Kerry's and Obama's labeling of Syrian war as a crisis, therefore strengthening her call to action with support from two of the most influential people in American foreign policy at the time. By connecting the crisis with Kerry and Obama, Richard strengthens her own argument for congressional support and argues the uniform position of those in the executive branch.

Similarly, other speakers invoked the crisis and scandal labels used by others in their speeches. For example, Representative Gerald Connolly (D-VA) repeatedly referred to the framing of the war in Syria as a crisis, referencing speeches made by President Obama, presidential candidates Trump and Clinton, and Secretary of State Kerry (C-SPAN, 2016d). Rather than passing the blame of the term onto these other speakers, this is a type of sign-system where the individual draws connections between the terminology and the status of others. Connolly gains credibility by citing these other speakers, rather than labeling the problem himself. His use of their language demonstrates his knowledge of the executive leadership as well as his understanding of the seriousness of the problems in a foreign country.

Second, speakers used the terms *crisis* and *scandal* comparatively and to draw connections between issues and events. For example, Connolly compared the crisis in Syria to the 1990s in Rwanda: "I know because I went to Rwanda for myself. I saw that crisis, it looks just like the Syrian one. Our lack of aid is the same scandal we faced two decades ago." Comparisons between crises and scandals reinforced the need for immediate action. Connolly implies that if Congress wants to avoid the same disastrous scandal of ignoring Rwanda during its genocide, they would need to take immediate action in Syria. This type of comparison again reinforces the need for action and uses the consequences of previous scandals to motivate the audience to avoid future scandals.

Similarly, Senator Lindsey Graham (R-SC) used the financial depression of the 1930s to motivate support for financial reform in 2009 (C-SPAN, 2015c). He stated, "The economic, personal, and social crisis of the Great Depression is perhaps imminent. We have to do something to fix our economy, or we too will face this same problem." Again, by connecting the issue to other issues within American history, he motivates support for action and reform.

Last, speakers use this discourse to connect the crisis or scandal to their own constituencies and the public. In 2015 Treasury Secretary Jack Lew reflected on the five-year anniversary of the Dodd-Frank Amendment, which was passed in response to the 2008 financial crisis (C-SPAN, 2015b). Lew reflected, "It's up to you [Congress] to remind your constituents why Dodd-Frank was necessary. It's an exhaustively long piece of legislation, so you must make it relevant. Remind them [about] the crisis, remind them that to do nothing would have been a scandal." Here, Lew tells Congress that the language of crisis and scandal can make even very complicated pieces of legislation relevant and interesting for citizens. However, he positions this as the task of Congress to use this language of crisis and scandal to inform constituents of the politics, not the actual policies themselves.

Lew's call to action is echoed by nonmembers of Congress, such as a 2015 speech by Secretary of Housing and Urban Development Julian Castro as he asks Congress for support explaining a recent Supreme Court ruling against housing discrimination (C-SPAN, 2015a). He states, "I know this decision isn't going to make for easy changes in each of your districts, that's why it's up to you to explain why this type of discrimination was problematic in the first place. Tell them it produced housing crises in Chicago and Oakland. Tell them this is how we fix it." Again, Castro asks Congress to make the Supreme Court ruling relevant through the language of crisis.

Crisis and scandal are used as terms of reference that can draw connections and sign-systems for later action and public engagement. Speakers used these terms discursively to demonstrate the interconnectedness of congressional action and federal government decision making. These connections help orient the implications and effects of issues, policies, and events taking place around the country for members of Congress and their constituents.

Discourse Three: Fostering Media and Public Attention

Finally, many members of Congress used the terms crisis and scandal to enact discourses of relationships and sign-systems within their audiences. In several cases, speakers reflected on the difficulty of gaining media and public support for their proposed policies without using the terms crisis or scandal. Senator Gary Peters (D-MI) reflected on his challenges in gaining public support for failing public schools in 2014 in his district: "No one cared until I called it a crisis. It was like the second I said our failing school crisis put our children's future in jeopardy, everyone wanted a piece of it. If I just said, 'our schools are failing,' crickets" (C-SPAN, 2016c). Peters's reflection that the term crisis was a pathway to gaining media attention and public support was echoed by other speakers who similarly reflected on their choice to phrase problems in their home districts as a crisis. For example, Minority Leader Nancy Pelosi (D-CA) suggested, "Let's just call everything a 'scandal' and be done with it. You want people to pay attention, tell them it's scandalous. That's human nature" (C-SPAN, 2016b). Quotes like Peters's and Pelosi's demonstrate the cognizant use of scandal and crisis to frame issues in such a way that the public understands and cares about them. This is what Gee (2010) calls a conscious discourse, where the choices to frame issues are active, reflective, and thoughtful. The speaker understands the impact of word choice and is willing to share the process by which the choice is made with the audience.

However, there were some critical members of Congress who disapproved of the commonality of the terms *crisis* and *scandal*. In December 2015, Secretary of State John Kerry spoke before a congressional committee regarding U.S.-Israel relations and the ongoing conflicts between Israel and Palestine (C-SPAN, 2015g). He noted, "I know you all see crises everywhere, I was a senator too, you know. But this is a real crisis, one that is life-and-death for some of the most vulnerable people around the world." Kerry's use of "real" demonstrates the challenges faced by members of Congress as they attempt to determine what events and issues must take priority. If the terms *crisis* and *scandal* were being used too frequently (as Kerry suggests), it is more difficult to separate "real crises" from rhetorical ones. Representative Kevin McCarthy (R-CA) seems to agree with Kerry's assertion, and in a 2015 press conference he criticized members for their liberal use of the term *crisis* (C-SPAN, 2015f). "We're dealing with one of the largest refugee crises in our history right now, and I just heard a senator, a prominent one, saying the lack of creamer in their office is a crisis. Are you kidding, we've got to rethink how we're using that word." Like Kerry, McCarthy is frustrated by the seeming ubiquitous nature of the words *crisis* and *scandal*. Kerry acknowledges that this is a function of the job of a member of Congress, to gain media and public support by articulating the crises that demand such attention. However, McCarthy is more critical, arguing that the use of these words in noncrisis situations has cheapened them and prevented more important issues from getting the attention they require.

It is important to note that there were also humorous reflections by members of Congress on the ABC hit drama *Scandal*. The prime-time show, featuring Kerry Washington working as a "fixer" for the DC and federal governments, was often used by members of Congress to show their knowledge of current pop culture trends while juxtaposing the seriousness of their job and responsibilities. In a 2016 address on the Flint water crisis, Representative Dan Kildee (D-MI) stated, "This isn't *Scandal*. I don't have Kerry Washington who can come in and fix this mess. You are the only ones who can fix this crisis" (C-SPAN, 2016a). Again, although *Scandal* is mentioned as a humorous departure from the seriousness of the Flint water crisis, its purpose is not just to make the audience laugh. Instead, it is to demonstrate Kildee's understanding of popular culture and also remind members of Congress why they have to act. Juxtaposing the ABC drama with the water crisis reminds Congress of the infinitely more serious crisis that can proliferate without their action.

DISCUSSION

The discourses identified within this data set suggest that there is no one consistent usage of the terms crisis and scandal within Congress. Rather, these terms are used strategically to draw the audience's attention to the relevance and importance of action or inaction on a topic, issue, or problem. For example, by referencing the Puerto Rican debt crisis, speakers deemed the issue consequential and eminently important. Throughout the data set, crisis and scandal are used as modifiers to draw audience attention to the severity of a problem. As an adjective modifies a noun, the terms crisis and scandal serve to modify the intensity and severity of a problem. Linguistically, this modification is critical to the nature of the discourses shared and used by Congress. Throughout the data set, the terms are used to draw attention or connection between members of Congress and contemporary political issues. The terms are vitally important to this identification process.

In addition, there are important differences between the use of crisis and scandal. Whereas crisis relates to the problem, scandal relates to Congress's reaction or response to the problem. Scandal is particularly important because of the connotation given by speakers within its use. Here, scandal is a type of threat that members of Congress rapidly attempt to avoid. Responding incorrectly to the problem or crisis, through approval or rejection of a suggested policy, could result in a scandal, which would jeopardize the member's position within the legislature.

This finding, that Congress members threaten scandals in order to motivate support, is a rather important discursive finding in this project. Its repeated use over the 24-year period suggests that this type of language is common within congressional speeches and has become a normative style of speech. While previous research has found that members of Congress threaten each other to motivate support, here these threats happen in public spaces. Importantly, there are no specific details given when a member of Congress threatens a scandal. For example, is this a professional threat to their reputation within the government, a personal threat to their interpersonal relationships, or another kind of scandal? Future research should look in more detail at how these threats resolve or are carried out in the aftermath of policy decisions.

Previous research also suggests that crisis and scandal are used in government to motivate public attention and possible media coverage. Although this study exclusively looked at speeches related to Congress (members and nonmembers), a cursory examination of the remainder of the C-SPAN Video Library reveals that footage of quotes on crisis and scandal appeared frequently within other forms of C-SPAN coverage, such as its daily *Washington Journal* show or its series *The Communicators*. In addition, it is clear from these speeches that the terms are used to demonstrate a legislative connection between the Congress member and the public. Through references to popular television, other legislation, and the personal stories of constituents, these terms appear to formalize a connection between the public audience and the speaker (Cigler, 2004; Jacobs, 2009).

Largely, this research supports Makropolous's (2012) model for the parts of a crisis. The diversity within the usage of crisis suggests that not all speakers referred to the term in the same way or referred to the same part of a crisis. Utah Republican representative Rob Bishop's discussion of the Puerto Rican debt crisis clearly referred to how the problems impacted members of the public.

There does not appear to be any partisan divisions regarding how the terms are used within the data set. For example, both Republicans and Democrats spoke against the quick adoption of reactionary policy without careful consideration of its quality and impact. It also does not appear to be topical in nature; for example, threats of scandal ranged from social issues such as abortion, to financial issues such as national debt, to global issues such as the War on Terror. This, in and of itself, is an important finding, suggesting the terms reflect a strategic approach to speech rather than a reflection of the characteristics of a problem. This strategic aim is reinforced through the pattern of argumentation, in which a problem is identified and labeled as a crisis, then a solution is suggested, and the audience's response or inaction is labeled as a potential scandal. The repeated appearance of this argument framework suggests that there is a normative pattern of speech associated with these two terms.

Future research should identify or seek out the consistency of this use across time and issue. For example, identifying the first appearances or labeling of crisis or scandal upon each issue could help analyze how the terms are used for political advantage. It could help answer the question of whether members of Congress are using the terms to cast blame upon others or deflect responsibility from their own actions. In addition, mapping the frequency of the terms within each issue could help juxtapose political communication research with public relations crises research and the phases of crisis communication.

CONCLUSION

The frequency of crisis and scandal throughout congressional speeches reinforces the need for a blend of discursive public relations research within political communication. As speakers construct issues and problems in Congress, their modification and labeling of these issues as crises and scandals impacts the audience's reception of and reaction to such discourses. Gee's (2010) discursive methodology proved useful in examining the context and patterns of crises and scandals. While empirical studies of the terms in other governmental contexts (such as local politics, debates, or campaign speeches) would help identify their frequency, more interpretive work is necessary to fully understand the mechanisms of this terminology's use. Through the three discourses we identified, this study provides the beginnings of a framework in which to examine how crises and scandals appear in congressional speeches; however, more research can lend further insight into the effects of such linguistic and discursive choices. For example, future work should examine the success rate of policies proposed within the context of scandals and crises. Studies such as these could lend further insights for politicians, campaign managers, and communication specialists.

REFERENCES

Andreaseen, T. (1994). Satisfaction, loyalty and reputation as indicators of customer orientation in the public sector. *International Journal of Public Sector Management, 7*(2), 16.

Ansolabehere, S., & Jones, P. E. (2010). Constituents' responses to congressional roll-call voting. *American Journal of Political Science, 54*(3), 583–597. https://doi.org/10.1111/j.1540-5907.2010.00448.x

Bodenheimer, T. (1996). The HMO backlash — righteous or reactionary? *New England Journal of Medicine, 335*(21), 1601–1604. https://doi.org/10.1056/NEJM199611213352112

Cigler, A. J. (2004). Enron, a perceived crisis in public confidence, and the bipartisan campaign reform act of 2002. *Review of Policy Research, 21*(2), 233–252. https://doi.org/10.1111/j.1541-1338.2004.00071.x

Cleeren, K. H. H., Heerde, v., H. J, & Dekimpe, M. G. (2013). Rising from the ashes: How brands and categories can overcome product-harm crises. *Journal of Marketing, 77*(2), 58–77.

C-SPAN (Producer). (1993, March 23). *Crisis in Russia* [online video]. Available from https://www.c-span.org/video/?38996-1/crisis-russia

C-SPAN (Producer). (2011, July 13). *News Review with Tim Kaine* [online video]. Available from https://www.c-span.org/video/?300495-5/news-review-tim-kaine

C-SPAN (Producer). (2014, May 30). *Representative Sheila Jackson Lee on veterans affairs mismanagement* [online video]. Available from https://www.c-span.org/video/?319624-7/washington-journal-rep-jackson-lee-va-mismanagement

C-SPAN (Producer). (2015a, June 26). *Newsmakers with Secretary Julian Castro* [online video]. Available from https://www.c-span.org/video/?326746-1/newsmakers-secretary-julian-castro

C-SPAN (Producer). (2015b, July 20). *Treasury Secretary Jack Lew on financial industry regulation* [online video]. Available from https://www.c-span.org/video/?327209-2/treasury-secretary-jack-lew-financial-industry-regulation

C-SPAN (Producer). (2015c, September 8). *Senator Lindsey Graham on the Iran Nuclear Agreement* [online video]. Available from https://www.c-span.org/video/?327968-1/senator-lindsey-graham-rsc-iran-nuclear-agreement

C-SPAN (Producer). (2015d, September 16). *News Review with Representative Gerald Connolly* [online video]. Available from https://www.c-span.org/video/?327991-4/washington-journal-representative-gerald-connolly-dva

C-SPAN (Producer). (2015e, November 6). *Newsmakers with Anne Richard* [online video]. Available from https://www.c-span.org/video/?400272-1/newsmakers-anne-richard

C-SPAN (Producer). (2015f, November 17). *Representative Kevin McCarthy on vetting Syrian refugees* [online video]. Available from https://www.c-span.org/video/?400901-101/representative-kevin-mccarthy-vetting-syrian-refugees

C-SPAN (Producer). (2015g, December 5). *Secretary of State John Kerry on U.S.-Israel relations* [online video]. Available from https://www.c-span.org/video/?401622-1/secretary-state-john-kerry-usisrael-relations

C-SPAN (Producer). (2016a, May 4). *Flint, Michigan, speech introductions* [online video]. Available from https://www.c-span.org/video/?409040-2/flint-michigan-speech-introductions

C-SPAN (Producer). (2016b, May 12). *House Minority Leader weekly briefing* [online video]. Available from https://www.c-span.org/video/?409467-1/house-minority-leader-nancy-pelosi-briefs-reporters

C-SPAN (Producer). (2016c, May 18). *State of the U.S. economy* [online video]. Available from https://www.c-span.org/video/?409266-4/washington-journal-senator-gary-peters-dmi

C-SPAN (Producer). (2016d, May 24). *Representative Bishop on the Puerto Rican debt crisis* [online video]. Available from https://www.c-span.org/video/?409733-1/representative-bishop-puerto-rican-debt-crisis

Eisenbeis, R. A. (2010). The financial crisis: Miss-diagnosis and reactionary responses. *Atlantic Economic Journal, 38*(3), 283–294. https://doi.org/10.1007/s11293-010-9235-1

Fink, S. (2013). *Crisis communications: The definitive guide to managing the message.* New York, NY: McGraw-Hill Education.

Fodor, A. (2014). Congressional arbitrage at the executive's expense: The speech or debate clause and the unenforceable stock act. *Northwestern University Law Review, 108*(2), 607.

Frey, H., & Noys, B. (2007). Introduction: Reactionary times. *Journal of European Studies, 37*(3), 243–253. https://doi.org/10.1177/0047244107080723

Gee, J. P. (2010). *An introduction to discourse analysis: Theory and method* (3rd ed.). New York, NY: Taylor and Francis.

Grebe, S. K. (2013). Re-building a damaged corporate reputation: How the Australian wheat board (AWB) overcame the damage of the UN "Oil for food" scandal to successfully reintegrate into the Australian wheat marketing regulatory regime. *Corporate Reputation Review, 16*(2), 118–130. https://doi.org/10.1057/crr.2013.5

Hansen, P. H. (2012). Making sense of financial crisis and scandal: A Danish bank failure in the first era of finance capitalism. *Enterprise & Society, 13*(3), 672–706. https://doi.org/10.1017/S1467222700010892

Jacobs, S. B. (2009). Crises, Congress, and cognitive biases: A critical examination of food and drug legislation in the United States. *Food and Drug Law Journal, 64*(4), 599–630.

Kim, S., Avery, E. J., & Laricsy, R. W. (2001). Reputation repair at the expense of providing instructing and adjusting information following crises: Examining 18 years of crisis response strategy research. *International Journal of Strategic Communication, 5,* 183–199.

Kim, S., & Sung, K. (2014). Revisiting the effectiveness of base crisis response strategies in comparison of reputation management crisis responses. *Journal of Public Relations Research, 26*(1), 62–78. https://doi.org/10.1080/1062726X.2013.795867

Kriner, D., & Shen, F. (2014). Responding to war on Capitol Hill: Battlefield casualties, congressional response, and public support for the war in Iraq. *American Journal of Political Science, 58*(1), 157–174. https://doi.org/10.1111/ajps.12055

Lodge, M. (2011). Risk, regulation and crisis: Comparing national responses in food safety regulation. *Journal of Public Policy, 31*(1), 25–50. https://doi.org/10.1017/S0143814X10000218

Makropoulos, M. (2012). Crisis and contingency: Two categories of the discourse of classical modernity. *Thesis Eleven, 111*(1), 9–18. https://doi.org/10.1177/0725513612453421

Novak, A. N., & Vilceanu, M. O. (2017). When crisis becomes policy: Credit card security crises and congressional speeches. *Electronic Journal of Communication, 27*(1).

Pearson, K., & Dancey, L. (2011). Elevating women's voices in Congress: Speech participation in the House of Representatives. *Political Research Quarterly, 64*(4), 910–923.

Quaglia, L. (2014). The Italian banking system: Banca Monte dei Paschi's scandal and the euro area's sovereign debt crisis. *Italian Politics, 29*(1), 216–232. https://doi.org/10.3167/ip.2014.290113

Ravenscroft, S., & Williams, P. F. (2005). Rules, rogues, and risk assessors: Academic responses to Enron and other accounting scandals. *European Accounting Review, 14*(2), 363–372. https://doi.org/10.1080/09638180500124889

Rocca, M. S. (2007). Nonlegislative debate in the U.S. House of Representatives. *American Politics Research, 35*(4), 489–505. https://doi.org/10.1177/1532673X07300233

Romano, R. (2005). The Sarbanes-Oxley Act and the making of quack corporate governance. *Yale Law Journal, 114*(7), 1521–1611.

Shank, J. (2008). Crisis: A useful category of post-social scientific historical analysis? *American Historical Review, 113*(4), 1090–1099. https://doi.org/10.1086/ahr.113.4.1090

Silva, C. L., Jenkins-Smith, H. C., & Waterman, R. (2007). Why did Clinton survive the impeachment crisis? A test of three explanations. *Presidential Studies Quarterly, 37*(3), 468–485. https://doi.org/10.1111/j.1741-5705.2007.02607.x

Thompson, J. R. (2017). Value shifts in public sector human resource management: A congressional perspective. *Review of Public Personnel Administration, 37*(4), 375–404. https://doi.org/10.1177/0734371X15605159

Vila, N., & Küster, I. (2014). Public versus private broadcasters' management. *Management Decision, 52*(8), 1368–1389. https://doi.org/10.1108/MD-05-2013-0295

Wilcox, D. L., Cameron, G. T., Ault, P. H., & Agee, W. K. (2003). *Public relations strategies and tactics* (7th ed.). New York, NY: Pearson.

CHAPTER **2**

EXPLORING CONGRESSIONAL "LAW ENFORCEMENT" TALK

Cody Blake Wilson and Joshua M. Scacco

One of the greatest assets of the C-SPAN Archives' online Video Library is the opportunity to electronically access the discourse of our elected officials. Words matter, even more so for those whose words become governing systems and laws. When drawing inferences from the political communication on a particular topic, however, studies often utilize public address or media literature, rather than the texts made available to the public by C-SPAN. Therefore, this chapter utilizes the Video Library to better understand the rhetorical nuances of congressional discourse on a particularly controversial topic on the contemporary public agenda: law enforcement.

Before long-festering concerns regarding racial bias in law enforcement actions reemerged in 2012 due to a string of high-profile incidents between police and persons of color, political elites in Congress faced both public opinion and a dominant narrative that saw police officers as positive, heroic forces in American life. Gallup polls show that the number of Americans reporting a great deal or quite a lot of confidence in the police rose steadily following the September 11, 2001, terrorist attacks to 64% of those polled (Newport, 2016).

By 2015, a slim majority (52%) reported the same level of confidence. A new "injustice" narrative had challenged the image of heroic law enforcement officers. Indeed, this nadir in public confidence for law enforcement matched public attitudes gauged shortly after the high-profile and controversial police actions taken against Rodney King in Los Angeles in 1993.

This chapter investigates how members of Congress navigated the changing currents of the law enforcement narrative from 2013 to 2015. The post–September 11 heroic law enforcement narrative was challenged by the much-publicized police actions against Michael Brown, Eric Garner, and Walter Scott and the protests organized by supporters of the Black Lives Matter social movement. These competing narratives may have been reflected in how members of Congress responded to these events and approached them as an issue to be solved in some legislative manner.

Analyzing the discursive construction of law enforcement narratives by members of Congress can give insight into how political leaders engage in a meaning-making process inherently wedded to policymaking. To explore the discursive territory walked by members of Congress during this time, this chapter uses a narrative perspective as a lens for examining congressional law enforcement talk. We first explore the mechanics of narratives in communicative discourse, offer details about the competing law enforcement narratives members faced during this time, and lay out our boundaries of inquiry for the automated textual analysis of more than 2,000 congressional statements regarding law enforcement between 2013 and 2015. The results shed light on the ways that the law enforcement "issue" offered points of narrative unity and division for members of Congress.

PREVIOUS RESEARCH

Narrative Perspective

The narrative perspective is a useful lens for inquiry since it allows for rich analysis of the spoken word. When narratives are used in discourse, we can evaluate how speakers place themselves in a story and assign meaning to protagonists and antagonists, problems and solutions, plots and settings. However, this perspective is more than an analytical tool.

Our humanity is tied to our awareness of and ability to place ourselves within a story (Fisher, 1987; Gottschall, 2012). Not only do we use stories to communicate, but we can interpret communication as narrative as well. How organizations, institutions, people, events, and places fit within our own narrative paradigm assigns unique, contextual meaning to each. With a storytelling lens, we can not only evaluate the spoken word, but also interpret its broader meaning and importance.

Humans as Storytellers

Storytelling is fundamental to the human and political experience. As Altman (2008) said, "among human endeavors, few are more widely spread or more generally endowed with cultural importance than narrative—the practice of storytelling" (p. 1). Furthermore, Fisher (1984) nicknamed the human race as "homo narrans (or storytelling animals)" (p. 2). Storytelling is an art form, used to record history, make meaning, and share experience.

We not only communicate in narratives, but also use narrative to interpret incoming information. Memory uses narrative structure as a package for our experiences. Thus, interpretations and reflections also happen within narrative form (Woodside, 2010). Story elements of our past experiences give connotational meaning to future experiences, serving as both a survival and social mechanism. Narratives are capable of such fundamental power because of their ability to verify and validate themselves.

Narrative Rationality

When presenting the narrative paradigm, Fisher (1987) relied heavily upon narrative rationality for his arguments. Narrative rationality is the ability of stories to produce their own kinds of logic, separate from scientific or other forms of rhetorical logic. Individuals rely on this logic to distinguish storytellers they can trust from those they cannot. If listeners find the narrative rational, it shapes and identifies elements of their reality. For instance, two individuals who lived in Ferguson, Missouri in 2014 following the fatal shooting of Michael Brown could rationally cling to completely separate narratives: Brown was a criminal who had just robbed a store or Brown was the victim of systemic racial bias in the Ferguson police department. The belief in these separate narratives may be based on individuals' prior experiences, as well as the narrative coherence and fidelity of new information they each received.

There are two pillars of narrative rationality: coherence and fidelity. Narrative coherence involves a story's internal logic. It is concerned with whether elements of the story match up or make sense in relation to one another (Fisher, 1987). In a court of law, testimony is scrutinized for coherence. One discrepancy in a retelling of an event could bring into question the entire case. On the other hand, narrative fidelity is how we judge a story's external logic. It is concerned with whether elements of the story match up or make sense with our own preconceived notions and experiences of reality. Narrative fidelity is why concepts like systematic inequalities in policing can be difficult to understand for some citizens of the United States. In this context, the objectivity narrative, the narrative of "equal justice under the law," and the "colorblind" narrative are so ingrained into the meta-narrative of culture, a story of one group receiving systematically unjust treatment from law enforcement receives heavy skepticism and doubt. Similarly, those whose life experience reinforces narratives of oppressive regimes, being put down by "the man," or class warfare, may have a hard time understanding how law enforcement become the heroes of a story. When these narratives come into conflict with life experience, they are often rejected from the meaning-making process. Thus, the narratives that are spoken in politics represent different (and often conflicting) realities experienced by different groups. One group may tell stories of law enforcement that seem incompatible with the stories of another group. However, both represent the lived realities of either group.

Together, fidelity and coherence allow for narratives to shape and define truth in the same way that scientific logic does. This can have profound implications on identity, persuasion, trust, and organizational constitution (Kent, 2015). For these reasons, storytelling has been an ever-present element of political discourse.

Political Discourse and the Law Enforcement Narrative

Our political discourse is predicated on the narratives and grand narratives we tell. In constructing a narrative, assumptions about reality create the story's foundation. Narratives give structure to meaning-making for both the teller and the hearer by acting as capsules to transport and communicate meaning. The meaning transported in political narratives can go on to set the reality for legislation, laws, campaigns, and political debates (Edelman,

1964, 1988). For instance, the discursive construction around the September 11 terrorist attacks forged a war frame including enemies to be confronted and heroes to be honored. President George W. Bush's first Saturday radio address following the attacks included the line "Those who make war against the United States have chosen their own destruction." In his address to a joint session of Congress six days later, Bush held up a police badge as a symbol of the heroism of those who "died at the World Trade Center trying to save others." These narrative moments helped to bookend a post-9/11 narrative that included legislation for an Authorization for the Use of Military Force, a Department of Homeland Security, and the Patriot Act.

Political narratives exist within a broader discursive context. In political communication, this discourse is constantly occurring as communicators seek to make meaning of topics and issues, as well as direct future decision-making and action. Debates on the congressional floor, testimony in committee hearings, presidential speeches, news articles, debates among family members, and water-cooler conversations all contribute to the discursive context. An important function of political narrative, then, is to discursively construct the reality and legitimacy of people, events, ideas, institutions, and policies (Edelman, 1964).

However, in order for political discourse to take place, a political issue must first exist. Public understanding of what is an "issue" is shaped by public and private communication. Edelman (1988) suggested that communication is necessary for the creation and dissemination of public issues. When discourse identifies a situation as a problem in need of a solution, it assigns dualistic meanings such as good and evil, important and unimportant, or change and stability (see also Hart, Jarvis, Jennings, & Smith-Howell, 2005). The conflict among different meanings in discourse can generate broader public debates around political issues.

The existing discourse around law enforcement in the United States features the necessary narrative conflict to constitute public debate. Public communication surrounding law enforcement routinely relies on the knowledge and experience of police and policing leadership, specifically following the September 11 terrorist attacks. The use of the term "first responder" nearly doubled between 2000 and 2006 (Google Books Ngram Viewer, 2017). Heroism became even more deeply married to the image of police as well. Figure 2.1 offers some evidence of the increased linkage between "law

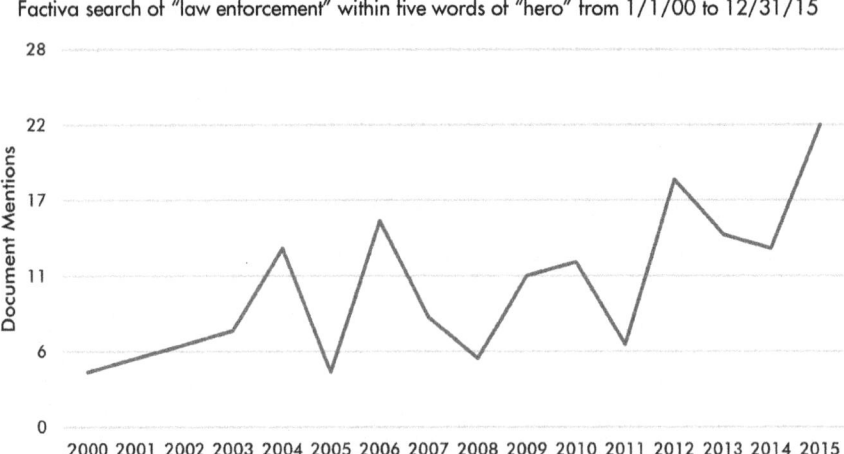

FIGURE 2.1 Associations between "law enforcement" and "hero," 2000–2015.

enforcement" and "hero" in media sources as found in the Factiva database between 2000 and 2015. These repeated discourses shape and alter the meta-discourse. Yet, this heroism narrative is challenged after high-profile police events involving White law enforcement and African American individuals. An "injustice" narrative comes to the fore, sparking the conflict necessary to form debate around a political issue. Figure 2.2 is a snapshot of this emerging "injustice" narrative as found in the Factiva database from

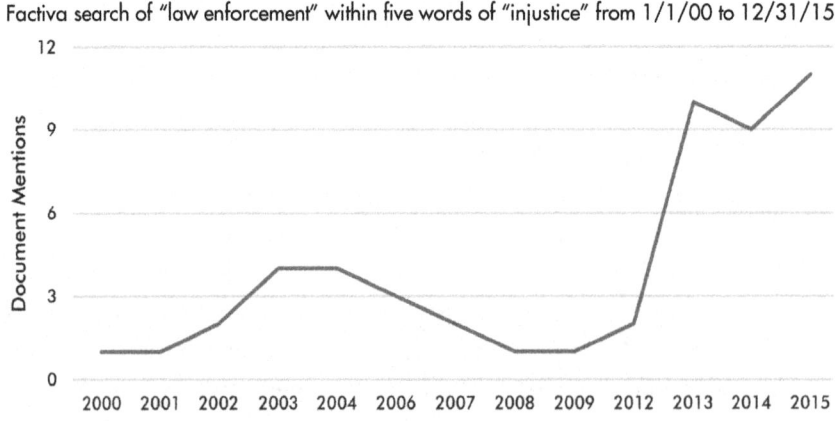

FIGURE 2.2 Associations between "law enforcement" and "injustice," 2000–2015.

2000 to 2015. Whether in news media sources, from political leaders, or in interpersonal conversations, every day political narratives work together to create and reinforce mass communicative narratives. Communication by members of Congress also is included in this narrative (co)production. Furthermore, members of Congress are in a unique position to codify these narratives into law, making it critical to understand congressional communication's stake in the law enforcement debate.

Congressional Communication

Congressional talk is an important element of discourse to study in understanding competing narratives and the creation of grand narratives. Members' voting records reveal a small part of the puzzle with regard to how 535 individuals can influence political reality and behavior (Sellers, 2010). We take a communicative perspective. The constitutional structure of Congress makes it the most democratic of political institutions in American politics (Morris & Joy, 2017; Sellers, 2010). Congress addresses and debates competing ideas and policies on a regular basis. In their study of public responses to congressional communication, Morris and Joy (2017) stated that Congress "was designed to promote extensive deliberation and factional conflict" (p. 3). Previous work looking at congressional speeches has focused on how often members choose to talk (Morris, 2001) as well as how different points in the legislative process, such as committee hearings and markups, influence communication (Morris & Joy, 2017). We build from these perspectives by choosing to focus on the content of congressional talk around an issue with multiple narratives.

When members speak in congressional settings, they not only define the issue, but also construct their relationship *to* the issue. Not all who participate in political discourse have experienced the problem under discussion; therefore, authority must be drawn from other actors. These actors, whom Edelman (1988) calls "experts," can be those who experience the issue, those who are "knowledgeable" about the issue, or those who hold the potential for its solution (pp. 20–21). Congressional representatives speak specifically as those who hold the potential for solution, varying their communication as "experts" based on the setting and medium. Members of Congress develop a "home style" with their constituencies that differs from official communication seen in Washington, D.C., for example (Fenno, 1978). To reach diverse and often factionalized constituencies, members communicate via direct mail, press conferences, and public statements in an attempt to set the public agenda (Lipinski, 2004; Sellers, 2010). This distinction thus requires researchers to investigate certain aspects of these "expert" communications separately. Yet experts can come to different conclusions, a reality that would be reflected in congressional language. In this chapter, we focus on individual, structural, and temporal factors that may contribute to differences in how members of Congress talk about law enforcement issues.

Individual Factors

A member's political party as well as affiliation with the Congressional Black Caucus (CBC) may influence law enforcement talk (Research Inquiry 1). Salient identities are critical to how congressional officials perform and communicate their job duties (Fenno, 1978; Lipinski, 2004; Sellers, 2010). As elites have become more polarized, Republicans and Democrats use increasingly different language to discuss policy (Gentzkow, Shapiro, & Taddy, 2017; Grindlife, 2016). Partisan divisions are particularly apparent on crime policy. Since the mid-1960s and continuing with varying emphasis to the present day, the Republican Party has advocated for punitive "law and order" police measures designed to combat crime (Flamm, 2005). Republican officials also have invoked crime with implicitly racial appeals about violent inner cities, gangs, and drugs at times (see Hurwitz & Peffley, 2005; Mendelberg, 2001). These perspectives may show up in how Republican congressional officials discuss law enforcement. Moreover, the tensions that emerged around controversial law enforcement actions from 2013 to 2015 implicate persistent racial issues in the body politic. We may see these tensions manifest between congressional officials in the CBC versus nonaffiliated members. Research has found that racial identity and experiences can influence congressional members to "pursue group-based politics" (Brown, Minta, & Sinclair-Chapman, 2016, p. 158). Because law enforcement issues touch on both partisan and racial dynamics, we may see individual differences in communication among members of Congress.

Structural Factors

Structurally, we examine cross-branch communication on law enforcement matters between the House of Representatives and the Senate as well as between floor and committee speeches (Research Inquiry 2). These structural factors lend themselves to different forms of communication, debate, and procedure. Compared to the U.S. House, the U.S. Senate is less restrictive on member communication due to its smaller size and egalitarian structure accommodating the rights of the minority party (Paletz, Owen, & Cook, 2011). Indeed, "individual senators hold incredible leverage over a majority leader intent on pursuing a party agenda," including blocking unanimous consent agreements to move legislation or threatening unrestricted debate through a filibuster (Binder & Smith, 1997, p. 12). Although the Senate has tightened restrictions around the filibuster and postfilibuster debate in the last 40 years, the Senate's tradition of extended debate is still valued by its members. Moreover, we explore potential differences between committee and floor remarks as each venue represents a critical point in the legislative process (Paletz et al., 2011).

Temporal Factors

Temporally, we examine the evolution of law enforcement talk between 2013 and 2015 (Research Inquiry 3). During this period, the counternarrative of unjust law enforcement practices came to the fore due to incidents involving White law enforcement and Black individuals. These events included the shooting deaths of Black men and women, including Michael Brown and Eric Garner. Additionally, political movements surrounding the issue of law enforcement (such as Black Lives Matter, Campaign Zero, and Blue Lives Matter) formed and caught significant traction during this time. Therefore, these years provide us a valuable window for investigating whether elite discourse reflected the increasingly contested narrative around law enforcement.

Analyzing Tone in Political Discourse

One tool for textual analysis that has become popular in communication studies is DICTION (Hart, 1984). This software uses a series of lexical dictionaries to assess the rhetorical tone and language characteristics of large amounts of texts. Using this program, researchers have analyzed texts associated with presidents (Hart & Scacco, 2014; Lim, 2008), entrepreneurs (Allison, McKenny, & Short, 2014), conflict managers (Feste, 2011), and more. DICTION operates on four assumptions: "(1) people use words to do things; (2) they use them in varying proportions; (3) audiences react to these deployments cognitively, socially, and emotionally; and (4) they are guided by implicit understandings of rhetorical form when doing so" (Hart, 2014, p. 153). The alignment of these four principles with the theoretical foundations of the narrative perspective and discursive constitution make DICTION an appropriate analytical tool.

The texts used for this study were drawn from the C-SPAN Video Library. Footage mentioning "law enforcement" was collected between 2013 and 2015, and the search was restricted to members of Congress during session or committee. Units of analysis consisted of transcripts of speech created by closed captioning. The unit itself began when the speaker started talking, and ended when he or she stopped talking. These units ranged in size from a single sentence to multiple paragraphs of text. Overall, 2,361 units with the mention of "law enforcement" were collected for analysis in DICTION. Each unit was analyzed individually by the DICTION program, as the program is designed to quantitatively analyze rhetorical tone from large amounts of data.

We use DICTION to look at three different discursive tones: narrative force, transcendence, and tradition to understand potential shifts in and conflict among narratives associated with law enforcement. First, *narrative force* measures the degree of storytelling within a text. As discussed, storytelling is a key rhetorical tool in political discourse, useful for reinforcing and/or challenging identity, socialization, and persuasion. As actors seek to battle for the power to define law enforcement, storytelling could be a useful tool for shaping macro-narratives. Storytelling language was analyzed using Hart's (2014) measure of narrative quality built on five separate lexicons containing embellishment, motion, human interest, temporal, and spatial terms.

Second, *transcendence* is "flying over" the subject by invoking collectivist or ideal language. Transcendence in many ways is the opposite of traditional storytelling in that it avoids focusing on one individual experience and instead broadens the focus to higher purposes or ideals (Hart & Scacco, 2014). It is a commonly used rhetorical tactic in crisis communication (Benoit, 1997), and therefore, it could potentially show up as a defensive strategy when a meta-narrative is challenged. The dictionary used to analyze text for this characteristic encompasses the addition of three lexicons (leveling, collectives, and cognition) and the subtraction of one dictionary (concreteness) in DICTION.

Third, *tradition* tone is language that lifts up the past and other symbolic elements of patriotism and country. A more traditional tone would accompany any discursive attempts to reinforce the historical meta-narrative, another possible responsive tactic to challenge. The tradition dictionary was created by the addition of two lexicons: patriotic and concern for the past (Hart, 2000).

FINDINGS AND DISCUSSION

Storytelling, Transcendence, and Tradition Language in Action

The characterizations of storytelling, transcendence, and tradition language are built upon carefully constructed multilexical searches through the texts. However, it can be difficult for readers to imagine what each of these might look or sound like. Therefore, the following sections provide brief examples of each to act as reference points.

Storytelling

The storytelling tone highlights the kind of descriptive, character-focused, and event-based language often found in narrative form. One example of storytelling language comes from Representative Tulsi Gabbard, a Democrat from Hawaii's 2nd District, speaking on May 15, 2013 in honor of National Police Week:

> In order to support the National Law Enforcement Memorial, my sister Davan, a deputy U.S. marshal, joined more than 1,800 officers last weekend in a 300-mile memorial bike ride from New Jersey to Washington, D.C. She honored the memory of three Hawaii officers killed in the line of duty last year: Eric Fontes, Chad Morimoto, and Garret Davis. They've been honored on the national memorial's wall; and in Hawaii, we're working to establish a local memorial, which will be the last State in the country to do so. Today, I honor these everyday heroes and their families for their unwavering dedication to the safety and service of others. (C-SPAN, 2013a)

In their simplest form, narratives consist of an object followed by the reader between two frames, or separate and significant moments in time (Altman, 2008). In other words, the most basic of narratives have at least one character and two actions by or about that character. In this excerpt, Representative Gabbard utilizes three different narratives: the story of her sister's race, the story of the three officers, and the story of Hawaii's local memorial wall. For example, the three officers were killed in the line of duty (first frame) and they are now being honored by a memorial bike ride (second frame) and a memorial wall in Hawaii (third frame). Beyond simple action, narratives are characterized by their use of descriptive detail, such as the use of spatial and temporal terms. Words such as "last," "weekend," "mile," "year," "Hawaii," "country," and "today" are all lexical clues that a narrative might be occurring. All three stories, though brief, use common humanizing, empathic, and persuasive elements for the structural purpose of narrative creation.

Transcendence

The transcendent tone captures language that avoids specific tangible detail and instead uses terms that indicate higher, more ambiguous and inclusive groups and concepts. One example of this comes from Representative Paul Ryan, a Republican from Wisconsin's 1st District and Speaker of the House, speaking on November 18, 2015 about the terrorist attacks that had just taken place in Paris:

> The events in Paris were horrifying. All of us were shaken by them. Yet we know that whenever terror like this strikes, the world community will rally together. Terror will not prevail. But these events should serve as a reminder: there is still evil out there. We cannot ignore it. We cannot contain it. We must defeat it. And we must protect our people. The country is uneasy and unsettled, and they have every right to be—not because of what they are hearing from politicians, but what they have seen with their own eyes. All of us here, Republicans and Democrats, are hearing these concerns in our offices. (C-SPAN, 2015c)

In this excerpt, we see many examples of leveling and collective words (e.g., "world community," "terror," "evil," "we," "country"). This kind of language serves to minimize group differences and focus instead on more general conceptions. "Flyover" language is one way to understand this trend, as the language seeks to take a bird's-eye view of a situation, rather than providing specific details.

Tradition

Tradition language is designed to potentially anchor dominant themes, providing legitimacy and continuity to narratives. An example of this comes from Representative Sheila Jackson Lee, a Democrat from Texas's 18th District, speaking on December 1, 2014 about the shooting of Michael Brown:

> As I started out in my remarks about the grand jury system, it is one that raises the fact question, and if the fact question is not answered, why were his hands up? Why was he shot these many times? Then you go to a jury of your peers. It is a criminal justice system that no matter what color, creed, race, or religion you are, abiding by the Constitution, you can clearly say a question has been raised, and justice needs to answer that question. Mr. Speaker, that is what we are asking for, a simple justice that allows everyone to stand at the table of opportunity, equality, and rightness. (C-SPAN, 2014)

In this excerpt, Representative Lee leans on traditional American ideographs and institutions to construct legitimacy and rhetorical power. She references the grand jury system, the criminal justice system, and the Constitution in ways that anchor the narrative she wants to tell in elements of the dominant narrative, thereby benefiting from their institutional legitimacy. She does the same for traditional ideographs such as justice, opportunity, equality, and rightness.

Each of these examples provides a snapshot of how the characteristics of storytelling, transcendence, and tradition can appear in the language of elected officials during "law enforcement talk." These tonal characteristics vary in interesting and important manners based on individual, organizational, and temporal factors, however. Understanding how these tonal notes systematically vary will assist in understanding the manners in which law enforcement talk unites and divides members of Congress.

To examine how a storytelling, transcendence, and traditional communicative tone would characterize "law enforcement talk" by members of Congress, we ran separate OLS regression models predicting tonal variation due to party affiliation (Republican = 1), house of Congress (House of Representatives = 1), setting (committee = 1, floor session = 0), year, and membership in the Congressional Black Caucus (membership = 1).

Differences in "Law Enforcement Talk" by Individual Factors (Research Inquiry 1)

The first research inquiry concerned how individual factors associated with a member of Congress's partisanship and membership in the Congressional Black Caucus (CBC) influenced the tonal measures of interest.

Turning first to partisanship, Republican officials were less likely to employ a storytelling tone compared to their Democratic and Independent counterparts in Congress (Table 2.1). Conversely, Republican members of Congress were more likely to use transcendent and traditional language than their more progressive colleagues. For example, the following excerpt of storytelling comes from Senator Cory Booker (D-NJ) speaking on November 13, 2013:

> I spent time with Jeh and I know this is something that he gets. The critical nature of these important partnerships. He understands that to keep community communities safe the relationship between federal law enforcement and local cops, first responders and elected officials is crucial. That's true for the mission where intelligence must be shared between cops and agencies at the federal and state level. It's true for work enforcing our nation's immigration laws as well and

TABLE 2.1 *Predictor Variables in Regression Models of "Law Enforcement Talk"*

Predictor Variables	Storytelling (B)	Transcendence (B)	Tradition (B)
Republican	0.008* (−)	<0.001* (+)	0.015* (+)
House	<0.000* (+)	<0.001* (+)	0.001* (+)
Committee	0.391	<0.001* (+)	<0.001* (−)
CBC	0.026* (−)	0.814	0.002* (+)
2013	0.198	<0.018* (+)	0.024* (+)
2015	0.331	0.170	0.739

*$p < 0.05$, (+) the named variable occurred significantly more, (−) the named variable occurred significantly less.

it's also true for its role in preparing for and responding to disasters. I witnessed that during Hurricane Sandy. During the response to that disaster, it was officials working together at every level to eliminate the loss of life and to begin the recovery process. There's still a long way to go as I discussed last week with administration officials. With Jeh at the helm of the desk I'm confident that New Jersey and communities all over America will have another partner and advocate here in Washington. (C-SPAN, 2013c)

In this excerpt, Senator Booker utilizes two narratives. First, he describes how law enforcement and administrative officials worked together after Hurricane Sandy to manage the crisis. Second, Senator Booker presents a hypothetical narrative, using then secretary of homeland security–designate Jeh Johnson as a specific character within the narrative. Narrative and storytelling readily bring to the front detail and role/character ascription. As can be seen in the above example, hypothetical storytelling can also be used alongside retelling as a communication tool.

The issue of police use of force and/or police targeting of minority communities became a widely discussed political issue during the time span analyzed, as did issues of law enforcement of undocumented immigrants. Storytelling might have occurred less as Republican congressional officials attempted to avoid discussing controversial situations in specific detail—a possibility that would make reliance on a transcendent tone more important. As a co-governing party with a Democratic president, blame also could be assigned to congressional Republicans for perceived deficiencies in law enforcement actions. Thus, this approach may be a form of image management—"flying over" an issue to pull attention away from details and refocus audiences on the things of higher priority (Benoit, 1997). Therefore, this might explain why Republicans demonstrated less storytelling, but more transcendence and tradition language than Democrats or Independents.

Turning next to membership in the CBC, we find that affiliation with this congressional organization also influences how individuals employ law enforcement talk (Table 2.1). Specifically, members of the CBC were less likely to use storytelling language, but more likely to use tradition language when discussing law enforcement than their congressional peers. Membership in the CBC did not significantly predict the use of transcendent language.

The CBC represents a different marker of social and political identity compared to partisan affiliation. Public and political discourse both identified the issue of law enforcement targeting people of color, making the organization's concerns salient both personally and politically. Presumably, the CBC represents the antithesis to the defensive position of law enforcement politics. However, members of the organization used less storytelling and more tradition language compared to nonmembers. In one manner, it could be surprising that members of the CBC did not use then-current events to discuss law enforcement policy. A common tactic for bringing underrepresented groups to light is the narrative (Clair, 1993). However, narratives that challenge the dominant narrative are often seen as illegitimate and more easily contestable; therefore, the testimony of victims who themselves faced potential law enforcement bias may not have been the best rhetorical tactic.

To guard against concerns about legitimacy, language highlighting tradition could be used to construct historic legitimacy—a pivot point to the credibility associated with tradition. One means of reframing current power frameworks for audiences is to make slight adjustments (Brown, 1986). In this case, the dominant narrative of "hero" law enforcement may have been too strong to counter politically with another narrative. Instead, using tradition language as a pivot to another point of view may have been the most appropriate option. For example, the following excerpt comes from Representative Keith Ellison, a Democrat from Minnesota's 5th District, speaking on June 6, 2013, as he proposes new legislation:

> Before the body is a simple amendment, leaders—we have four separate caucuses members of the body, the Congressional Progressive caucus, the Congressional Black Caucus, the Congressional Hispanic American Caucus, and the Congressional Pacific Islander Caucus, it's important to point out—they worked to together to bring this amendment. It's important to remember that the hard-working staff of D.H.S. work hard to keep us safe and we appreciate that we appreciate all law enforcement, especially when they put their lives on the line for us. No one questions the drive of them every day. However, we occasionally hear about racial profiling and too many Americans have been discriminated against because of race, color or ethnicity. It's not what America is all about. This amendment would simply help

to put an end to it. Our amendment is straightforward and cites the Constitution and antidiscrimination laws no funds can be used to engage in ethnic, religious profile. It was the former Bush administration said this is not good policing. We ask this amendment receive the support of the body and that we again affirm our nation which believes in equality under the law and behavior that should inform law enforcement decisions and not simply identity. (C-SPAN, 2013b)

In this excerpt, Representative Ellison cites four congressional caucuses, the Department of Homeland Security, the Constitution, laws, and equality as institutions, traditions, and ideographs to anchor his legislation as part of a dominant, traditional narrative. This positioning then allows him to challenge the narrative by citing racial profiling and discrimination.

Differences in "Law Enforcement Talk" by Structural Factors (Research Inquiry 2)

Organizational and structural factors also played an important role in how members of Congress discussed law enforcement. Specifically, members of the House of Representatives used a more storytelling and transcendent tone compared to their cross-branch colleagues in the U.S. Senate. Conversely, House members' talk was less likely to feature a traditional tone. Organizational setting also mattered for how members of Congress discussed law enforcement. Members' talk about law enforcement in congressional committees contained a more transcendent and less traditional tone compared to members' law enforcement talk during floor proceedings. The storytelling tone did not vary between committees and the floor.

On all three tonal indicators, members of the House used language significantly different from that of members of the Senate. This trend reveals the initial watermarks of a communicative genre, whereby particular ways of symbolic construction reflect and constitute situational constraints (Campbell & Jamieson, 1978; Harrell & Linkugel, 1980). Hart and Scacco (2014), when speaking of the recurring communicative approaches associated with the presidential press conference, note that genres contain "distinguishing characteristics, approaches, and strategies" (p. 79). Quite a bit of scholarly attention has focused on genres of presidential discourse (for example, see Campbell & Jamieson, 2008; Scacco, 2011), with less focus on genres of congressional discourse. We see here that different speaking constraints in the House, as well as representational factors (shorter terms and lack of news attention compared to the U.S. Senate), could explain some of these differences with their cross-branch senatorial colleagues. These results illustrate the efficacy of further research involving cross-branch communicative differences.

Differences in Law Enforcement Talk by Year (Research Inquiry 3)

Research inquiry 3 examines how law enforcement talk may have changed between 2013 and 2015 as the topic evolved in the political sphere. As noted in Table 2.1, members of Congress used a more transcendent and traditional tone when speaking about law enforcement in 2013 compared to 2015. No change occurred in tonal storytelling during that period.

Events involving police between 2013 and 2015 held a significant place in how average Americans and members of Congress discussed law enforcement. Although storytelling language did not change significantly between 2013 and 2015, use of transcendent and tradition language did. From a rhetorical perspective language that attempted to "fly over" the issue and bolster dominant narratives decreased in frequency. For example, this example comes from Republican representative Ralph Abraham from Louisiana's 5th District in 2015:

> I rise today to pay my respect for law enforcement officers, who put your lives on the line to protect our communities and to applaud these men and women who take part in their selfless actions every day. We sleep safely at night because we know the men and women who wear the badges are on the streets looking out for us. They look out for our families, our communities, our country, and words cannot convey how grateful we are to them. (C-SPAN, 2015b)

The next example also comes from 2015, from Democratic representative Chaka Fattah from Pennsylvania's 2nd District:

> On a serious note, for those who are in law enforcement, who are out in dark alleys and who have to confront circumstances that they don't know the exact dangers that they're going to face, the fact that

we want to have weapons that suppress the sound, now we want to have bullets that can pierce armor, and that we want to make sure that under the guise of the Second Amendment that you can have all manner of armament, you know, without any type of reasonable speed bumps that might protect the American public is not something that I'm sure that the majority would want to take such an enthusiastic effort around. (C-SPAN, 2015a)

Both of the examples use some transcendent language by talking about collective groups, but also include specific narrative details. As the dominant hero narrative of law enforcement was challenged, transcendence and tradition language may have become less effective at bolstering. Instead, other rhetorical strategies may have been employed. It is difficult to suggest why storytelling language did not change. Further research should investigate whether time influenced the use of storytelling for different groups within Congress as events unfolded.

The decreased use of transcendence and tradition language is important for a variety of reasons. As discussed earlier in this chapter, the way we talk about a concept shapes it ontologically. When those in power do so, there are very real policy and legal implications. If law enforcement talk becomes less transcendent and traditional throughout this time, it could shape how law enforcement officers are viewed culturally and the law enforcement policy shaped during the legislative process.

A decline in use of transcendence language could decrease the salience of the values, mission, and purpose of law enforcement. This could have many implications, including how the public comes to understand law enforcement actions. Furthermore, less use of tradition language can either legitimize or delegitimize new narrative perspectives. If the dominant narrative of law enforcement is "to serve and protect," tradition language could be used to shut out stories of law enforcement officers being positioned to harm or endanger citizens. However, if a communicator utilizes tradition language to legitimize peripheral narratives, it could position marginalized groups as protagonists within the American historical context. While these outcomes are possibilities of changing language, more research is needed to discover the specific ways dominant narratives of law enforcement have been influenced by changing discourse.

CONCLUSION

This study sought to understand how members of Congress responded to high-profile events involving police between 2013 and 2015, including the changing narrative of law enforcement. Understanding congressional communication is critical for illuminating facets of the legislative process, regardless of topic. Based on narrative theory, we grounded this chapter in the belief that these public communications matter not only for legislative purposes, but also for their potential influence on how law enforcement is discussed in public discourse. The tragic and much-discussed events involving White law enforcement actions in Black communities during this time not only took a prominent place on the public agenda, but also the congressional discursive agenda as well.

Communication literature has shown that the way we communicate about topics shapes their constructed reality. When in the hands of powerful people, these realities can become laws and legislation. If law enforcement represents the protagonist of a hero narrative, legislation is not necessary regulating its behavior or protecting citizens from abuses of power. However, if other narratives begin to powerfully shape the discourse (such as with a fallen angel story, a prodigal son story, or a totalitarian regime story), then not only does the conversation change, but so does the role of law enforcement and law enforcement legislation. It is imperative that communication scholars engage with and analyze how political discourses evolve and change in order to foresee and better understand resulting legislation.

The public pressure placed on police departments, as well as the movement response and resistance to law enforcement actions, have created competing ways of understanding law enforcement's place in civil society. Our findings reveal important variation in how members of Congress discuss law enforcement based on individual, organizational, and temporal factors. Divisions that emerged in social discourse regarding police actions in majority-minority communities found their way into the halls of Congress as well. In the process, our data present the possible first stages of a narrative shift. Specifically, if transcendent language has been key to bolstering dominant narratives of law enforcement, its decreased usage may signal an extended period of narrative contestation. As a result, the stories that counter dominant narratives about heroism may become powerful tools for arguing future legislation.

Time will tell if these competing narratives have a long-standing impact on the dominant law enforcement narrative, and whether this will result in legislative implications. Nonetheless, our findings demonstrate clear shifts and divisions in how law enforcement is discussed even at the highest levels of government. Future research should investigate how these same discourse shifts happen to other political issues and topics, and how these shifts create legal system changes. Future research should also continue to monitor the results of observable changes and tensions, as well as future changes and tensions in discussions of law enforcement in Congress.

Grand gestures—such as rioting, protesting, or waving a blue-striped flag from the back of a truck—can have an incredible impact on the social world, but so can simple conversations. The conversation on law enforcement, at both macro and micro levels, is changing. This harkens a change in the role and regulation of law enforcement, and the narrative that results. This chapter sought to explore these communicative phenomena utilizing the C-SPAN Video Library. In doing so, this chapter acts as an example of the importance and value of the Archives for political and communication research and exploration.

REFERENCES

Allison, T. H., McKenny, A. F., & Short, J. C. (2014). Entrepreneurial rhetoric and business plan funding. In R. Hart (Ed.), *Communication and language analysis in the corporate world* (pp. 21–35). Hershey, PA: IGI Global.

Altman, R. (2008). *A theory of narrative.* New York, NY: Columbia University Press.

Benoit, W. L. (1997). Image repair discourse and crisis communication. *Public Relations Review, 23*(2), 177–186.

Binder, S. A., & Smith, S. S. (1997). *Politics or principle? Filibustering in the United States Senate.* Washington, D.C.: Brookings.

Brown, N. E., Minta, M. D., & Sinclair-Chapman, V. (2016). Personal narratives and representation strategies: Using C-SPAN oral histories to examine key concepts in minority representation. In R. X. Browning (Ed.), *Exploring the C-SPAN*

Archives: Advancing the research agenda (pp. 139–164). West Lafayette, IN: Purdue University Press.

Brown, W. R. (1986). Power and the rhetoric of social intervention. *Communication Monographs, 53*(2), 180–199.

Campbell, K. K., & Jamieson, K. H. (1978). Form and genre in rhetorical criticism: An introduction. In K. K. Campbell & K. H. Jamieson (Eds.), *Form and genre: Shaping rhetorical action* (pp. 9–32). Falls Church, VA: Speech Communication Association.

Campbell, K. K., & Jamieson, K. H. (2008). *Presidents creating the presidency: Deeds done in words.* Chicago, IL: University of Chicago Press.

Clair, R. P. (1993). The use of framing devices to sequester organizational narratives: Hegemony and harassment. *Communication Monographs, 60*(2), 113–136.

C-SPAN (Producer). (2013a, May 15). *House session, Part 2* [online video]. Available from https://www.c-span.org/video/?312666-3/house-session-part-2

C-SPAN (Producer). (2013b, June 6). *House session, Part 2* [online video]. Available from https://www.c-span.org/video/?313136-2/house-session-part-2

C-SPAN (Producer). (2013c, November 13). *Homeland Security secretary nomination hearing* [online video]. Available from https://www.c-span.org/video/?316213-1/homeland-security-secretary-nomination-hearing

C-SPAN (Producer). (2014, December 1). *House session, Part 3* [online video]. Available from https://www.c-span.org/video/?322957-3/us-house-congressional-black-caucus-speeches-ferguson-decision

C-SPAN (Producer). (2015a, June 3). *House session* [online video]. Available from https://www.c-span.org/video/?326244-2/us-house-debate-fy-2016-spending

C-SPAN (Producer). (2015b, September 8). *House session, Part 3* [online video]. Available from https://www.c-span.org/video/?327590-3/us-house-legislative-business-general-speeches

C-SPAN (Producer). (2015c, November 18). *House session* [online video]. Available from https://www.c-span.org/video/?400926-101/us-house-legislative-business

Edelman, M. (1964). *The symbolic uses of politics.* Champaign, IL: University of Illinois Press.

Edelman, M. (1988). *Constructing the political spectacle.* Chicago, IL: University of Chicago Press.

Fenno, R. F. (1978). *Home style: House members in their districts.* Boston, MA: Little, Brown.

Feste, K. (2011). *America responds to terrorism: Conflict resolution strategies of Clinton, Bush, and Obama.* New York, NY: Palgrave/Macmillan.

Fisher, W. R. (1984). Narration as human communication paradigm: The case of public moral argument. *Communication Monographs, 51,* 1–22.

Fisher, W. R. (1987). *Human communication as narration: Toward a philosophy of reason, value, and action.* Columbia, SC: University of South Carolina Press.

Flamm, M. (2005). *Law and order: Street crime, civil unrest, and the crisis of liberalism in the 1960s.* New York, NY: Columbia University Press.

Gentzkow, M., Shapiro, J. M., & Taddy, M. (2017). Measuring polarization in high-dimensional data: Method and application to congressional speech (Working paper). *National Bureau of Economic Research Working Paper Series.* Retrieved from https://www.nber.org/papers/w22423.pdf

Google Books Ngram Viewer. (2017). Search for first responder. Retrieved from https://books.google.com/ngrams/graph?content=%22first+responder%22&year_start=2000&year_end=2009&corpus=15&smoothing=3&share=&direct_url=t1%3B%2C%22%20first%20responder%20%22%3B%2Cc0

Gottschall, J. (2012). *The storytelling animal: How stories make us human.* Boston, MA: Houghton Mifflin Harcourt.

Grindlife, S. (2016). Expressive polarization in political discourse. In R. X. Browning (Ed.), *Exploring the C-SPAN Archives: Advancing the research agenda* (pp. 77–102). West Lafayette, IN: Purdue University Press.

Harrell, J., & Linkugel, W. A. (1980). On rhetorical genre: An organizing perspective. In B. L. Brock & R. L. Scott (Eds.), *Methods of rhetorical criticism: A twentieth-century perspective* (2nd ed., rev.) (pp. 404–433). Detroit, MI: Wayne State University Press.

Hart, R. P. (1984). *Verbal style and the presidency: A computer-based analysis.* New York, NY: Academic Press.

Hart, R. P. (2000). *Campaign talk: Why elections are good for us.* Princeton, NJ: Princeton University Press.

Hart, R. P. (2014). Genre and automated text analysis: A demonstration. In J. Ridolfo and W. Hart-Davidson (Eds.), *Rhetoric and the digital humanities* (pp. 152–168). Chicago, IL: University of Chicago Press.

Hart, R. P., & Scacco, J. M. (2014). Rhetorical negotiation and the presidential press conference. In R. P. Hart (Ed.), *Communication and language analysis in the public sphere* (pp. 59–80). Hershey, PA: IGI Global.

Hart, R. P., Jarvis, S. E., Jennings, W. P., & Smith-Howell, D. (2005). *Political keywords: Using language that uses us.* Oxford, UK: Oxford University Press.

Hurwitz, J., & Peffley, M. (2005). Playing the race card in the post–Willie Horton era: The impact of racialized code words on support for punitive crime policy. *Public Opinion Quarterly, 69,* 99–112.

Kent, M. L. (2015). The power of storytelling in public relations: Introducing the 20 master plots. *Public Relations Review, 41,* 480–489.

Lim, E. T. (2008). *The anti-intellectual presidency: The decline of presidential rhetoric from George Washington to George W. Bush.* New York, NY: Oxford University Press.

Lipinski, D. (2004). *Congressional communication: Content & consequences.* Ann Arbor, MI: University of Michigan Press.

Mendelberg, T. (2001). *The race card: Campaign strategy, implicit messages, and the norm of equality.* Princeton, NJ: Princeton University Press.

Morris, J. S. (2001). Reexamining the politics of talk: Partisan rhetoric in the 104th House. *Legislative Studies Quarterly, 26*(1), 101–121.

Morris, J. S., & Joy, M. W. (2017). Congressional process and public opinion towards Congress: An experimental analysis using the C-SPAN Video Library. In R. X. Browning (Ed.), *Advances in research using the C-SPAN Archives* (pp. 1–31). West Lafayette, IN: Purdue University Press.

Newport, F. (2016, June 14). "U.S. confidence in police recovers from last year's low." Gallup. Retrieved from http://www.gallup.com/poll/192701/confidence-police-recovers-last-year-low.aspx

Paletz, D. L., Owen, D., & Cook, T. E. (2011). *American government and politics in the information age* (version 1.0). Irvington, NY: Flat World Knowledge.

Scacco, J. M. (2011). A weekend routine: The functions of the weekly presidential address from Bill Clinton to Barack Obama. *Electronic Media & Politics, 1*(4), 66–88.

Sellers, P. (2010). *Cycles of spin: Strategic communication in the U.S. Congress.* New York, NY: Cambridge University Press.

Woodside, A. G. (2010). Brand-consumer storytelling theory and research: Introduction to a psychology & marketing special issue. *Psychology and Marketing, 27*(6), 531–540.

CHAPTER **3**

COMMUNICATION AS AN ECONOMIC TOOL AND CONSTITUTIVE FORCE: CHAIRMAN GREENSPAN'S TALK ABOUT UNCERTAINTIES IN FUTURE U.S. CONDITIONS

Lauren Berkshire Hearit and Patrice M. Buzzanell

A previous chairman, Alan Greenspan, cast himself for a time in the role of protagonist, single-handedly driving the action forward. He clearly didn't read about the inevitable destiny of the tragic hero; after decades of being revered around the world, he saw his hubris lead to the near collapse of the entire global economy. (Lin-Manuel Miranda, please call me; I just got a really good idea for your next hip-hop musical.) Greenspan's successors, Ben Bernanke and Janet Yellen, have reverted to the Fed norm of trying to be the human embodiment of an Excel spreadsheet: gray, data-driven, personality-less, passion-free decision makers. (Davidson, 2013, p. MM18)

While the Federal Reserve has evolved over time and is important in the day-to-day enactment of U.S. monetary policy, many everyday Americans do not fully understand the role of the Federal Reserve System, their role as stakeholders, or how to influence the Federal Reserve's actions (Davidson, 2013). However, a growing body of empirical evidence points to a real, tangible effect that monetary news released on Federal Open Market Committee (FOMC) meeting days has on the U.S. financial system, with material effects for the average citizen (e.g., Gurkaynak, Sack, & Swanson, 2005; Rosa, 2011a, 2011b, 2013). Under Chairman Alan Greenspan, the quantity of communication from the Federal Reserve greatly increased. Greenspan's reported use of communication highlights the need for a greater understanding of how communication functions within the Federal Reserve not simply as a tool but also as a constitutive force for creating realities.

One potential purpose of Federal Reserve communication is to manage the uncertainty of financial markets. While scholars have begun to extend uncertainty management to organizational settings (e.g., Kramer, 1999, 2004), it has been done with an eye toward organizational members and their management of job transfers and other kinds of uncertainties related to career and workplace dynamics.

This chapter, conversely, takes a macro-level view of organizational uncertainty management and examines whether an organization itself can manage uncertainty about the future through the content of its messages. Specifically, we ask: What does Federal Reserve chairman Alan Greenspan talk about during his opening statements to Congress? Not only are we interested in the content of such talk but we also investigate how such discourse might be related to the management of uncertainty.

The practice of congressional testimony is common in our democratic government. Congress seeks testimony from other individuals for a variety of purposes. These testimonies can be held to inform legislation, investigations, and/or oversight. Testimonies are given publicly by the individuals called before Congress or congressional committees. The chairman of the Federal Reserve is routinely called upon to report to Congress and a variety of congressional committees on U.S. monetary policy. As chairman of the Federal Reserve, this context for monetary talk was a routine practice for Alan Greenspan (Sicilia & Cruikshank, 2000). (See Figure 3.1.)

Moreover, Greenspan was a unique figure in Federal Reserve history, and he arguably enjoyed higher status and recognition than his modern counterparts (Conti-Brown, 2016). Part of his unique ethos was the reliance that the government had on his testimony and insights. For example, while campaigning during the 2000 presidential election, John McCain went so far as to

FIGURE 3.1 Federal Reserve Board chairman Alan Greenspan appears before the Joint Economic Committee to testify on economic policy.

say he would pull a *Weekend at Bernie's* if Chairman Greenspan died while McCain was president ("Presidential Debates," n.d.). *Weekend at Bernie's* was a comedy film released in 1989 in which one of the main characters, Bernie, is killed. When Bernie's colleagues discover his dead body, they maintain the illusion that Bernie is alive. McCain's comment that he would pull a *Weekend at Bernie's* if Greenspan died—in other words, attempt to maintain the illusion for all that Greenspan was still alive and in control—underscored not only the public's perceived importance of Greenspan and his role as chairman of the Federal Reserve, but also that Greenspan was both highly trusted and transformative. Yet the content of his communication was difficult to understand, and Greenspan "prided himself on 'mumbling with great incoherence'" (Blinder, Goodhart, Hildebrand, Lipton, & Wyplosz, 2001, p. 911); Greenspan himself wrote in his memoir that his style of communication was intentional, designed to prevent jolts to the market (Greenspan, 2007).

Therefore, this chapter examines the content of Chairman Alan Greenspan's communication during hearings before Congress to provide an interesting case study to explore *how* the Federal Reserve, under a widely recognized chairman, communicated expectations about the future performance of the economy. To do so, we first present an overview of scholarship on uncertainty management and the Federal Reserve's economic communication. Then, we use the C-SPAN Archives' online Video Library videos and transcripts and the Federal Reserve Archives to illustrate how a coding schema was created and subsequently used to examine a corpus of data. Finally, we discuss the implications of this project.

PREVIOUS RESEARCH

This section first explores the current literature on uncertainty management as it relates to organizational communication. Then, we position the Federal Reserve's communication within the Federal Reserve System and the broader context of economic policy communication (EPC). Economic policy communication is conceptually based in the fields of political science, economics, and communication, and seeks to understand the Federal Reserve's communicative relationship to monetary policy.

Uncertainty Management

Uncertainty management theory (UMT) is considered a contemporary update and extension of uncertainty reduction theory (URT), as uncertainty reduction theory was considered overly simplistic in its initial formulation and with its emphases (e.g., Babrow, Hines, & Kasch, 2000; Babrow, Kasch, & Ford, 1998). Originally an interpersonal theory developed by Berger and Calabrese (1975), URT posited that within a dyadic interaction, both individuals are motivated either to reduce or maintain their level of uncertainty regarding the future actions of their partner through information-seeking strategies. URT is comprised of two prediction and explanation phases: an individual will try to predict the most likely alternative actions his or her partner might take by asking the partner questions, and after the interaction, an individual will try to make retroactive sense of the partner's behavior.

As the theory was originally conceptualized, Berger and Calabrese (1975) argued that increased communication can reduce levels of uncertainty, given that they assumed that uncertainty in its positive forms as excitement and stimulation would only be rewarding to a certain point. For example, if someone could completely predict his or her partner's behavior, there may be costs to the interpersonal relationship, like boredom. As proposed by Berger and Calabrese (1975), uncertainty likely would be reduced over time, meaning that uncertainty typically is highest at the beginning of a relationship.

Uncertainty Management in Organizational Contexts

Although scholars have applied uncertainty management to organizational contexts (e.g., McPhee & Zaug, 2001), the work of Kramer (1993, 1999) and his colleagues (e.g., Kramer, Dougherty, & Pierce, 2004; Kramer, Meisenbach, & Hansen, 2013) is perhaps the most systematic application and extension of uncertainty management in organizational contexts. For example, Kramer, Dougherty, and Pierce (2004) examined the uncertainty of airline pilots during a major airline merger and acquisition. In this study, they examined organizational members (in this case, airline pilots) and the sources of information (e.g., the union, colleagues, and the media) that these members sought and used during periods of organizational uncertainty.

Later work conceptually decoupled the importance of information seeking and uncertainty management/reduction, extending URT in important ways. For example, Kramer and colleagues (2013) examined the ways in which volunteers navigated uncertainty. Because volunteers have a unique status within organizations given their contributions to the work itself but they are positioned outside of organizational hierarchies and official roles, their status might contribute to perceptions of uncertainty about their roles within an organization. Although focused on volunteers, this study extended URT to more complex organizational contexts and may be transferable to others who are in boundary-spanning roles and positions in hybrid organizations for which traditional lines of authority and role are assumed to be less straightforward, clear, and unambiguous. Furthermore, throughout the corpus of his work, Kramer (1999) argues that "people may reduce uncertainty through cognitive processes rather than by seeking information or act based on motives that supersede uncertainty reduction" (p. 96).

Whereas this body of literature on uncertainty management has broadened and deepened understanding of these communication process, it remains limited in its application to organizations per se and in its examination of discourse, specifically economic discourse, for uncertainty management. First, existing scholarship examines the process of managing organizational *member* uncertainty, but not how the organization *itself* communicates uncertainty to its members. To expand scholarship on organizational uncertainty management, we take as our starting point the conceptualizations of organizations as having social personae, or in other words, as holding legal, social, and juristic status in society (e.g., Cheney, 1983). In this extension, the communication of an organization itself during periods of significant uncertainty is worth studying to see whether the propositions advanced by uncertainty management scholars about formation, advantages and disadvantages, and/or lessening and managing uncertainties originally formulated for interpersonal and organizational interactants prevail among organizations as actors. Therefore, this study works to extend uncertainty management to the Federal Reserve and look at the ways in which an organization *itself* can manage uncertainty through its communicative messages.

An organization is communicatively constituted; it is any body of members bound together by a set of norms, rituals, and rules that are set, communicated, and reinforced over time. Moreover, as it is communicatively constituted, its members bring the organization into being and enter and exit over time, crossing boundaries of knowledge, legitimacy, and connection (Miller, 2015). An organization also communicatively positions itself to interact with other organizations (Miller, 2015). This chapter constitutes the Federal Reserve as an organization in order to explore the ways in which it communicates with its various stakeholders, specifically, in its external communication to Congress. This study provides a unique case in which to understand how an organization with an economic identity like the Federal Reserve communicates about the future performance of the economy. Of note to this study, Scacco (2014) examines how presidents shape expectations and develops a typology to identify sentences in presidential communication that reference the future. He uses future-tense verbs (e.g., "will," and "should"), coupled with a specific expectation in his content analysis of presidential signing statements, State of the Union addresses, and tweets. This study utilizes and extends his typology to the context of the Federal Reserve and how it shapes expectations regarding the future performance of the economy by using it to identify instances where Chairman Greenspan discusses the future of the U.S. economy.

Second, this study extends emphases on discourse, particularly economic discourse, as playing an important role in alleviating concerns about the future (Smith, 1795/2013). Economists have pointed to the technical and difficult language of economics for noneconomists and have gone so far as to recommend that economists adapt their rhetoric to work with, for example, policymakers who may only have a basic understanding of the ways in the which the economy reacts to change, is shaped, or can be managed (Goodwin, 1988). Studies on how economic actors such as the president of the United States shape public opinion on the economy argue that the sentiments of these economic actors ("the relative optimism of presidential remarks about the economy and its specific dimensions," Wood, 2007, p. 19) help to establish a climate for the economy and help economic actors to interpret economic processes and to affect economic confidence.

If any president is considered an important economic actor that can affect economic confidence, we argue that so, too, can the Federal Reserve chairman affect economic confidence. While a president has a much broader reach than a Federal Reserve chairman who seems to communicate to economic elites, one way that the president can affect economic confidence is through the framing of the economy. Therefore, this chapter develops a schema for a quantitative content analysis using the C-SPAN Video Library for the purpose of understanding *what* the Federal Reserve chairman says about the future performance of the economy, and *how* he or she talks about the future performance of the economy. These two aims are necessary steps with which to begin studies that can explore the management of economic uncertainty. This aim and our review of the literature led to this chapter's research question: How does Greenspan talk about and frame the future performance of the U.S. economy?

METHOD

To examine the ways Greenspan speaks about the future performance of the U.S. economy and to understand the sentiment with which he speaks about the economy (i.e., is he positive, negative, or neutral in his framing of the future of the economy), this chapter employs content analysis.

Content analysis is a quantitative method designed for a systematic, reproducible, and valid reading of a corpus of texts (Krippendorff, 2012). The scientific technique of content analysis allows—to an extent—for the separation of the researcher from the text, but the conceptualization of the content analysis and interpretation of the results can never be fully divorced from the researcher (Krippendorff, 2012).

To conduct a quantitative content analysis on a sample of 20 transcripts of Alan Greenspan's congressional testimony during his term as chairman of the Federal Reserve (1987–2006), we used the C-SPAN Video Library. When selecting Greenspan's testimony before Congress as Federal Reserve chairman, we found 241 videos in the C-SPAN Video Library. We deliberately chose to include the first, midpoint, and final congressional testimonies to capture potential variation over time. Uncertainty reduction theory (URT) argues that within an interpersonal context, uncertainty is a function of time. Based on work by Hart (1987) on presidential communication changes over the course of an administration, this emphasis on time holds for organizational contexts as well. In other words, the longer Greenspan served as chairman of the Federal Reserve, the more likely (according to URT) uncertainty regarding Federal Reserve communication should decline. Therefore, after identifying Greenspan's first, midpoint, and final congressional testimonies, a random sample of Greenspan's testimony at different points during his tenure as chairman was chosen for the remaining 17 testimonies so that time could be controlled in the analyses, yielding 20 total congressional testimonies for analysis, or 2,934 sentences for coding. To code, we used the closed captioning transcripts as much as possible, but in some instances, closed captioning was unavailable for our use. In those instances, we went to the Federal Reserve Archives and used the written testimony submitted by the Federal Reserve to Congress.

To develop our codebook, we watched several of Greenspan's testimonies in the C-SPAN Video Library and qualitatively coded for themes. Once we had a large number of themes, we met to condense individual themes (e.g., stability, security, strength, growth) into broader ideas and conceptualizations (e.g., stability). We coded and discussed codes in ways that represented the spirit of Greenspan's language, or in other words that had validity, and began to test our codebook for reliability.

Specifically, 10% of the data set (294 sentences) was randomly sampled for reliability as recommended by Krippendorff (2012). A minimum score of .68 (Krippendorff, 2012) was obtained for all codes before coding moved from the reliability stage to full coding. Intercoder reliability for each code is included in Table 3.1.

Greenspan only referenced the future performance of the U.S. economy 17.9% of the time ($n = 524$). Within the 17.9% that Greenspan referenced the

TABLE 3.1 *Intercoder Reliability*

Greenspan: N = 2,934	Krippendorff's Alpha
Economic future mentioned	0.88
Improvement	0.78
Uncertainty	0.68
Stability	0.77

future of the U.S. economy, he mentioned economic improvement 21.6% of the time ($n = 112$), uncertainty about the future of the economy 30.1% of the time ($n = 156$), and economic stability only 13.9% of the time ($n = 72$). Overall, his tone indicated that he was negative only 19.3% of the time ($n = 567$) and positive 53.6% of the time ($n = 1571$). These percentages and sentences indicated that he was neutral in tone for 27.1% of the time ($n = 796$). Following is the coding schema we used and a description and example for each of these codes.

Development of the Codebook

To code at the sentence level, we had to identify which sentences might shape the public's expectation about the economy (see Table 3.2). To do so, we first identified sentences that made a direct mention of the economy using future-tense verbs like "will," "should," "can," or "expect" in conjunction with an economic reference (see Scacco's 2014 typology). For example, during testimony before the Senate Committee on Banking, Housing, and Urban Affairs on July 13, 1988, Greenspan said:

> A more serious *long-run threat to price stability could come from* government actions that introduced structural rigidities and increased costs of production. ... Protectionist legislation, inordinate hikes in the minimum wage, and other mandated *programs that would impose costs* on U.S producers *would adversely affect* their efficiency and international competitiveness. (C-SPAN, 1988, emphasis added)

Several phrases in this comment by Greenspan referenced the future performance of the economy. When he says "could come from government actions," Greenspan was making a reference to the future of the economy

TABLE 3.2 *Intercoder Reliability*

Code	Sentence-Level Variables
Economic future mentioned	Future-tense verbs (e.g.: "will," "would," "shall," "should," "can," "could," "expect," "anticipate," "forecast," "foresee," or "predict"; Scacco, 2014) and a reference to the economy/entitlement program impact on economy
Improvement	Coded "improvement," "resilience," "strength," "growth," "better," "develop," "expand," "depend," and a reference to the future performance of the economy
Uncertainty	Coded "uncertainty," "weakness," "fragility," "unsure," "doubt," "contraction," "threaten," "volatility," "cautious," and a reference to the future performance of the economy
Stability	Coded "stable," "smooth transition," "no change," "steady," "static," "sustained," and a reference to the future performance of the economy

and the impact government actions and/or policies could have on it. Later in this testimony, Greenspan goes on to say:

> The fall in the dollar we have already experienced over the last few years, even allowing for the dollar's appreciation from the lows reached at the end of last year, has set in motion forces that should continue to narrow our trade and current account deficits in the years ahead. The associated loss of foreign-funded domestic investment is likely to adversely affect overall investment unless it can be replaced by greater domestic investment financed by domestic saving. *Such a fiscal cutback should help counter future tendencies* for further increases in U.S. interest rates and declines in the dollar, partly by instilling confidence on the part of international investors in the resolve of the United States to address its economic problems. (C-SPAN, 1988, emphasis added)

When he stated, "Such a fiscal cutback *should* help counter future tendencies," Greenspan is setting an expectation about the future of the economy and, to an extent, what actions the Federal Reserve could take to meet this expectation.

Greenspan's testimony often made reference to the future performance of the U.S. economy, but we also wanted to know what topics Greenspan mentioned in talking about the U.S. economy. We found three major themes in Greenspan's testimony: improvement, uncertainty, and stability.

Coding Improvement

Improvement references any type of economic improvement, growth, or expansion. For example, Greenspan said, "A small persistent rise in some of the indexes *would be tolerable,* given the inadequate adjustment for trends in quality *improvement* and the tendency for spending to shift toward goods that have become relatively cheap" (C-SPAN, 1988, emphasis added). As this sentence was coded for economic future ("would be tolerable"), we then examined the statement for other content. In this case, improvement was coded.

But this code could also reference negative improvement, too. For example, Greenspan testified, "It is important to recognize as I indicated earlier that the negative effects of federal deficits on growth in the capital stock *may be attenuated for a while* by several forces in the private sector" (C-SPAN, 1989, emphasis added). In this sentence, economic growth "may be attenuated for a while," meaning that economic growth may not happen. Rather, there may be stagnant economic growth in the future. While this is technically coded under our coding scheme, this does illustrate a limitation to this method: in attempting to maintain the reliability of our codebook, this requires a balance with validity. This is why using a sentiment code (conducted through computerized coding) helps shape and provide color for these findings and codes.

Coding Uncertainty

Uncertainty was the second code we examined once we established mentions of the economic future. To code uncertainty, we looked for mentions of words like "uncertainty," "weakness," "doubt," "contraction," and "volatility." For example, Greenspan ended his testimony by saying, "But allowing deficits to persist courts a dangerous corrosion of our economy and *risks potentially significant reductions* over time in our standard of living" (C-SPAN, 1989, emphasis added). His statement indicates that there may be economic volatility in the future. His wording, "risks potentially significant reductions," indicates uncertainty—the words "risk" and "potentially" allowed us to code for uncertainty.

A second example of our uncertainty code comes from testimony before the Joint Economic Committee in 1990. Greenspan testified, "Looking forward, recent data are offering mixed signals about future capital spending. For example, orders for nondefense capital goods received in November and December show a bounceback from the decline that had occurred in the third quarter. Other indicators of capital spending, however, give the impression of *softness ahead*" (C-SPAN, 1990a, emphasis added). The words "softness ahead" indicate some uncertainty and potentially change to the future of the economy and its performance, making reference to a slight worsening or change to current economic conditions.

Coding Stability

The final code used to demarcate when Greenspan mentioned the future of the economy was "stability." To code for stability, we looked for references to stability, smooth transitions, no change, steady, static, or sustained (e.g., sustained growth) in Greenspan's language. During a May 8, 1990, testimony before the Senate Agriculture, Nutrition, and Forestry Committee, Greenspan said:

> We believe some changes to the existing regulatory system are necessary to avoid the prospect that jurisdictional disputes among regulators will impede innovation in our financial markets, but consolidation of jurisdiction is not necessary to achieve this objective Federal Margin Regulation. A prominent area of disagreement among those interested in the *smooth functioning of our capital markets* has been the appropriate level of margins for stock index futures and the need for federal authority over such margins. (C-SPAN, 1990b, emphasis added)

The language "smooth functioning of our capital markets" indicates economic stability in the context of changing regulatory systems in the financial markets. The assurance of stability is especially important as investors and market-watchers alike would take note of Greenspan's testimony and respond to language indicating instability or uncertainty.

A second example of this code is from a February 27, 1997, testimony before the Senate Banking, Housing, and Urban Affairs Committee. In his testimony, Greenspan stated:

> As always, with resource utilization rates high, we would need to watch closely a situation in which demand was clearly *unsustainable* because it was producing escalating pressures on resources, which could *destabilize* the economy. And we would need to be watchful that the *progress* we have made in keeping inflation expectations damped was not eroding. (Greenspan, 1997, emphasis added)

Language like "unsustainable," "destabilize," and "progress" meant both these sentences were coded for stability. However, just like with the "uncertainty" code, a sentiment score is needed to answer if this a positive or negative reference to stability.

Therefore, after we coded our entire data set of 20 randomly selected testimonies from Chairman Greenspan's tenure at the Federal Reserve, we also used a computer-run sentiment analysis to create sentence-level and testimony-level sentiment scores. Importing the data into RStudio, we used the "tidytext" package to isolate each word from the sentence column, giving it its own column. Common English stopwords were removed. Then, using Bing Lexicon, a sentiment analysis indexed each word by the date. There were more than 19,000 words. RStudio identified 176 positive words (e.g., advanced, ample, applaud, exceptional, extraordinary) and 195 negative words (e.g., endanger, erode, difficult, detriment, trouble unavoidably, undermine). In other words, we could identify whether an individual sentence was positively or negatively emotionally charged; this analysis gave insights into the net positive and net negative sentiment for the entire testimony.

RESULTS

After obtaining reliability on our codebook, we coded the full data set and then ran a series of chi-square tests, crossing negative sentiment and mentions of the future performance of the U.S. economy, and crossing positive sentiment and mentions of the future performance of the U.S. economy. The results of the chi-square test are included in Table 3.3.

TABLE 3.3 *Chi-Square Results for Alan Greenspan*

Variable	Chi-Square	df	p	n
Neg*Economic Future	0.43	1	.84	2,933
Neg*Economic Improvement	11.96	1	.001**	518
Neg*Economic Uncertainty	10.33	1	.001**	519
Neg*Economic Stability	.09	1	.77	517
Pos*Economic Future	6.78	1	.008*	2,933
Pos*Economic Improvement	41.40	1	.001**	518
Pos*Economic Uncertainty	17.17	1	.001**	519
Pos*Economic Stability	7.02	1	.008*	517

*$p < .05$; **$p < .001$.

Notably, results revealed a statistically significant difference between negativity and economic improvement ($X^2(1) = 11.96$, $p = .001$, $\Phi = .15$), and negativity and economic uncertainty ($X^2(1) = 10.33$, $p = .001$, $\Phi = .14$). Conversely, a statistically significant difference between positivity and economic future ($X^2(1) = 7.98$, $p = .008$, $\Phi = .05$), positivity and improvement ($X^2(1) = 41.40$, $p = .001$, $\Phi = .28$), positivity and uncertainty ($X^2(1) = 17.17$, $p = .001$, $\Phi = .18$), and positivity and stability ($X^2(1) = 7.02$, $p = .008$, $\Phi = .12$) emerged.

DISCUSSION

This chapter worked to understand the content of Alan Greenspan's congressional testimony and to explore what, if any, association existed between the content of Greenspan's communication and the sentiment with which he spoke about the economy. To examine this relationship, we used the C-SPAN Video Library to create a coding schema. Several examples of each code were provided to illustrate how the coding schema was created, and also to demonstrate how the coding took place.

Then, a series of chi-square tests examined how Greenspan spoke when framing the future performance of the U.S. economy. Greenspan spoke both positively and negatively about future economic improvement and future economic uncertainty. Conversely, he only spoke positively about economic stability. This tendency toward speaking positively might indicate his and others' expectations that negative sentiment about economic stability could have negative repercussions on the U.S. economy. This reasoning seems to be an intuitive result, yet such trends in our data and their interpretations could highlight Greenspan's awareness about the sensitivity and positivity with which he needed to speak about future economic stability.

Besides developing and using a codebook for economic uncertainty content, this study contributes to the academic literature by positioning the organization itself as an actor in uncertainty management, noting that communication operates both as a tool and as a constitutive force in public economic discourse by using the content of Greenspan's communication as an illustration. This extends work on uncertainty management within organizational communication as previous scholarship has not linked organizational and economic communication to examine the talk itself—what was said and how it was said—in these specific contexts over time. Furthermore, the utilization of the C-SPAN Video Library in an organizational and economic communication context further extends the ways in which the Video Library can be used in academic research in the discipline of communication.

This study worked to extend Kramer's (1999, 2004) findings on uncertainty management. Specifically, this study sought to understand how the chairman of the Federal Reserve communicated uncertainty in his testimony about the economy before Congress. Other organizational communication studies have found that that organizational members faced with uncertainty go to the media, colleagues, and other sources to manage their uncertainty levels (e.g., Kramer et al., 2004; Kramer et al., 2013). Understanding how Greenspan communicated uncertainty about the economic future is important. Not only does this study extend Kramer's (1999, 2004) work to another aspect of organizations (namely, how a CEO or head of an organization communicates about future uncertainty or future expectations), but this study has practical implications for everyday individuals who have a part in the stock market.

While future research should work to confirm these findings, future analysis of Federal Reserve chairman communication (and potentially CEOs when conveying financial performance information) should recognize that a relationship exists between economic performance indicators, economic topics discussed, and the valence with which they communicate this information. The schema developed in this chapter provides a starting point for these studies. Moreover, additional work to examine the extent to which Federal Reserve chairmen are reacting to economic performance measures during their testimony may further inform how sentiment helps shape public expectations about future economic performance or make sense of current economic trends.

Limitations and Future Directions

A limitation of this chapter is that only 20 congressional testimony transcripts were coded. Future studies would want to take this limitation into account in order to have sufficient power to detect significant effects.

A second limitation of this chapter is that findings can only be extended to a broader corpus of Chairman Greenspan's testimony. In other words, these results are not generalizable. Therefore, scholars and practitioners should acknowledge the unique position and ethos Greenspan enjoyed and recognize that these results should be applied only tentatively to other chairmen of the Federal Reserve System.

A final limitation of this chapter is the method itself. Although content analysis provides a useful tool for researchers to systematically interrogate the content of a text, trade-offs between reliability and validity exist. Therefore, these results should be interpreted with caution, and future experimental projects should work to validate or confirm these results.

Future studies should expand the number of congressional testimonies and chairman studied in order to look for differences over time, differences based on congressional committee, and other interesting patterns. Ambitious studies should consider the ways in which economic volatility data may indicate the ways in which the U.S. economy is reacting to the content of the chairman's communication and incorporate these data for an added level of sophistication. Further studies should use the entire video segments available through the C-SPAN Video Library so that nonverbal communication such as facial expressions, paralinguistic cues, posture, and other aspects could be included in a more embodied sense of economic uncertainty management.

In closing, this chapter presents a first look at how a well-regarded chairman of the Federal Reserve attempted to manage uncertainty about the economy through the content of his talks. Although uncertainty management would not be the only goal that Chairman Greenspan would have wanted to pursue, it functions as a primary part of his role. In investigating how Greenspan spoke about the future performance of the U.S. economy, this study opens the doors for other research that integrates organizational and economic communication as a tool and as a constitutive force in economic policy and everyday economic discussions.

ACKNOWLEDGMENT

We would like to thank C-SPAN for the grant that enabled us to pursue this research and its presentation. Lauren would like to express her gratitude to Josh Scacco, Cody Wilson, and Elizabeth Hinz for their thoughtful comments on earlier iterations of this project.

REFERENCES

Babrow, A. S., Hines, S. C., & Kasch, C. R. (2000). Managing uncertainty in illness explanation: An application of problematic integration theory. In B. B. Whaley (Ed.), *Explaining illness: Messages, strategies and contexts* (pp. 41–67). Hillsdale, NJ: Erlbaum.

Babrow, A. S., Kasch, C. R., & Ford, L. A. (1998). The many meanings of uncertainty in illness: Toward a systematic accounting. *Health Communication, 10,* 1–23. https://doi.org/10.1207/s15327027hc1001_1

Berger, C. R., & Calabrese, R. J. (1975). Some explorations in initial interaction and beyond: Toward a developmental theory of interpersonal communication. *Human Communication Research, 1,* 99–112. https://doi.org/10.1111/j.1468-2958.1975.tb00258.x

Blinder, A., Goodhart, C., Hildebrand, P., Lipton, D., & Wyplosz, C. (2001). *How do central banks talk?* Geneva Reports on the World Economy, No. 3. London, UK: International Center for Monetary and Banking Studies.

Cheney, G. (1983). The rhetoric of identification and the study of organizational communication. *Quarterly Journal of Speech, 2*(69), 143–158. https://doi.org/10.1080/00335638309383643

Conti-Brown, P. (2016). *The power and independence of the Federal Reserve.* Princeton, NJ: Princeton University Press.

C-SPAN (Producer). (1988, July 13). *Federal monetary policy* [online video]. Available from https://www.c-span.org/video/?3353-1/federal-monetary-policy

C-SPAN (Producer). (1989, January 31). *1989 economic outlook* [online video]. Available from https://www.c-span.org/video/?6007-1/1989-economic-outlook

C-SPAN (Producer). (1990a, January 30). *Economic outlook for 1990* [online video]. Available from https://www.c-span.org/video/?10821-1/economic-outlook-1990

C-SPAN (Producer). (1990b, May 8). *Jurisdiction of the SEC and the CFTC* [online video]. Available from https://www.c-span.org/video/?12234-1/jurisdiction-sec-cftc

Davidson, P. (2013, Oct. 9). Ben Bernanke helped lead nation out of crisis. *USA Today*. Retrieved from https://www.usatoday.com/story/money/business/2013/10/09/bernanke-steps-down/2897829/

Goodwin, C. D. (1988). The heterogeneity of the economists' discourse: Philosopher, priest, and hired gun. In A. Klamer, D. N. McCloskey, & R. M. Solow (Eds.), *The consequences of economic rhetoric* (pp. 207–220). New York, NY: Cambridge University Press.

Greenspan, A. (1997). *The Federal Reserve's semiannual monetary policy report*. Retrieved from https://www.federalreserve.gov/boarddocs/hh/1997/february/testimony.htm

Greenspan, A. (2007). *The age of turbulence: Adventures in a new world*. New York, NY: Penguin.

Gurkaynak, R., Sack, B., & Swanson, E. T. (2005). Do actions speak louder than words? The response of asset prices to monetary policy actions and statements. *International Journal of Central Banking, 1*(1), 55–93.

Hart, R. P. (1987). *The sound of leadership*. Chicago, IL: University of Chicago Press.

Kramer, M. W. (1993). Communication and uncertainty reduction during job transfers: Leaving and joining processes. *Communication Monographs, 60*, 178–198. https://doi.org/10.1080/03637759309376307

Kramer, M. W. (1999). Motivation to reduce uncertainty: A reconceptualization of uncertainty reduction theory. *Management Communication Quarterly, 13*, 305–316.

Kramer, M. W. (2004). *Management uncertainty in organizational communication*. Mahwah, NJ: Lawrence Erlbaum Associates.

Kramer, M. W., Dougherty, D. S., & Pierce, T. A. (2004). Managing uncertainty during a corporate acquisition: A longitudinal study of communication during an airline acquisition. *Human Communication Research, 30*(1), 71–101. https://doi.org/10.1111/j.1468-2958.2004.tb00725.x

Kramer, M. W., Meisenbach, R. J., & Hansen, G. J. (2013). Communication, uncertainty, and volunteer membership. *Journal of Applied Communication Research, 41*(1), 18–39. https://doi.org/10.1080/00909882.2012.750002

Krippendorff, K. (2012). *Content analysis: An introduction to its methodology* (3rd ed.). Thousand Oaks, CA: Sage.

McPhee, R. D., & Zaug, P. (2001). Organizational theory, organizational communication, organizational knowledge, and problematic integration. *Journal of Communication, 51*(3), 574–591. https://doi.org/10.1111/j.1460-2466.2001.tb02897.x

Miller, K. (2015). *Organizational communication: Approaches and processes* (7th ed.). Stamford, CT: Cengage Learning.

"Presidential Debates." (n.d.). *The American Presidency Project.* Retrieved from http://www.presidency.ucsb.edu/ws/?pid=105436

Rosa, C. (2011a). Words that shake traders: The stock market's reaction to central bank communication in real time. *Journal of Empirical Finance, 18*(5), 915–934. https://doi.org/10.1016/j.jempfin.2011.07.005

Rosa, C. (2011b). The high-frequency response of exchange rates to monetary policy actions and statements. *Journal of Banking and Finance, 35*(2), 478–489. https://doi.org/10.1016/j.jbankfin.2010.09.008

Rosa, C. (2013). The financial market effect of FOMC minutes. *Federal Reserve Bank of New York Economic Policy Review, 19*(2), 67–81.

Scacco, J. M. (2014). *Presidential prediction: The strategic construction and influence of expectation frames* (Doctoral dissertation). Retrieved from Texas ScholarWorks. Stable URL: http://hdl.handle.net/2152/25959

Sicilia, D. B., & Cruikshank, J. L. (2000). *The Greenspan effect: Words that move the world's markets.* New York, NY: McGraw-Hill.

Smith, A. (2013). *Essays on philosophical subjects.* Memphis, TN: General Books. (Original work published 1795)

Wood, D. B. (2007). *The politics of economic leadership.* Princeton, NJ: Princeton University Press.

CHAPTER 4

REFLECTIONS ON THE C-SPAN VIDEO LIBRARY AND THE STUDY OF CONGRESS

Janet M. Martin

The papers emerging from the conference The Research Possibilities of the C-SPAN Archives provide a foundation for mining data available through the C-SPAN Archives' online Video Library. With gavel-to-gavel coverage of all House and Senate floor proceedings, coverage of many hearings, interviews, call-in programs, and policy conferences, the Video Library remains a largely untapped resource for researchers. The chapters included in this volume by Alyssa A. Wildrick and Alison N. Novak ("Constructing Congressional Discourses: C-SPAN Archives and Congressional Speeches on Crises and Scandals"), Cody Blake Wilson and Joshua M. Scacco ("Exploring Congressional 'Law Enforcement' Talk"), and Lauren Berkshire Hearit and Patrice M. Buzzanell ("Communication as an Economic Tool and Constitutive Force: Chairman Greenspan's Talk About Uncertainties in Future U.S. Conditions") use different methodologies in focusing on the rhetoric of policymakers. Each chapter looks at how the use of language may shape policy. While all of the work is in preliminary stages, the research contributes to an understanding of how members of Congress and executive branch officials can selectively choose words that can bring about a change in policy.

The authors all come from the field of communications, but the research presented opens up methodologies that can also be easily adapted to research questions by those in such disciplines as political science, policy studies, and economics. The studies are all imaginative in identifying research questions and in mining the Video Library. The authors' use of different methodologies in focusing on the rhetoric of policymakers suggests the many ways in which the Archives can be used to glean information heretofore rarely tapped.

The chapter by Alyssa A. Wildrick and Alison N. Novak provides interesting research in how the words "crisis" and "scandal" are used by members of Congress. The authors set out to see if and when members of Congress use these words, and then if there is an identifiable distinction in how the terms are used. And, they ask, what is the impact of that distinction?

Wildrick and Novak find that in fact there is a difference in how the words "crisis" and "scandal" are being used. "Crisis" is used to bring attention to an issue; "scandal" adds a normative dimension in that the word is being used strategically to force some type of response. The response might be in suggesting that one has a responsibility in seeing that there is a resolution to the crisis, or that one will be held accountable for a disaster that might result if a scandal isn't taken seriously.

The use of the word "scandal" goes one step beyond that of "crisis." Wildrick and Novak note the impact of this distinction. In the chapter the authors suggests that perhaps the word "crisis" has been used to such a large extent that it doesn't set off the alarm bells that the word "scandal" can in bringing attention to an issue. The author notes that Minority Leader Nancy Pelosi (D-CA) and Secretary of State John Kerry each have found the use of the word "crisis" to be overdone, to the point that when the word "crisis" is used there is no response on the part of Washington policymakers.

The chapter gives us a look at the richness of the C-SPAN Archives in that scholars can look at how issues are framed by members and in what setting. With all floor speeches available for study, the C-SPAN Video Library is ideal for this type of analysis. In this study, we see how floor speeches may lead members of Congress to use the word "crisis" in a way that, perhaps, party leaders might not.

The analysis suggests a number of different areas ripe for research. The data in this study could be easily expanded. Similar research could be done on the rhetoric of different members—do party leaders or committee chairs identify issues as crisis or scandal when they speak on the floor? Or would a committee chair invoke the same words in bringing an issue to the floor? Given that the term "scandal" seems to have a normative association, in that action or responsibility is to be taken if a crisis moves in the direction of a scandal, either by specific actions or through neglect, it might be unlikely for a leader in the majority party to move an issue onto a "scandal" agenda. Former Speaker and Minority Leader Nancy Pelosi (D-CA) is quoted in the chapter as saying, "let's just call everything a 'scandal' and be done with it. You want people to pay attention, tell them it's scandalous. That's human nature." And perhaps committee members, with an eye on the needs of the institution, might forgo framing an issue as a scandal if in doing so it would compel a substantive response by the committee.

This study helps one ferret out nuances between the terms "crises" and "scandals" as used by members of Congress. The authors suggest an agenda for future researchers to look at the "success rate of policies proposed within the context of scandals and crises." It might be that the oversight role of Congress more readily lends itself to the use of such data. Policy proposals might not be as much an end goal as would be oversight by a committee, with appropriate hearings.

It might be that a different set of words could take the findings in a different direction. Along with "crisis" members of Congress also talk of "emergencies" or "dire emergencies." The term "scandal" might appear more frequently in the context of ethics violations, rather than in terms of addressing policy needs. And "emergencies" are built into congressional statutes (e.g., "The National Emergencies Act"). Imminent government shutdowns, as appropriations bills miss target dates with the start of a new fiscal year, are viewed by members as "emergencies." Declaring a situation an "emergency" can hasten a response. But it is also a term that can't be used lightly.

Whether "emergency" would yield different results is not known, but the term is one that members of Congress might use if action was sought in a particular area. If "crisis" was paired with "emergency" rather than with "scandal," it could be that the researchers would find more examples in the areas of policy; and perhaps oversight, linked to scandal, would add a new dimension to oversight studies.

In Cody Blake Wilson and Joshua M. Scacco's chapter, "Exploring Congressional 'Law Enforcement' Talk," the focus is on the "content of congressional talk around an issue with multiple narratives" (p. 27). The focus of analysis is on the narrative. Storytelling is a "key rhetorical tool in political discourse" (p. 30). Specifically, they look at "how members of Congress navigated the changing currents of the law enforcement narrative" (p. 22). Law enforcement covers a wide range of individuals, from those working in the area of homeland security, with a focus on terrorism, to those working in border control, customs, and immigration. "Law enforcement" also covers federal, state, and local officials and activities. The variation in the use of the term "law enforcement" warrants study in and of itself, especially since September 11, 2001.

The authors set out an interesting and ambitious research line to see if the narrative surrounding talk on "law enforcement" has changed. Does Congress reflect changes in the public narrative? Can the narrative be used to influence policy and goals?

If the focus is on race relations and law enforcement, it might prove more fruitful to look at members speaking about "police" and variants such as "policing," which more directly get at measurements of change in the narrative. For example, while the authors focus on Representative Keith Ellison's use of "a dominant traditional narrative" in positioning his introduction of new legislation regarding ethnic and religious profiling, it is important to note Ellison's pivot from a narrative on law enforcement to one linking the issue to the Bush administration and "policing."

The authors note potential benefits in "further research involving cross-branch communicative differences" (p. 38). They find that House and Senate members use language that is "significantly different." In part this may reflect the structured nature of House floor debate, with the Rules Committee's use of rules setting forth time for debate as well as amendments allowed, which both limits and structures debate. Speaking on the floor of the House would not be at all comparable to Senate debate structured by unanimous consent agreements that often are modified. It might be that House "One Minutes" would have more in common with Senate "Morning Business." Or a focus on the type of speech—for example, "One Minutes" in the House—may provide a needed control in order to detect more variation in the content of speeches over time.

In the chapter by Lauren Berkshire Hearit and Patrice M. Buzzanell, "Communication as an Economic Tool and Constitutive Force: Chairman

Greenspan's Talk About Uncertainties in Future U.S. Conditions," the authors provide an interesting variable for scholars of the Federal Reserve Board and the U.S. economy to consider. Using regular testimony before Congress, their analysis opens up a new way to study the rhetoric of the Federal Reserve chair. And Congress, with the availability of the C-SPAN Video Library, provides the vehicle for systematically examining the impact of this discourse between the chair and the committee. Their research convincingly examines how the statements made by Federal Reserve chairs, in regular testimony before Congress, might manage uncertainty by "communicat[ing] expectations about ... future performance of the economy" (p. 48).

Future scholars can look at confirmation hearings and subsequent testimony to see if there is a similar effect on the markets. Or confirmation hearings can be mined to see if early and subsequent indicators of monetary and fiscal policy can be gleaned in the testimony given in the confirmation hearing. Moreover, the discourse between a chair-designate and committee members might shed light on congressional response to the Federal Reserve, and any influences that might be had on fiscal policy.

One aspect of the data collected by the authors allows for a test to see if the opening statements of the chair of the Federal Reserve Board, read from prepared remarks and available through the archives of the Federal Reserve, is the same as the remarks read live, recorded, and available through the C-SPAN Video Library. The additional materials prepared and submitted to the committee might extend beyond the actual recorded remarks.

All of these chapters contribute to a better understanding of a public strategy in the rhetoric of political leaders. C-SPAN, as an unmediated resource, provides an ideal way to look at the public strategy of political leaders in different settings and with different targeted audiences. While some authors are presenting a first cut at the data in using the C-SPAN Archives, all are building on prior research of others demonstrating how research involving the Archives can create new data sets that allow familiar topics to be examined with different methodologies.

I am writing this in December 2017 as the 115th Congress nears the end of the first session, awaiting the fate of a major tax code overhaul. In reflecting upon the commonalities and differences in how one describes action in Congress, one is struck by how often budget stalemates are described as a "crisis." And one is also struck by an inability on the part of members to use the term "scandal" in describing the Senate's stealth vote, near 2 a.m. on a Saturday morning (December 2, 2017), on the largest tax overhaul in over thirty years on a bill cobbled together with handwritten notes in the margins, not even available in a printed copy before the bill was amended and passed on the Senate floor. Congress fails to use the term "scandal." Over the years Congress comes up with legislative proposal after legislative proposal to find a solution to growing debt, yet in the dead of night greatly expands that debt. Somehow budget crises avoid becoming self-described "scandals."

It becomes apparent in reading about Congress that when Congress appears to be heading over the "fiscal" cliff, due to partisan gridlock or failure to reach agreement on an omnibus appropriations bill, we never refer to the situation surrounding political leaders as a "scandal." The impasse is referred to as a "fiscal crisis." And perhaps, by using the term "crisis," an opportunity for the type of response needed and seen when a "scandal" is identified is deliberately missed.

CHAPTER 5

USING C-SPAN TO EXAMINE THE POLITICAL DISCOURSE OF HIV/AIDS, 1985–1987

Nancy E. Brown

In the 1980s, the AIDS crisis challenged the resilience of gay and lesbian activists. Friends, family members, and loved ones died from an unknown syndrome as activists fought to secure funds for research, services, and education. In 1981, the first media reports of unusually lethal cancers and pneumonias sensationalized the patients' drug use and homosexuality. By the summer of 1982, scientists had identified possible transfusion-associated immune problems in the heterosexual population. In 1983, AIDS became a cover story that was difficult to ignore as conflicting reports on the safety of the blood supply and the potential for casual communicability circulated. The public reacted with fear and uncertainty. Some responded with blame and anger toward gay men. Others demonstrated compassion toward people with AIDS. The media hype of 1983 dissipated in 1984 but surged again in 1985 with increased attention on the spread of AIDS in the heterosexual population. Medical discoveries gave hope of a vaccine or treatment but also revealed that people who tested positive could remain symptom-free and transmit the virus unknowingly. Some called for mandatory testing for all in high-risk groups and quarantine for any who tested positive. Parents organized to keep children with the AIDS virus out of their children's schools. Meanwhile, 12,529 people had succumbed to the opportunistic infections associated with AIDS (Thirty Years, n.d.).[1]

While struggling to meet the immediate needs of people with AIDS, activists continued to fight for protection of their rights. The newly formed Human Rights Campaign Fund (HRCF), the first national political action committee dedicated to lesbian and gay issues, promoted a national civil rights bill. They sought to bring their message of gay and lesbian rights as human rights into the "mainstream." As the AIDS crisis grew, HRCF attempted to use its nascent political connections to influence federal AIDS policies and funding. They also educated activists at their annual leadership conference (see Figure 5.1). Community-based AIDS service groups formed the Federation of AIDS Related Organizations (FARO) at the Second National AIDS Forum in Denver (1983). Under the name AIDS Action Council, FARO became the only national lobbyist group dedicated solely to AIDS issues. The council attempted to broaden the public's compassion for all people with AIDS. The messaging of HRCF and the AIDS Action Council intersected and placed human rights and health care in the same framework. My investigation considers the organizations' strategies and reach during the period 1985–1987 when fear and uncertainty were high. My research question considers whether the activists' messaging entered public and political conversations and how the messages were received during this period of high anxiety.

The C-SPAN Archives' online Video Library affords a unique glimpse into both the public and the political realm. Programming includes legislative hearings, call-in programs featuring legislators, political figures, activists and journalists, and political event coverage such as national meetings, organizational panels, and speeches. The variety of program formats provides examples of political positions as well as the voices of the public and activists. As a primary source, the C-SPAN Video Library offers an unmediated glimpse of multiple points of view. For this chapter, I examined the available videos that mentioned gay and lesbian rights or AIDS from July 1985 through October 1987 for evidence that the activists' messages circulated in the public and on Capitol Hill. Although an analysis of C-SPAN videos does not denote the full reach or impact of HRCF and AIDS Action Council messaging, the broad swath of coverage types does provide an indication of the depth to which their objectives circulated.

FIGURE 5.1 C-SPAN televises a conference of the Human Rights Campaign Fund.

THE HUMAN RIGHTS CAMPAIGN AND POLITICAL POWER

The first section of this chapter considers the Human Rights Campaign Fund (HRCF) and perceptions of gay and lesbian political power. The HRCF board promoted their goal of a national civil rights bill "by supporting and educating candidates for federal elective offices" (By-laws, 1982). Early on, they established working relationships with key figures in Washington including Representatives Henry Waxman (D-CA) and Ted Weiss (D-NY) and Senators Alan Cranston (D-CA) and Lowell Weicker (R-CT), leaders who sponsored the national civil rights bill and later chaired congressional committees on AIDS testing, drug development, and funding. These political relationships included campaign contributions.

In his memoirs, organization founder Steve Endean described the early funding distribution strategy HRCF applied throughout the 1980s. "We decided we would make only small contributions, rather than major ones, to safe incumbents ... [that] would leave us with resources for the really big races" (Endean & Eaklor, 2006, p. 112). By 1982, HRCF had raised enough money to distribute $140,000 to 118 congressional candidates (25 Years, n.d.). Also in 1982, they convinced former vice president Fritz Mondale to speak at a major HRCF fund-raiser. The audience applauded Mondale's remarks about the Democratic Party's commitment to "eliminate all laws, rules and regulations which discriminate against individuals on the basis of sexual orientation" (Smothers, 1982). The dinner raised $400,000. Referring to the 1982 election, Endean asserted, "[It] helped us start to turn the corner—bringing the gay and lesbian rights movement into the mainstream" (Endean & Eaklor, 2006, pp. 106, 116).

The political impact of the HRCF campaign contribution strategy is difficult to assess. Sources claim the HRCF won 81% of the 1982 races and 69% of the 1984 races it contributed to (Endean & Eaklor, 2006, p. 116; HRCF, 1984). A 1984 HRCF newsletter broadly interpreted the success of the election: "The victory goes far beyond the election of men and women who will continue to speak out in the Congress for human and civil rights. A more important underlying result is that support for the issue of human rights is spreading." The report balanced the celebratory remarks with an acknowledgement that incumbency played a critical role in many of the races—both won and lost. Despite a few points of discouragement, the election summary concluded, "But taken as a whole, the 1984 election was a solid victory for gay rights" (HRCF, 1984). The small donation strategy allowed the HRCF to claim sponsorship of many campaigns and thereby associate more candidates with gay and lesbian civil rights; however, the policy of providing small sums to "safe" candidates diminishes the significance of the success rate.

The AIDS crisis complicates the evaluation of HRCF's victory claims. Videos in the C-SPAN Video Library suggest the perceived political clout of those who supported gay and lesbian civil rights. Callers, activists, reporters, political groups, and legislators mentioned the gay community's power; however, fear and uncertainty over the communicability of AIDS shaped the perceptions of power. Some blamed the spread of AIDS on government inaction due to the political influence of gay activists. Often, those in strongest opposition to gay rights credited activists with the greatest political influence. Three 1985 call-in programs bared the intensity of the response.

In the summer of 1985, *Life* magazine published a dramatic cover story on AIDS titled "Now No One Is Safe From AIDS"; beloved movie star Rock Hudson announced he had AIDS and died shortly after; and children with AIDS were entering schools. The newly developed blood test for the HTLV-III virus amplified concern as the public began to understand that people could transmit the virus prior to having any symptoms of AIDS. In September, *Newsweek* correspondent Mary Hager spoke to C-SPAN host Brian Lamb about her experiences covering the AIDS story. In general, callers wanted to discuss medical and social issues rather than media coverage. Several expressed hostility toward the gay population's perceived political power. A male caller from Reno, Nevada, argued that extreme precautions including quarantines used for hepatitis and measles should apply to AIDS. He forcefully concluded, "I don't see why we are suddenly being urged not to worry about it—everything's just fine—because it happens to attack a politically powerful segment of the society." A few minutes later, a caller from Yonkers, New York, complained about the defense of "the homos" and the leniency of the liberal press. Hager responded by describing two extreme views she had heard as a reporter. The first claimed, "One reason AIDS has gotten so much attention is because it is in the homosexual community and this was a very well-organized lobbying group." The other asserted a solution would have been found by now if the afflicted were from the Chamber of Commerce. Hager placed her opinion in the middle of the two (C-SPAN, 1985a). These AIDS conversations reveal a divide between the gay community and a segment of the population that was angry and fearful about the spread of AIDS. Whether or not the gay lobby had succeeded in influencing government policies on AIDS, some concluded they had the power to do so.

A few weeks later, Representative William Dannemeyer (D-CA), a strong critic of same-sex relationships, discussed his legislative goals to protect Americans from AIDS on a C-SPAN call-in program. Dannemeyer spoke directly of his resistance to elevating the "status of male homosexuality to a civil right." Several times, he complained that public health officials' concern for "homosexual sensitivities" had resulted in poor public health decisions. Referring to San Francisco, he claimed, "The political authorities of that city are so beholden or fearful of the political backlash of the male homosexual community that they're just standing around doing nothing." He continued, "Because they don't want to complicate or impair their ability to get political contributions from a very powerful, small special interest group." The next caller, from Richmond, California, complained that the media did not show both sides of the issue due to the "extremely powerful" homosexual community (C-SPAN, 1985c). Dannemeyer heightened the intensity of his moral complaints and his comments about medical uncertainty with fearmongering about the ability of the gay community to influence public officials to make poor decisions that would endanger the public's health.

The C-SPAN Video Library also included videos featuring leaders from gay activist organizations. In November, C-SPAN offered a call-in program with Nancy Roth, the executive director of the Gay Rights National Lobby (GRNL). Roth fielded questions from often antagonistic callers. Roth maintained an even demeanor as she asserted, "The rest of society has chosen to make the gay and lesbian lifestyle a political issue by making it perfectly legal to discriminate against us because we are gay men and lesbians. If it were not legal to discriminate against us, it would no longer be a political issue." C-SPAN host Brian Gruber asked Roth about conservative Democrats who felt the Democratic Party lost votes in the 1984 election because of the platform support for "groups such as yours." In reply, Roth discussed GRNL efforts to educate both parties. "And they're beginning to understand that there's tremendous voting power and tremendous disposable income within the gay and lesbian community. We were named the seventh largest voting bloc in the United States last year at the height of the 1984 election hype. So that begins to tell you what kind of political hype we can have." In additional answers, Roth advanced GRNL strategies and goals, and asserted political strength (C-SPAN, 1985d). C-SPAN covered other activists sharing messages about gay rights including Jeffrey Levi, executive director of the National Gay Task Force (NGTF); Paul Popham, a founder of the Gay Men's Health Crisis and of AIDS Action Council; and Marguerite Donoghue, spokesperson for AIDS Action Council. In a sense, C-SPAN assisted activists' efforts to share their message with the public.

The three 1985 call-in programs demonstrate that HRCF's assumption of political victory was acknowledged by others; however, the reaction to the perceived political strength created a backlash when applied to the AIDS crisis. Fear drove some of the responses. While activists had decried the federal government's limited response to the AIDS crisis for several years at this point, some people now blamed the activists' political power for interfering with the government's response to the crisis.

The C-SPAN coverage of the chief justice confirmation hearings of Associate Justice William Rehnquist affords a glimpse of attitudes about gay and lesbian rights outside of the AIDS discourse (1986b, 1986c). Activist Jeffrey Levi firmly opposed Rehnquist's promotion to chief justice because of his previous rulings restricting freedom of speech and freedom of association. He placed his rebuke of Rehnquist's record on civil liberties for gay and lesbians in the broader context of rights for every American. Levi cautioned, "These positions are threats to all Americans, not just homosexuals, because once we start making exceptions to fundamental constitutional rights for one group, it becomes increasingly easy to allow the government to intrude on the freedom of others" (C-SPAN, 1986b). Levi's ability to testify demonstrates that the message of gay and lesbian rights as commensurate with civil and human rights had crossed a threshold of political viability.

Activists succeeded in getting their message heard but still faced significant opposition. Watching the video clip adds nuance to the available written testimony. A brief exchange between Levi and Hearing Chair Strom Thurmond (R-SC) reveals Thurmond's disregard for the gay community. Thurmond asks if gays and lesbians can receive treatment to "change them and make them normal like other people?" He follows up with another question about whether "they could be converted to be like other people?" (C-SPAN, 1986b). While the written words could be interpreted as uninformed questions, on the video, the countenance and vocal inflection of both men indicate a pointed verbal sparring match. Thurmond did not engage in Levi's testimony on civil and human rights; rather, he pressed Levi to acknowledge that gays and lesbians were not "normal."

As the confirmation process continued the next day, Representative Ted Weiss (D-NY) also spoke in opposition to Rehnquist's confirmation. Weiss delivered his erudite comments with force and conviction. He argued, "[Rehnquist] will further divide this country between the privileged and the poor, between black and Hispanic and white, between men and women, between homosexual and heterosexual, between the majority and the minorities." By placing potential division between homosexual and heterosexual people in the same framework as economic, racial, gender, and political division, Weiss indicates gay and lesbian men and women were one of several minorities that could be at risk rather than an exceptional minority at risk. Later during questioning, he again placed "sexual orientation" in the same category as minority and women's rights. Weiss's overall testimony condemned Rehnquist's failure to protect the civil rights of all citizens (C-SPAN, 1986c). By embedding "homosexual" rights within the civil rights movement, he located gays and lesbians in the larger struggle for a cohesive America. His inclusion demonstrated his open support of the gay and lesbian struggle for civil rights extended beyond sponsorship of the national rights bill.

C-SPAN's coverage of the hearing testimony gave the public an opportunity to evaluate Associate Justice William Rehnquist's nomination to chief justice far beyond that available in newspaper articles or the evening news broadcasts. Although only a small fraction of the total testimony, Levi's and Weiss's statements asserted the significance of gay and lesbian civil rights as a determining factor in the promotion of a Supreme Court justice and demonstrated the political resonance of the gay and lesbian rights movement without specifically discussing its power.

Republicans had lost the Senate majority in the 1986 midterm election. In August 1987, C-SPAN offered a behind-the-scenes view of the Republican campaign process as the party anxiously planned for the 1988 presidential election. The program exposed conservative dismay over the power of the gay lobby and displayed the antigay climate that motivated HRCF's continued efforts. Similar to the content of the 1985 call-in programs, the AIDS discourse negatively intersected with the conversation on gay and lesbian rights.

The group Young Americans for Freedom sponsored a panel on AIDS that featured Representative Newt Gingrich (R-GA) and Joseph Sobran, senior editor of the conservative *National Review*. Gingrich labeled Senator Ted Kennedy (D-MA) and Representative Waxman as "princes of power" who led a community of the "radical values" Left in which Gingrich declared the homosexual rights advocates were a significant faction. Gingrich called Waxman (a politician supported by the HRCF) a "chief prince" and warned the audience that "The princes of power in order to keep their power will do what their radical allies insist because that's how their community works." Sobran's remarks condemned liberal sexual values he referred to as the "sex and drug networks" and the "fluids exchange networks." He denounced President Reagan's appointment of an "avowed homosexual and gay activist" to the President's Commission on the HIV Epidemic and expressed surprise at the power of the "homosexual lobby" as the "most embarrassing and ludicrous example of a special interest lobby in American politics." Both Gingrich and Sobran implied that political expediency caused liberals to make irresponsible and expensive decisions regarding AIDS (C-SPAN, 1987a). Although not mentioned by name, the panel members characterized efforts by groups such as the HRCF as immoral and dangerous.

Returning to the Human Rights Campaign Fund's hope that the 1984 election portended gay and lesbian acceptance into the "mainstream," one can use the C-SPAN Video Library to sample some of the messages circulating in the public discourse in the following years. Lists of campaign contributions and candidate success rates do not clearly demonstrate the political power of activist organizations; however, claims of gay political power originating from both the opposition to and support for gay rights add weight to assumptions of gay activist power. The HRCF did not achieve its goal of a national gay and lesbian civil rights bill; nevertheless, the message of protecting gay and lesbian civil rights had entered the wider political discourse. The ability of activists such as Roth and Levi to address the national audience of C-SPAN suggests the HRCF message did reach the mainstream; however, videos also demonstrate that acceptance of the message, particularly in reaction to the AIDS crisis, was limited.

AIDS ACTION COUNCIL AND THE PUBLIC HEALTH CRISIS

Gary MacDonald, the first executive director of AIDS Action Council, saw his role as an ambassador for AIDS. Although many of the board members represented gay rights organizations, MacDonald asserted, "The council had deliberately decided not to position itself as a gay organization" (Andriote, 2011, p. 202). AIDS service organizations and gay and lesbian rights groups including the Gay Men's Health Crisis, the National Gay Task Force, and AIDS Project Los Angeles funded AIDS Action Council's lobby project (FARO update, 1983, p. 3). The NGTF and the GRNL worked through the AIDS Action Council to coordinate congressional lobbying (*AIDS Action Update*, 1984b, p. 15).

The AIDS Action Council communicated the organization's goals and strategies in a series of newsletters. Efforts to increase AIDS funding dominated the issues. The newsletters also encouraged members to build coalitions in their local community and shared information about how to organize grassroots letter-writing campaigns to support the council's efforts. The articles confined discussion of civil rights to matters related to AIDS. Topics of concern such as the soon to be released HTLV-III antibody blood test and member success stories rounded out the issues. In this chapter, I will confine my investigation of AIDS Action Council's message to one goal—shifting the public's view of AIDS to recognize it as a global public health crisis rather than a gay problem.

The council adopted several strategies to reframe AIDS including coalition building and messaging that linked AIDS to the larger public. The first newsletter noted, "A little creative discussion of actual interests and the wide-ranging impact of AIDS on virtually every sphere of American life goes a long way toward convincing people of the urgency of this crisis." The council offered members talking points to promote public support of AIDS research and education. The points highlighted the applicability of AIDS research to cancer, infectious diseases, and immune disorders research. They concluded, "Solving the AIDS mystery through intensive research will thus definitely benefit the overall health of the nation." Funding for public education would also have social benefits for all. During 1984 and 1985, the public was uncertain about AIDS transmission vectors. The council argued that education would reduce the hysteria of those not at risk and potentially "demystify homosexuality" by providing opportunities for heterosexuals to meet gay people (*AIDS Action Update*, 1984a, pp. 5–7).

In a later newsletter, MacDonald argued that the council needed to convince people that AIDS is "a disease to which everyone is potentially vulnerable" and that "AIDS ... is in fact a very dangerous general public health emergency" (*AIDS Action Update*, 1985, p. 7). In reflection 10 years later, Jean McGuire, AIDS Action Council executive director (1988–1990), commented, "'De-gaying' the epidemic, and playing upon the fears of heterosexuals that they were also at high risk became the main strategy of gay AIDS advocates, including the AIDS Action Council" (Andriote, 2011, p. 205). During the news lull and perceived complacency of 1984 and early 1985, the council's strategy of calling attention to public vulnerability seemed reasonable to its members.

C-SPAN videos reveal that the message of AIDS as a public health crisis gained political traction but also generated resistance. In legislative hearings on AIDS funding, research, and testing, committee chairs expressed undifferentiated support for people with AIDS; however, some committee members and panel speakers still viewed the crisis in terms of innocent victims versus gay men and IV drug users. In 1987, C-SPAN programs on media coverage of AIDS provided opportunities for public response. Similar to the interactions observed in the 1985 call-in programs discussed earlier, callers often strayed from the intended topic of discussion. Their comments reveal how some negatively applied the message of AIDS as a public health emergency.

Senator Lowell Weicker sat as chair on a Senate Appropriations Subcommittee regarding funding for AIDS. In a 1985 session, he concluded his opening remarks with a strong statement of expectation. "Today we do not have the cure for AIDS. But neither do we have the ignorance of our ancestors who cast lepers in the sea and the mentally ill in the dungeons. As our society presses the attack on AIDS with vigor and resoluteness, those among us who suffer this disease deserve understanding and help. We in the United States are one people. And by fact or law there will be no pariahs among us" (C-SPAN, 1985b). Representative Ted Weiss, chair of the House Subcommittee on Intergovernmental Relations and Resources, opened a 1986 hearing on the status of AIDS drug development with remarks that did not identify the sexuality of people with AIDS. He frankly stated, "Twelve thousand men, women, and children have died from the disease and over 100,000 are believed to exhibit ARC—AIDS Related Complex " (C-SPAN, 1986a). The people were not homosexuals or heterosexuals, high-risk groups or innocent victims; they were Americans who had died. A year later, Representative Henry Waxman, chair of the subcommittee on Health and the Environment, supported legislation to protect the confidentiality of people with AIDS and to diminish discrimination. At a hearing on AIDS testing, he presented his position as apolitical and scientific: "This is not liberal or conservative, it is not a Democratic or Republican position, it is the position of the experts in medicine and public health... and every professional group that has looked at AIDS" (C-SPAN, 1987b). All three chairs presented AIDS as a national public health concern in line with AIDS Action Council strategy.

Representative William Dannemeyer sat on the 1987 committee on AIDS testing chaired by Waxman. The video clearly revealed the tension between those who supported voluntary testing with confidentiality protection measures and Dannemeyer, who had introduced legislation requiring mandatory testing for marriage licenses, all hospital patients, and prostitutes. The intensity of the disagreement comes to fore with the first witness, June Osborn, dean of the School of Public Health at the University of Michigan. Osborn warned that mandatory measures could shake society's "pluralistic foundations." Waxman followed up with a series of questions. He asked why the government could not mandate people to get testing and whether mandatory testing for marriage and driver's licenses would reach more people. Without the cues that tone of voice, facial expressions, and body language provided by the video, one might assume Waxman's rhetorical questions supported mandatory testing; however, he spoke with a pleasant inflection and Osborn smiled and nodded as they interacted (C-SPAN, 1987b).

Osborn's comportment changed as she answered Dannemeyer's questions. Although he began his questioning with a smile, Dannemeyer quickly became frustrated with Osborn's responses. She was critical of his questions and deflected them with a lecturing tone on medical technicalities. At times, he interrupted and talked over her answers. Dannemeyer concluded with strong words that accused Osborn of defying logic and supporting unsound policy, and then mocked her expertise. The uncomfortable exchange ended as Waxman called the next speaker (C-SPAN, 1987b). Although the conversation centered on the medical, financial, and social issues regarding AIDS testing, the underlying dispute placed those who recognized the health needs and civil rights protection of all people living with AIDS in conflict with those who felt the general public needed protection from people living with AIDS and others deemed to be engaged in unacceptable activities. In the two years since the 1985 call-in program, Dannemeyer had certainly learned more about the limited communicability of AIDS and heard messages about AIDS as a public health crisis. He continued to view AIDS as a gay health crisis that could be kept out of the public with restrictive measures.

In 1987, C-SPAN offered a few programs that evaluated media coverage of AIDS. Panel members at a Radio-Television News Directors Association meeting offered poignant reflections of the frustrations they encountered. Journalist Jim Merriam, who had written many of the early AIDS stories for United Press International, related how people often assumed there had already been enough AIDS media coverage. He discussed the continued hysteria and fear and urged journalists to write "story after story" to get the message across. Merriam echoed AIDS Action Council strategies to bring AIDS closer to the public. He concluded, "Unfortunately, the other thing that will help bring people around is that as there are more and more people with AIDS, more and more people will get to know somebody who has AIDS or know somebody who knows somebody who has AIDS and that's going to help change attitudes, I think" (C-SPAN, 1987d).

Robert Bazell, science and medical correspondent for NBC, followed Merriam on the panel. Bazell discussed how difficult it had been to convince producers and editors to include AIDS stories in 1982 and 1983. He described their standard response: "Why would we want to put on a story about a disease that is affecting gays and drug addicts ... there's not that many of them, it's not that big of a deal, there're not many cases." He tied his next anecdote to Merriam's remarks: "Then Rock Hudson died and suddenly America knew somebody who died of AIDS. Well, here was a communal experience, we all knew Rock Hudson.... So that kinda shocked people and suddenly there was an endless appetite of stories for AIDS" (C-SPAN, 1987d). Merriam and Bazell mirrored the council's talking point on "demystifying homosexuals" and AIDS through familiarity.

The conflicting messaging about compassion for people with AIDS and the "very dangerous general public health emergency" generated mixed results. Panelist Laurie Garrett from National Public Radio expressed a different opinion. She urged the audience of reporters to avoid sensationalizing AIDS stories with emotional community responses that validated fears. At one point, she specifically disagreed with Merriam's idea that more cases would help change attitudes.

> I think when there are more cases around, hysteria will get worse. People will start feeling it closing in on them. They start feeling "ooh"—it's in our town in Ohio. My god, it's in Oklahoma. It's come to Memphis. It's here in North Dakota. When that's starts happening, there will be a greater and greater temptation to resort to authoritarian means to solve the problem, to resort to vigilante means to solve the problem. (C-SPAN, 1987d)

Garrett concluded her remarks by urging reporters to educate their audiences (C-SPAN, 1987d).

Polls conducted in 1987 reveal the continued need for education. A Gallup Poll found 30% of those surveyed believed insects could transmit AIDS with another 15% uncertain. At least a quarter of those surveyed responded that people could catch AIDS from donating blood, food handling, drinking glasses, and coughs (Gallup, 1987). A separate qualitative analysis concluded, "Underlying respondents' attitudes and behaviors regarding AIDS was a strong current of perceived personal vulnerability and confusion which should not be underestimated" (Kaplan, 1987). C-SPAN call-in programs vividly reflect the anxiousness and anger this uncertainty created. For example, in a program meant to discuss the challenges journalists faced as they wrote about the AIDS crisis, Robert Engelman, correspondent for Scripps Howard News Service, and Philip Boffey, deputy editor of the *New York Times,* spoke to more than 20 callers from 12 states. Callers wanted to discuss insect transmission; AIDS as a right-wing plot to get rid of undesirables; AIDS as an international biologic weapon; media conspiracies; Haiti and cheap gay sex; why the media ignored the Christian interpretation of AIDS—referring to the punishment of God; why media reports conflicted; LaRouche's claims; sexual acts and transmission; mandatory testing and quarantine. Some demonstrated a lack of knowledge about the state of AIDS medical research and a distrust of official sources (C-SPAN, 1987c). Similar to Mary Hager's responses to callers in 1985, Engelman and Boffey's answers educated the public on medical and policy issues and debunked speculative claims.

Additionally, the journalists challenged viewers who condemned the gay community or suggested mandatory testing or quarantine. Boffey asserted that the issue of testing should be treated as a civil rights issue. In response to a caller who argued that if the government could ban smoking, they should stop homosexuals, he gave a lengthy reply. After explaining how the presence of the AIDS virus in the gay community was a historic accident, he informed viewers, "I think the public should always look upon it as from the point of view—even if I am from a heterosexual family—this could be my son, my daughter, and it could be spreading like herpes did" (C-SPAN, 1987c). Boffey effectively articulated the message AIDS Action Council had proposed in 1984; however, the call-in program demonstrated the message was not accepted by all.

In the 1985 call-in programs discussed earlier, some voiced anger over the political power of the "homosexual" lobby. They did not trust experts' assurances on the limited communicability of AIDS and demanded the government provide better protection from accidental exposure. In 1987, callers expressed resentment about the government's civil rights protection of people with AIDS in regard to mandatory testing and quarantine. By this time, the public understood that a person could transmit the HIV virus prior to exhibiting any symptoms of AIDS. Although the language of the complaint had shifted from political power to civil rights, the impetus and intent remained the same. Some callers feared people who had AIDS and felt the government should identify, regulate and possibly remove them.

During 1984, when it seemed the public did not care about AIDS, the AIDS Action Council conceived a message similar to the HRCF message of "gay rights are human rights." They advocated for recognition of AIDS as a universal health crisis rather than just a gay crisis. The council's strategy broadened the appeal for support of AIDS funding by promoting AIDS research as applicable to broader medical research. It amplified the urgency by elevating AIDS to a global health emergency. On one hand, the broadened scope increased compassion as more people became aware of the human suffering. C-SPAN videos indicate the political reach of the message. Archives footage of hearings show that key legislators recognized AIDS as a national problem. Additionally, programs allowed reporters to educate the public and correct myths. On the other hand, fear of AIDS led to blame and a backlash. Videos demonstrated that some callers and members of Congress supported harsh measures of mandatory testing and quarantine to stop the "homosexuals" from spreading the disease.

As the participants in the 1987 March for Gay and Lesbian Rights gathered in Washington, activist Jeffrey Levi spoke to the National Press Club. In his presentation, Levi brought together many of Human Rights Campaign Fund and AIDS Action Council's messages. The March organizers had built coalitions with other civil rights groups. Additionally, Levi recognized the diversity within the community: "There are gay Republicans, gay conservatives, gay liberals, gay Democrats." In the body of his speech and in the question session following, Levi explained how AIDS had increased familiarity and understanding. Although he concluded the chances of a federal gay and lesbian civil rights bill in the near future was "slim to none," Levi described the "quiet revolution" in city councils and state legislatures and predicted members would advance to Washington positions "ready and willing to move these issues to the national level." He noted, "Doors to member of the Senate and the House have been open because of the AIDS crisis—people we would not have otherwise talked to but for their role on health policy." He continued, "As they come to understand our community, as they come to see us as real people rather than some stereotype they may have read or seen in the media, I think their support will increase" (C-SPAN, 1987e). Levi's speech

86 CHAPTER 5

echoed the message of inclusion found in the HRCF campaign strategy and early AIDS Action Council newsletters. Despite the political backlash and staggering death rate of 1985–1987, Levi looked forward to the march on Washington with hope.

As I conclude, I would like to consider the similarities between the Human Rights Campaign Fund and the AIDS Action Council's messages and strategies. Both organizations promoted a message of inclusion. The messages sought to pull gay and lesbian concerns out of the periphery and into the center or mainstream of public discourse. The similarity in messaging intertwined the objectives of expanding human rights and of expanding access to health care. My analysis of C-SPAN videos strongly suggests that the organizations succeeded in disseminating their messages in the public and political spheres. The HRCF adopted a strategy of funding candidates who supported gay and lesbian rights. They interpreted their candidates' success as progress toward a more inclusive society that recognized gay civil rights as human rights. Although it is difficult to weigh the impact of the financial contributions, my analysis shows their efforts contributed to a perception of political power; however, those opposed to gay and lesbian civil rights used affirmations of their political power as fearmongering. The AIDS Action Council adopted a strategy of broadening the appeal of AIDS in order to increase compassion and secure federal funding for AIDS education, services, and research. They framed AIDS as an inclusive national and global health crisis. My investigation found examples of compassion and recognition of the global nature of AIDS; however, focus on the state of emergency contributed to heightened anxiety. The videos in the C-SPAN Video Library establish a range of responses to both strategies, from acceptance and support to rejection and resistance.

HISTORIANS AND C-SPAN

In a recent chapter, historian David Greenberg asked, "Do Historians Watch Enough TV?" He comments that historians of the postwar period often avoid television as a source and notes that those who do examine television often prefer reading the transcript over the time-consuming process of watching TV (Greenberg, 2012). Most of the videos in the C-SPAN Video Library do have transcription available. Reading transcripts certainly takes less initial time than watching the video version of a broadcast. I had intended to rely on the transcripts for this chapter; however, I found the transcripts of material from C-SPAN's early years were incomplete. My brief investigation of the AIDS crisis demonstrates what is lost when relying solely on transcripts. Most obviously, video includes interpretive aids such as vocal inflection, facial expression, and body language absent from print sources. If I had confined my research to transcripts, I would have missed the composure Nancy Roth and Jeffrey Levi exhibited when asked provocative questions that condemned their "lifestyle" and the assertiveness of Philip Boffey as he countered calls for quarantine. Historians can find additional congressional hearing transcripts that also include the submitted written material at Hathi Trust Digital Library; however, the transcript versions do not include the visual and aural clues that indicate humor, rhetorical questions, or sarcasm. These interpretive aids are particularly informative when analyzing committee members as they questioned witnesses and interacted with each other. Similarly, the language of parliamentary procedure can mask goodwill, annoyance, and anger. One does not need to watch a video to understand that Representatives Waxman and Dannemeyer held different positions on mandatory AIDS testing; however, a video of their interaction exposes the intensity of their disagreement. Overall, I feel that the opportunities to hear and view the individuals and events I investigated enhanced my evaluation of attitudes and relationships.

Historians can use C-SPAN call-in broadcasts to add context to quantitative study and survey results. For instance, the 1987 Gallup poll results indicated a significant portion of Americans were unclear about what the "transmission of bodily fluids" entailed. Twenty-five percent thought a person could catch AIDS from a cough or sneeze; another 10% did not know. The survey summary noted, "Many Americans still cling to mistaken ideas about its [AIDS] transmission." Callers' responses suggest why people continued to hold views that "[had] been entirely discounted by health officials" (Gallup, 1987). Callers mention the confusion caused by contradicting reports. Several reference newspaper or magazine articles that supported fears of insect transmission or casual contact. The doubt contributed to fear. During the 1987 broadcast, Boffey responded to a caller who suggested all travelers should take an AIDS test before they enter the United States. In his rebuttal, he remarked, "So many of the callers—seem to me that there is an undertone that they are at risk." Call-in conversations about mandatory testing and quarantine exposed hostility toward gay men and disregard for the civil rights of people with AIDS but also expressed mistrust of the medical information received. For instance, a caller from New Jersey in favor of quarantine regardless of the cost or consequence argued, "If AIDS is so hard to get, why do so many people have it?" (C-SPAN, 1987c). The callers' responses suggest these mistaken ideas identified in the survey could have been the result of the circulation of contradictory information and may have contributed to the support of extreme measures such as mandatory testing and quarantine.

In evaluating call-in programs, historians should consider the demographic limits of the caller sample. C-SPAN solicited a variety of callers by providing separate numbers for different geographic regions and adopting a rule that limited caller participation to once in 30 days. The host typically identified callers by city and state. In the videos I sampled, more callers came from California and New York but just as many callers from other states in the Midwest, South, and West joined the conversations. Callers seldom mentioned their age but at times their comments included clues. Similarly, gender is often left unspoken but remarks provided clues. The videos I viewed included calls from men, women, activists, people with AIDS, people with medical backgrounds, people who identified as gay or lesbian, and people with various religious and political opinions. Anonymity may have encouraged more truthful and/or more extreme statements. Although not a random representative sample and likely to express the views of those motivated by public engagement, the callers' statements shed insight on the public's concerns and responses to policy issues.

Programs in the C-SPAN Video Library also provide an unmediated view of political discourse. Almost every video I viewed included interaction between guest and host; guest and callers or audience members; political figures and callers or audience members; legislators and witnesses; or legislators with each other. The participants discussed various issues and expressed multiple points of view. C-SPAN viewers also heard unedited testimony on the discrimination and medical challenges faced by people with AIDS. For those investigating congressional floor proceedings, the videos show the unedited dialogue prior to any revisions added to or subtracted from the account published in the *Congressional Record*. Historians relying on printed sources or commercial television for accounts of debates and events must first unpack the authors' or producers' selection of evidence and argument with a critical eye toward reliability and bias. While C-SPAN provides uncensored content, discourse alone does not provide a full view of the AIDS crisis. Journalists and reporters entered homes and hospitals with cameras and video equipment to more poignantly show the daily lived experiences of people with AIDS. Still, the Video Library affords the historian a selection of unabridged social and political dialogues.

For my research, one of the benefits of using the C-SPAN Video Library was the variety of programming available, especially considering that the time period I investigated occurred before C-SPAN routinely preserved their tapes. In addition to call-in programs, hearings, and political events, I evaluated campaign interviews, a U.S. Conference of Mayors panel on AIDS, presentations related to the President's Commission on HIV, two events featuring Surgeon General C. Everett Koop, an Association of American Medical Colleges conference panel, and a program on the psychology of AIDS prevention. The scope of programming offered samples of the expected political positions as well as opinions of activists and viewers. I watched Newt Gingrich use fear of AIDS to rally supporters and Robert Kunst use the slogan "Cure AIDS Now" to define his campaign. I viewed mayors sharing their communities' concerns about AIDS and U.S. representatives and senators discussing what the government should do about AIDS. I observed numerous witnesses condense their expertise into concise presentations in hopes of influencing public policy decisions. Activists spoke with intensity as did callers. In the process of evaluating the videos, I became better acquainted with many of the political figures, experts, and activists I had previously read about.

C-SPAN strives to provide "a balanced presentation of points of view" and "a direct conduit to the audience without filtering or otherwise distorting their [elected and appointed officials and others who would influence public policy] points of view" (C-SPAN, n.d.). Historians should still assess the program selection for unintended bias, particularly in consideration of the category of "others who would influence public policy." In my research, I did not assume the videos contained every point of view or individual integral to AIDS public policy decisions. By mission and resource, the wealth of material did not delve into local and state government. Based on the videos, I could not measure the extent to which HRCF and AIDS Action Council's messages reached their intended audiences or the specific effect of their messages. I do argue that their messages were present and considered in public policy debate. The backlash evident in some callers' comments suggests the messages also circulated in the public sphere. Much of what I discovered will find a place in the larger research project that includes this chapter.

As part of "The Research Possibilities of the C-SPAN Archives" conference, participants toured the Archives facility at Purdue Research Park. The behind-the-scenes tour included a meeting with C-SPAN website developers. Since I began my research in the library, the website interface has added features. The developers shared plans for continued enhancements. I appreciate the option to search for congressional videos based on committee, members, votes, bills, or elections. Users can also search by Series, Executive Branch, and Supreme Court as well as employ advanced search features for people or topics. The video clip feature allows users to create, save, comment, and share video segments, an especially useful tool when analyzing longer videos such as congressional hearings. It could also be a useful classroom tool. The bulk of available material suits historians of the 1980s and forward; however, C-SPAN's American History TV series includes videos on American artifacts, lectures, topical programs, oral histories, early 20th-century clips, and historians talking about their work, which could be of interest. I encourage researchers of American history to investigate the C-SPAN Video Library for content related to their research needs and to consider the benefits of incorporating video as a primary source.

NOTE

1. The Centers for Disease Control adopted the name Acquired Immune Deficiency Syndrome (AIDS) in the summer of 1982. French scientists identified a virus they named LAV in 1983 and American scientists identified a virus they named HTLV-III in 1984 as the cause of AIDS. In 1986, an international committee decided both names should be replaced with the name Human Immunodeficiency Virus (HIV). During the period under discussion in this chapter, the term AIDS was often used to refer to the virus, the syndrome, and the cause of death. For simplicity, my use of "AIDS" reflects the use of the time.

REFERENCES

AIDS Action Update [newsletter]. (1984a, November). Retrieved from (Folder, "AIDS Action Council 1984–1986," Box 332) Gay Men's Health Crisis records, New York Public Library Manuscripts and Archives Division, New York, NY.

AIDS Action Update [newsletter]. (1984b, December). Retrieved from (Folder, "AIDS Action Council 1984–1986," Box 332) Gay Men's Health Crisis records, New York Public Library Manuscripts and Archives Division, New York, NY.

AIDS Action Update [newsletter]. (1985, May). Retrieved from (Folder, "AIDS Action Council 1984–1986," Box 332) Gay Men's Health Crisis records, New York Public Library Manuscripts and Archives Division, New York, NY.

Andriote, J. M. (2011). *Victory deferred: How AIDS changed gay life in America.* Chicago, IL: University of Chicago Press.

By-laws of the Human Rights Campaign Fund. (1982). Retrieved from http://rmc.library.cornell.edu/HRC/

C-SPAN. (n.d.). Our mission. Retrieved from https://www.c-span.org/about/mission/

C-SPAN (Producer). (1985a, September 17). *AIDS* [online video]. Available from https://www.c-span.org/video/?49634-1/aids

C-SPAN (Producer). (1985b, September 26). *AIDS funding* [online video]. Available from https://www.c-span.org/video/?125690-1/aids-funding

C-SPAN (Producer). (1985c, October 8). *AIDS* [online video]. Available from https://www.c-span.org/video/?49748-1/aids

C-SPAN (Producer). (1985d, November 4). *AIDS awareness* [online video]. Available from https://www.c-span.org/video/?49889-1/aids-awareness

C-SPAN (Producer). (1986a, July 1). *Status of AIDS drug development* [online video]. Available from https://www.c-span.org/video/?150141-1/status-aids-drug-development

C-SPAN (Producer). (1986b, July 31). *Chief justice confirmation hearing* [online video]. Available from https://www.c-span.org/video/?150259-1/chief-justice-confirmation-hearing

C-SPAN (Producer). (1986c, August 1). *Chief justice confirmation hearing* [online video]. Available from https://www.c-span.org/video/?150275-1/chief-justice-confirmation-hearing

C-SPAN (Producer). (1987a, August 7). *AIDS issues* [online video]. Available from https://www.c-span.org/video/?151007-1/aids-issues

C-SPAN (Producer). (1987b, August 7). *Pending AIDS legislation* [online video]. Available from https://www.c-span.org/video/?57419-1/pending-aids-legislation

C-SPAN (Producer). (1987c, August 24). *AIDS reporting* [online video]. Available from https://www.c-span.org/video/?98631-1/aids-reporting, 1987

C-SPAN (Producer). (1987d, September 3). *Covering AIDS* [online video]. Available from https://www.c-span.org/video/?151082-1/covering-aids

C-SPAN (Producer). (1987e, October 10). *Gay rights movement* [online video]. Available from https://www.c-span.org/video/?903-1/gay-rights-movement

Endean, S., & Eaklor, V. L. (2006). *Bringing lesbian and gay rights into the mainstream: Twenty years of progress.* New York, NY: Harrington Park Press.

FARO update [report]. (1983, October). Retrieved from (Folder, "FARO update 1983–1984," Box 10) Human Sexuality: National Lesbian and Gay Health Association records 1978–1992, Cornell University Library, Ithaca, NY.

Gallup, G., Jr. (1987, November 26). *Public aware of how AIDS is spread but misconceptions are common.* Retrieved from (Folder, "Public Opinion Polls 1987," Box 53) Gay Men's Health Crisis records, New York Public Library Manuscripts and Archives Division, New York, NY.

Greenberg, D. (2012). Do historians watch enough TV? Broadcast news as a primary source. In C. B. Potter & R. C. Romano (Eds.), *Doing recent history: On privacy, copyright, video games, institutional review boards, activist scholarship, and history that talks back* (pp. 185–199). Athens: University of Georgia Press.

Human Rights Campaign Fund: 1984 election round-up [newsletter]. (1984). Retrieved from (Folder, "1984 Camapign Contributions," Box 17) Human Sexuality: Human Rights Campaign Records 1975–2005, Cornell University Library, Ithaca, NY.

Kaplan, B. (1987). *Confusion and concern: Middle Americans, AIDS, and public policy.* Retrieved from (Folder, "Public Opinion Polls 1987," Box 53) Gay Men's Health Crisis records, New York Public Library Manuscripts and Archives Division, New York, NY.

Smothers, R. (1982, September 30). Mondale tells homosexual group Reagan record is biased on rights. *New York Times.* Retrieved from http://www.nytimes.com

Thirty years of HIV/AIDS: Snapshots of an epidemic [website]. Retrieved from http://www.amfar.org/thirty-years-of-hiv/aids-snapshots-of-an-epidemic/

25 years of political influence: The records of the Human Rights Campaign [website]. Retrieved from http://rmc.library.cornell.edu/HRC/exhibition/changingroles/

CHAPTER 6

TREATMENT OR GUN CONTROL? CONGRESSIONAL DISCOURSE ON MENTAL ILLNESS AND VIOLENCE

Elizabeth Wulbrecht

As the nation mourns the tremendous loss of life in Charleston, South Carolina, from another mass shooting, details of what drove someone to commit this terrible act remain elusive. But if history is any indication, the shooter most likely has a history of severe mental health issues that have either gone untreated or undiagnosed.
—Matthew Lysiak, *Newsweek,* June 2015

Alarming and terrible acts of violence such as the mass shootings at Newtown, Virginia Tech, and Orlando shock and paralyze the American public. People want answers. They want to know what, if anything, can compel someone to commit such an atrocious deed. The media, when reporting on these acts of violence, often blame the crime on the perceived mental illness of the shooter (McGinty, Webster, Jarlenski, & Barry, 2014; Metzl &

Macleish, 2015). The dictums of newsworthiness require reporters to focus on the most sensational of news. However, the idea of a mentally ill individual committing an appallingly violent act is more than just sensational; it is incomprehensible. Despite this, the practice is stigmatizing for the majority of individuals with mental illness who are not violent and will never commit a violent crime (Elbogen & Johnson, 2009).

The framing of mental illness in news and entertainment media is often negative and stereotypical. Researchers have explored the framing of mental illness in cable TV, newspapers, films, and even children's television (Beveridge, 1996; Wahl, 1992, 1995; Wahl, Hanrahan, Karl, Lasher, & Swaye, 2007). However, no one has yet addressed the framing of mental illness by members of Congress, who as opinion leaders are often an important source of information for news media. Through both negative and positive portrayals of mental illness, members of Congress contribute to the social construction of mental illness and mentally ill people. Congressional portrayals directly impact both the debate and the creation of policies targeted at mentally ill individuals, whether punitive in nature, such as gun control, or treatment based.

The mass shootings of this century have sparked an intense debate surrounding gun control. In some states the gun control debate has focused on restricting access to weapons only among those suffering from a serious mental illness (SMI) (McGinty et al., 2014; Metzl & Macleish, 2015). This has important implications for the continuing stigmatization of mentally ill persons as violent and dangerous criminals and who have access to firearms.

The goal of this chapter is to analyze congressional discourse during a time when mass shootings became especially prevalent. Between 2011 and 2014, the number of mass shootings tripled in rate (Cohen, Azrael, & Miller, 2014). Because of this, I choose to analyze discourse beginning within this timeframe. During the interval of my study, members of Congress largely emphasized the treatment needs or the dangerousness of the mentally ill populace. I hypothesize that the framing of mental illness in congressional sessions will differ depending on the subject under consideration: child, adult, veteran, and mass shootings. Through a logistic regression, I analyze whether the frame of discourse (danger or treatment) differs depending on the subject(s) discussed.

FRAMING

Framing is a process through which an issue is communicated to the public or more specialized audience members, such as members of Congress. Frames present an issue as a package, often including a "particular problem definition, causal interpretation, moral evaluation, and/or treatment recommendation" (Entman, 1993, p. 52). The audience not only receives a certain message regarding a policy issue (mentally ill people commit mass shootings), but the important policy action that should accompany the message (background checks for individuals with mental illness). Framing is an important phenomenon to study because "framing effects" contribute to changes in public opinion, which can and does impact policy creation (Burstein, 2003). Chong and Druckman (2007) describe framing effects as "when (often small) changes in the presentation of an issue or an event produce (sometimes large) changes of opinion" (p. 104).

Creating successful frames, or frames that alter public opinion, is an important tool for policymakers. Whether they seek to promote a certain policy or bring an issue to the public's attention, framing can help policymakers achieve their goal. Political elites emphasize a certain definition of a problem either to promote a certain policy solution or prevent one. For example, gun control is often framed as a threat to individual liberty because gun rights, according to this frame, are ensured by the Constitution (Callaghan & Schnell, 2001). However, citizens will only accept the frame's policy solution if they believe the problem definition to be legitimate. Not everyone agrees that gun control is a threat to individual liberty and instead may believe that it is a necessary and important measure to promote public safety. Thus whether a policy is enacted or not depends on whose frame or interpretation of the policy issue is most successful (Gamson & Modigliani, 1989, p. 2). The definition that succeeds is often the one that is most convincing to the public. As Raymond (2016) argues, this depends on the norm(s) a frame is based on and the strength of the normative fit to the issue at hand.

Individuals are bombarded with competing frames and conflicting information, yet they weigh some norms/considerations/beliefs/values more heavily than others (Nelson, Oxley, & Clawson, 1997). The value citizens weigh most heavily when evaluating an issue, such as individual liberty in the gun control debate, becomes their "frame in thought" (Chong & Druckman, 2007, p. 105). If elites want to galvanize the citizens concerned with individual liberty behind their policy platform of limited to no gun control, they will use the frame "individual liberty" in their rhetoric. When this occurs, individual liberty becomes a "frame in communication" (Chong & Druckman, 2007; Druckman, 2001).

In this chapter, I am analyzing the frames in communication employed by members of Congress in congressional sessions. There is a dearth of research on the construction of frames by political elites as most framing studies concern experiments on the frames employed in mass media sources (Chong & Druckman, 2007; Nelson, Bryner, & Carnahan, 2011). Mass media frames are often attributed to political elites, even though the construction of frames by politicians is not systematically studied (see Callaghan & Schnell, 2001, pp. 186–187). Callaghan and Schnell (2001) find that the media often fail to accurately communicate or even include elite messages in their coverage of issues. They compare elite discourse on gun control, analyzed through use of the *Congressional Record,* to reports on gun control in the mass media. Members of Congress employed a "sensible legislation" frame in 47.9% of the cases the authors coded, whereas the mass media employed the same frame in 11.2% of cases. The dominant frame used by their mass media sources was a "culture of violence" frame, found in 47.6% of the cases versus 23% of cases in the *Congressional Record.* Thus, elite discourse is not always reflected in the mass media, and scholars cannot assume that the media are faithfully reporting the opinions of elites and the issue frames they employ. It is important to analyze the framing of issues by political elites and how their construction differs or converges with media sources.

It is important to study members of Congress because in addition to influencing the mass media, they help set the national policy agenda (Kingdon, 2011, pp. 36–38). The topics that members of Congress discuss influence what both the public and the president believe to be important policy issues. A phenomenon such as mental health care in the United States is not a political issue until someone, such as a member of Congress, frames it to be one (Baumgartner & Jones, 2009; Kingdon, 2011). Members of Congress are important in the agenda-setting and issue-definition process because not only do they have access to publicity and the mass media, they also, and most significantly, make laws (Kingdon, 2011, p. 37). In addition to placing an issue on the national policy agenda, members of Congress propose policy alternatives to solve the issue at hand (Kingdon, 2011). The framing of mental illness by members of Congress has the potential to result in a concrete outcome: legislation. Thus, it is important to study members of Congress because they directly influence the construction of mental illness frames and legislation that impacts mentally ill people.

FRAMING OF MENTAL ILLNESS AND GUN VIOLENCE

Recent mass shootings have led to a proliferation of media coverage on the events themselves, the perpetrators, and reflections on the potential causes and consequences of such horrendous violence. Within the mass media, discourse surrounding mass shootings, mental illness, and violence has increased (McGinty, Kennedy-Hendricks, Choksy, & Barry, 2016; McGinty et al., 2014). McGinty and colleagues (2016) found that between 1994 and 2004, only 9% of stories on mental illness included discussion of mass shootings. Between 2005 and 2014, this increased to 22%.

Policymakers and the media highlight serious mental illness (SMI) as one potential and important cause of these violent acts. This has led to policy initiatives seeking to reduce gun access among those with a serious mental illness, but not necessarily the public at large (McGinty et al., 2014). McGinty and colleagues (2014) assessed mass media coverage of mass shootings and SMI and attributions of responsibility for the violent events, either "dangerous people" or "dangerous weapons," during the period 1997–2012. Drawing on the work of Iyengar (1991) on framing and causal attribution, they argue that the first frame blames gun violence on those with serious mental illness and the latter on guns. The former causal attribution is consistent with stereotypes concerning people with mental illness that have persisted for hundreds of years—that they are violent and dangerous (Foucault, 1965). McGinty and colleagues found that the dangerous people frame was more prevalent than the dangerous weapons frame. The former frame was present in 22.5% of the news stories and the latter in 14.6%. The most common policy proposal news stories presented was restricting access to weapons among those with serious mental illness. This policy proposal was mentioned in 18% of news stories, while mental health policy proposals were mentioned in 12% of cases. The authors coded for policies that encompassed improving the mental health care system or increasing the ability of mentally ill individuals to be involuntarily committed to inpatient or outpatient treatment.

The framing of mentally ill people as dangerous is not a new phenomenon with movies portraying this stereotype since the silent film era (Hyler, Gabbard, & Schneider, 1991). Wahl (1995) explains, "The popularity of mentally ill villains—they attract large audiences and sometimes even critical industry acclaim—helps to ensure their continued appearance" (p. 58). Mentally ill villains have characterized news stories for decades, even before our current era of mass shootings (Day & Page, 1986; Shain & Phillips, 1991; Wahl, 1992). The portrayal of mental illness in newspapers and entertainment media is problematic because many people gain information from the mass media. In a representative television survey, 87% of individuals cited television, 74% magazines, and 76% newspapers as an information source on mental illness (Borinstein, 1992). As consumers of television, movies, and other forms of media, political elites are arguably also impacted by the stereotypes surrounding mental illness found in these sources. As discussed below, I found that members of Congress often emphasize the dangerousness and potential violence of the mentally ill populace. They are not immune to the ubiquitous stereotypes that surround mental illness and their discourse reflects this.

THE SOCIAL CONSTRUCTION OF MENTAL ILLNESS

The way that members of Congress frame mental illness is impacted by the social construction of the mentally ill as a group. Schneider and Ingram's (1993) social construction framework explains why some groups, known as target populations, are the recipients of resources, punitive policy, or nothing at all. A target population is a group of individuals with shared characteristics, such as single mothers, homeless persons, Black Americans, or those with mental illness. Target populations are the potential recipients of resources through policies directed at them. The content of the policy often depends upon the group's social construction, which, according to Schneider and Ingram (1993), are "stereotypes about particular groups of people that have been created by politics, culture, socialization, history, the media, literature, religion, and the like" (p. 335).

Depending on the images and stereotypes associated with them, groups, according to Schneider and Ingram (1993), can be characterized into one of four social constructions: advantaged, contenders, dependents, and deviants. The elderly and veterans are advantaged groups. They are positively constructed, politically powerful, and the recipients of beneficial policy. Contenders are powerful politically, but negatively constructed, such as unions and corporations. Dependents are not powerful politically but positively constructed such as children and mothers. Deviants are both negatively constructed and politically powerless, such as criminals, drug addicts, and in some cases the mentally ill population. Many Americans also view welfare recipients as deviants and often blame them for their own plight (Gamson & Lasch, 1983; Seccombe, James, & Walters, 1998). As Nelson and Kinder (1996) show, many Americans view the poor as having a "suspect moral character" and thus aren't supportive of welfare spending (p. 1063).

Support for policies that benefit or harm groups will depend on their social construction. The public does not generally endorse policies that benefit deviant groups because they are perceived as immoral and undeserving (Nelson & Kinder, 1996; Schneider & Ingram, 1993). Analyzing the 1996 General Social Survey module on mental health, McSween (2002) uncovered less support for spending on mental health than general health care, attributing her findings to the negative construction of mental illness.

People have multiple identities and the positive construction of one may deemphasize the stigma of the other. I hypothesize that this is the case for children and veterans with mental illness. Children and veterans are both positively constructed populations that are seen as deserving by the public (Schneider & Ingram, 1993, 2005). Jensen (2005) argues that veterans were first constructed as deserving citizens in the 19th century. She writes, "Members of the U.S. military forces have been considered deserving of public benefits for so long that veterans' entitlements seem an almost natural part of the American social policy landscape" (p. 35). I hypothesize that this discourse extends into discussions of mentally ill veterans, with members of Congress emphasizing their treatment needs.

Compared to veterans and children, the majority of adults with serious mental illness are viewed negatively. There is evidence that belief in the dangerousness of those with serious mental disorders is actually increasing, even as knowledge about mental illness grows (Phelan, Link, Stueve, & Pescosolido,

2000). Mentally ill people have been subjected to a number of punitive policies over the years, including restrictions on their ability to vote, serve on juries, and have families, contributing directly to their construction as incompetent and deviant (Corrigan et al., 2005; Hemmens, Miller, Burton, & Milner, 2002). Excluding persons with mental illness from full citizenship began in the 19th century when states started to enfranchise more and more of their citizens than just propertied males, but disenfranchised those labeled "idiot," "lunatic," and "insane" (Schriner, 2005). Schriner (2005) argues, "new suffrage laws both reflected the social constructions of mental illness and intellectual impairment that were emerging in the 19th century and shaped these constructions—resulting in the political marginalization and stigmatization of persons with these impairments" (p. 65). This stigmatization and the social construction of mentally ill adults as incompetent persists today.

Because of the different social constructions of children, veterans, and mentally ill adults, I hypothesize that members of Congress will frame veterans, active-duty military, and children differently than the average citizen with mental illness. I uncovered two prevalent frames in my data set. The first, which I titled "treatment frame," emphasizes the treatment needs of individuals with mental illness and expanding their access to care. The second, which I titled "danger frame," focuses on the perceived dangerousness of individuals with mental illness and preventing dangerous mentally ill people from committing violent acts. The following are my hypotheses:

H1: If adolescents are a subject of discourse, a treatment frame will be used.
H2: If veterans/military members are a subject of discourse, a treatment frame will be used.
H3: If adults are the subject of discourse, a danger frame will be used.

The main variable of interest in my study is the subject of the discourse (adult, veteran, child), but I control for other factors as well, including whether a mass shooting is mentioned. I believe discussions of mass shootings and mental illness are less likely to invoke the treatment frame, but rather emphasize the dangerousness or potential dangerousness of the mentally ill populace. Thus, I hypothesize that if a mass shooting is mentioned, a danger frame will be used.

METHODOLOGY

The data for my study were collected from the C-SPAN Archives' online Video Library, a public database available electronically. The C-SPAN Archives was founded at Purdue University in 1987 with videos available from this date to the present. Upon request, text transcripts of the videos are available for research projects. I requested and received transcripts for cases in which mental illness or some iteration of the term arose, such as mental health problem, mentally ill, and mentally unstable. The appendix to this chapter includes information on each term I searched for and the number of observations associated with it.

Each observation is a floor speech in the House or Senate or a speech made in a House or Senate hearing by a member of Congress (MC). I received text output from the C-SPAN Archives for every mention of mental illness and my other search terms from January 1, 2013, to December 31, 2015. I chose this period because multiple high-profile mass shootings occurred during this time frame, such as the Charleston church shooting, a second shooting at Fort Hood, and shootings at Isla Vista, Washington Navy Yard, Colorado Springs, and San Bernardino. In addition, the Sandy Hook massacre occurred in December 2012, and members of Congress talked about this event multiple times throughout my observations.

I received text output for all my search terms during this time period, starting with 498 observations. Many of these were repeat cases in which more than one of my search terms was mentioned such as "mental illness" and "mentally ill." I received text output for the words "insanity" and "insane," but the majority of these cases had nothing to do with mental illness. Many of these observations involved Republicans and Democrats accusing the other party of having "insane" policies or ideas. After accounting for repeat observations and observations where mental illness was not actually discussed, my cases amounted to 254. In the study's timeframe, many members of Congress spoke multiple times, such as Tim Murphy (R-PA), who is a staunch advocate of mental health care and introduced H.R. 3717 Helping Families in Mental Health Crisis Act of 2013 (see Figure 6.1). When the legislation did not pass in the 113th Congress, he introduced it again in the 114th and frequently visited the floor to discuss the bill's purpose and provisions.

FIGURE 6.1 Rep. Tim Murphy (R-PA) introduces H.R. 3717 Helping Families in Mental Health Crisis Act of 2013.

Some of my observations correspond to short one- or five-minute speeches or special orders, which can last up to an hour. Each observation encompasses the entire length of the speech before the member exited the floor or another MC started speaking.[1] If a speaker spoke multiple times in one congressional session on mental illness, each speech is a separate observation. For hearings, I coded each question and answer session by a MC as one observation. For example, at most hearings, members of Congress who participate have up to five minutes to either speak or direct questions at the witnesses. I coded each of those five minutes as one observation. I did not code any of the responses of the witnesses, since this study is focused on the framing of mental illness by members of Congress.

DEPENDENT VARIABLE

The study's dependent variable is the frame used in discourse. I identified two prominent frames: danger and treatment. A danger frame emphasizes the potential dangerousness of those with mental illness or discusses episodes of violence attributed by the speaker to mentally ill persons. The most discussed episodes of violence perpetrated by or blamed on mentally ill persons was mass shootings. Members of Congress highlighted other bizarre cases of violent acts committed by mentally ill persons, including a young man who murdered his mother with a hatchet in 2006. The following is an example of a danger frame:

> We know these tragic events almost always occur in instances where somebody's unstable and they are terribly violent and they are able to get a gun easily and use it to carry out these terrible attacks. We know this, yet we fail to pass and approve federal laws placing distance between mentally ill, violent people, and guns. (C-SPAN, 2015e)

A treatment frame emphasizes the treatment needs of the mentally ill populace, including how their needs are not being met. Other topics include increasing funding for research on mental illness, eradicating stigma and discrimination, providing housing for people with mental illness, and mental health parity. The following is an example of a treatment frame:

> As a nation our goal must be to ensure that veterans get the best mental health care possible and that they get it in a timely, nonbureaucratic way. How that health care is delivered is of enormous consequence. I want to commend the VA for its work in this area. The department has made important strides forward in providing mental health to our veterans. In fact, in many ways, the VA is leading [the] nation in terms of PTSD research, but clearly with all of the accomplishment, much, much more must be done. (C-SPAN, 2013b)

A treatment frame and a danger frame can appear in the same speech. In many of my observations, expanding access to mental health care was promoted as a means to prevent future instances of violence. When this occurred, I coded the observation as containing both a treatment and danger frame. The study resulted in 47 observations that included both frames. The following is an example of a treatment and danger frame:

> The events that transpired in Lafayette last week are a reminder of the long road we must take to reform our mental health system. Too many innocent lives are being taken in senseless attacks in movie theaters, schools, churches, and other places where we should feel safe. The common denominator in these tragedies is all too often

TABLE 6.1 *Frames, C-SPAN 2013–2015*

Frame	No.	% (N = 254)
Treatment frame only	114	44.9
Danger frame only	63	24.8
Both danger and treatment frames	47	18.5
Other	30	11.8

untreated mental illness. As public servants we should seek to keep the public safe, but our mental health system is badly broken and fails to do so and reforms are coming too slowly. It doesn't make sense that parents caring for a mentally ill child cannot be part of the medical decision-making that could prevent horrendous tragedies. (C-SPAN, 2015b)

There were a number of cases that did not contain elements of either a treatment or a danger frame. In these instances, I coded the observation as "other." The following is an example of an "other" frame:

Senator Franken told a story at a recent hearing about an 8-year-old boy who was told by an immigration judge that he had the right to cross-examine the government's witness, an 8-year-old boy. And, sadly, those with mental illness in this process many times never understand what they're going through. There was an example of a U.S. citizen, a U.S. citizen with a severe mental illness deported from this country because he didn't understand the fact that he just had to explain he was an American. (Dick Durbin, 2013c)

The frames are all dummy variables coded as "1" frame present and "0" not present. Table 6.1 shows the distribution of frames in my observations.

INDEPENDENT VARIABLES

For each speaker, I coded for his or her race, gender, and party. The majority of the speakers were white and male. There were 254 observations, but only 132 unique speakers, with multiple members of Congress speaking

TABLE 6.2 *Subjects, C-SPAN 2013–2015*

Subject	No.	% (*N* = 254)
Adults	33	12.99
Adolescents	56	22.05
Veterans/military	59	23.23
Prisoners	63	24.8
Mass shootings	86	33.86

in more than one observation. Thirty-five of the 132 unique speakers were women, 77 were Democrats, and only 20 were minorities.[2] The variable minority includes members of Congress of Asian, Hispanic, and African American descent.

I also coded for the subject of the discourse. As with frames, there could be more than one subject mentioned in a speech, but in many, there was no mention of a specific subject. I coded for mentions of mass shootings, non-veteran adults, adolescents, veterans/active-duty military, and mentally ill people who had come in contact with law enforcement, such as prisoners. Adolescents included both children and young adults of university age. Table 6.2 shows the distribution of subjects in my observations.

I also coded for whether a member of Congress admitted to having a personal experience with mental illness or being close to someone who had. In only 11 of the observations did a speaker discuss a personal experience with mental illness. I expect that having a personal experience with mental illness will be correlated to the use of a treatment frame, since studies have found that people close to those with a mental disorder view mental illness less negatively (Alexander & Link, 2003; Angermeyer & Dietrich, 2006; McSween, 2002). In addition, I coded for whether gun control was discussed. All the independent variables are dummy, with "1" coded as the variable present and "0" with the variable not present.

ANALYSES

To measure for intercoder reliability, another researcher coded 65 of my observations. I use Cohen's kappa, a conservative measure developed for calculating intercoder reliability on nominal data. It is frequently employed in mass communication studies and controls for chance agreement between coders (Lombard, Snyder-Duch, & Bracken, 2002). According to McHugh (2012), the kappa statistic is interpreted as 0.61–0.80 indicating "substantial" agreement between coders and 0.81–1.00 as "almost perfect agreement" between coders. Using a method developed by Cantor (1996), I calculated the sample size I would need to reach an agreement of 0.8 or higher on my most important variables (adults, adolescents, and veterans), finding that a sample size of 65 would be sufficient. The results of the inter-rater reliability test are in the appendix to this chapter. The kappa statistics for treatment frame, danger frame, adults, adolescents, mass shootings, and prisoners are in the "almost perfect agreement" category, and the kappa statistic for veterans, personal story, and gun control are in the "substantial agreement" category.

The time period of my study included 254 observations in which mental illness was discussed. There were only 132 unique speakers with 44 members of Congress appearing multiple times throughout the observations. Because of this, I analyze my data using a logistic regression with clustering on the speaker to correct for bias. I include three separate models. In the first, treatment frame is the dependent variable with the subject of discourse, party, gender, personal story shared, mass shooting, and discussion of gun control as explanatory variables. The dependent variable also includes observations in which both the treatment and danger frame were used. In the second, danger frame is the dependent variable with the same explanatory variables as Model 1. The dependent variable also includes observations in which both the danger and treatment frame were used. In the third, the dependent variable is the use of both a danger and treatment frame (danger-treatment) only. This allows me to understand whether the use of a danger-treatment frame is qualitatively different from the use of a treatment or danger frame alone.

The data also include hearing and debates from the same day, such as the hearing on veterans' mental health care cited in the above example of a treatment frame. This could also bias the results, and so I ran the same models clustering on date to capture whether observations on the same day (e.g., a hearing on gun control or mental health) would result in different findings. The findings were the same. Clustering on date yielded similar results as the models that clustered on speaker.

Results

Tables 6.3 and 6.4 show logistic regressions of danger and treatment frames for 2013–2015. In Model 1 (Table 6.3), adults, veterans, adolescents, and gun control are all statistically significant, with the first three positively and gun control negatively related to the use of a treatment frame. The odds of a treatment frame being used is 5.9 times higher with mention of adults, 10.6 times higher with mention of veterans, and 15.4 times higher with mention of adolescents than if these subjects were not discussed. The odds of employing a treatment frame when gun control is considered is 7.9 times less than the odds when gun control is not debated.

In Model 2 (Table 6.3), adults, mass shootings, and gun control are all statistically significant and positively related to the use of a danger frame. Sharing a personal experience with mental illness is negatively related to the use of a danger frame, consistent with my expectations. The odds of

TABLE 6.3 *Logistic Regression of Treatment and Danger Frames, C-SPAN 2013–2015*

	Model 1 (Treatment Frame)			Model 2 (Danger Frame)		
	Odds Ratio	Robust Std. Error	P > z	Odds Ratio	Robust Std. Error	P > z
Adults	5.878	3.683	0.005	6.353	3.284	0.000
Veterans	10.605	5.751	0.000	0.403	0.233	0.116
Adolescents	15.357	11.507	0.000	0.732	0.343	0.506
Prisoners	1.663	0.830	0.309	1.306	0.679	0.607
Democrat	0.728	0.348	0.507	0.876	0.340	0.732
Female	1.639	0.866	0.350	0.856	0.476	0.780
Minority	0.338	0.205	0.074	0.197	0.177	0.070
Personal	1.181	0.954	0.837	0.127	0.097	0.007
Mass shooting	1.028	0.482	0.953	8.189	3.394	0.000
Gun control	0.126	0.612	0.000	22.423	13.875	0.000
Constant	1.310	0.530	0.501	0.238	0.099	0.001
$N = 254$						
MacFadden's R^2	0.39			0.48		

employing a danger frame when adults are mentioned is 6.4 times higher, 8.2 times higher with mentions of mass shootings, and 22.4 times higher with mention of gun control then if these subjects were not discussed. Neither veterans nor adolescents are statistically significant in this model. In the third model, adults, adolescents, prisoners, and mass shootings are all positively related and statistically significant to the use of a danger-treatment frame, complicating the findings in Models 1 and 2. These subjects aren't related to discourse espousing either the treatment or dangerousness of mentally ill persons only. Rather, the treatment needs of mentally ill persons and their perceived dangerousness are often discussed together, especially in the case of adults, where the results are significant across all three models. And contrary to my expectations and hypothesis 1, adolescents are also framed negatively, with members of Congress employing the danger-treatment frame when adolescents with mental illness are considered.

TABLE 6.4 Logistic Regression of Danger-Treatment Frame, C-SPAN 2013–2015

	Model 3 (Danger Treatment Frame)		
	Odds Ratio	Robust Std. Error	$P > z$
Adults	6.227	2.765	0.000
Veterans	1.146	0.678	0.818
Adolescents	4.025	1.927	0.004
Prisoners	3.715	2.039	0.017
Democrat	0.651	0.375	0.455
Female	1.341	0.877	0.654
Minority	0.334	0.274	0.181
Personal	0.102	0.091	0.010
Mass shooting	13.734	7.392	0.000
Gun control	0.580	0.315	0.316
Constant	0.032	0.019	0.000
$N = 254$			
MacFadden's R^2	0.36		

The discussion of a personal experience is also statistically significant in Model 3 (Table 6.4), but negatively related to the use of a danger-treatment frame. The second model fits the data better with a McFadden's R^2 of 0.48 compared to a McFadden's R^2 of 0.39 in the first and 0.36 in the third. The demographic information was not significant in any of the three models. Being a female or Democrat or a male or Republican does not predict the use of a treatment or danger frame. The variable minority approached significance in Models 1 and 2 (Table 6.3) at $p < 0.07$ with a negative relationship to the use of both frames, indicating that minorities are using a different frame when discussing mental illness.

DISCUSSION

All three of my hypotheses concerning the subject of discourse were correct. The use of a treatment frame was statistically significant for speeches in which veterans and adolescents were discussed. These target groups were viewed as both deserving of treatment and entitled to it. Discussing the Veterans Mental Health Accessibility Act, Matt Cartwright (D-PA) explains:

> I believe we owe a great debt to those war fighters who serve our country through military service, including those who stood ready at a moment's notice to fight for our freedom. As long as I'm a member of Congress, I will be working to increase knowledge on this subject, to correct the shortcomings of the VA system, and to ensure that the men and women of our armed forces who bravely serve this country receive all the benefits to which they are *entitled*. (C-SPAN, 2015c)

A frequent theme in speeches on veterans and mental illness was the deserving nature of veterans and how they are not receiving the care they are entitled to. Veterans are a positively constructed population, and the mentally ill among them are not framed in the same way as nonveteran adults. A similar sentiment was expressed for children. In 2015, Heidi Heitkamp (D-ND) proposed an amendment to promote the mental health needs of children, including those living on reservations. She explained:

> My amendment would simply preserve a voluntary program that helps schools provide children's stability and the tools necessary to handle mental stress.... I hope the Senate will similarly protect this program by helping schools coordinate with wealthy professionals specializing and addressing the effects of traumatic events and mental stress; we will secure our most disadvantaged *the equal opportunity that they deserve,* that equal opportunity to learn and to achieve. (C-SPAN, 2015a)

Contrary to my expectations, adolescents were significant in Model 1, but also in the third model where the independent variable was the use of both a danger and treatment frame. The variable adolescent includes children and young adults. There were multiple cases in which "young men" were associated with violence. For example, John Cornyn (R-TX), at a gun control legislation markup in the Senate Judiciary Committee, spoke on the intersection of mental health, gun violence, and mass shootings. He explained: "No one wants disturbed young men or women, for that matter, to have access to firearms" (C-SPAN, 2013a). In his speech, he advocates for both mental health care and background checks to prevent mentally ill individuals from buying guns. In a March 5, 2013 hearing on mental illness and violence, Diana DeGette (D-CO) talks about the mentally ill "young men" who committed mass shootings. Many of the high-profile mass shootings in recent years have been perpetrated by young men and this, as well as their mental state, was discussed in Congress. Thus, in many cases the variable adolescent was associated with violence.

Although there were not enough mentions of adolescents and the use of a danger frame for adolescents to be significant in Model 2, adolescents were significant in Models 1 and 3, where the treatment frame was used. However, the treatment needs of adolescents were not only discussed because they were perceived as deserving of treatment, but because their dangerousness required it. Thus, the co-occurrence of the frames adds more complexity to the findings. Veterans were the only population constructed as truly deserving of treatment. The treatment needs of veterans were not justified due to their perceived dangerousness or capacity for violence.

The use of a danger frame was statistically significant for speeches in which adults were discussed. However, mention of adults was also statistically significant to the use of a treatment frame, contrary to my expectations, and mentions in which both frames were used. Mentally ill persons are framed as a group in need of treatment, but adults were not framed as deserving of treatment in the same way as veterans and in certain cases adolescents. Multiple members of Congress argued that individuals with mental illness should receive treatment to prevent them from becoming dangerous in the future or stop their violent behavior in the present. For example, in a House session on June 10, 2014, Jackie Speier (D-CA) went to the floor to discuss America's recent mass shootings and one of the "common denominators" that unites them: mental illness. After discussing the "troubled" adults, the recent U.S. Santa Barbara shooting, and their "history of mental illness," she asks her colleagues:

> What's it going to take ... is the problem too many guns? Is it mental health? Is it guns in the wrong hands? The answer to all these questions is yes. ... the threshold for taking someone against their will for psychiatric evaluation needs to be reviewed. Police need better mental health training. It must become easier to intervene when there are risks. (C-SPAN, 2014)

Congresswoman Speier then goes on to say that the majority of those with mental illness are not violent, but she has already linked the phenomenon of mass shootings in the United States to untreated mental illness. Speier called for improved mental health as one avenue to prevent mass violence from occurring. She is not alone. A similar sentiment is expressed by multiple members of Congress throughout my study. Mention of mass shootings was statistically significant and positively related to the use of a danger frame, but also a danger-treatment frame. The discourse in Congress reflects recent findings by Barry, McGinty, Vernick, and Webster (2013) on public attitudes toward mental illness, mental health, and gun control. They found that 60% of the survey respondents supported increased government spending on mental health care "as a strategy to reduce gun violence" (p. 1080). The general population of mentally ill adults is not framed as a group deserving of treatment because they have a right to be healthy, but rather as a population in need of treatment to protect others.

However, adults were significant in Model 1, with the treatment frame as the independent variable. The dangerousness of mentally ill adults was not always discussed, even if this was a common theme in my observations. Members of Congress promoted the treatment of mentally ill adults even in cases where gun control or mass shootings were not debated. This was an unexpected and important finding, indicating that members of Congress do not always espouse the dangerousness of mentally ill nonveteran adults when promoting their treatment needs. The stereotype of the dangerous and violent mentally ill individual was still present in my observations, but there were many cases in which this stereotype was not. There were many cases in which this stereotype was present but also argued against, such as in Congresswoman Speier's speech mentioned above. In another observation, Senator Chris Murphy (D-CT), on September 24, 2015, discusses mass shooter Adam Lanza and others like him, who he argues have mental illness, are violent, and "exist in the fringes of their mind." However, he then goes on to argue, "There's no inherent connection between being mentally ill and being violent. There's no greater incidence of mental illness in the United States than anywhere else in the world, and yet we have these epidemic rates of gun violence" (C-SPAN, 2015d).

Mass shootings were mentioned in 34% of my observations. In their analysis of news stories on mental illness, McGinty and colleagues (2016) found that between 2005 and 2014, 22% were reports on mass shootings attributed to mentally ill individuals, an increase in coverage from 1995 to 2004. With the increase in mass shootings over the past five years, so has discourse on violence, mental health, and gun control increased. Angus King (I-ME) explains,

> In all of these mass shooting incidents, it appears that the perpetrators had some significant mental health issues, and we have to deal with that, and we have to have a better system that finds people in advance before they act out their violent fantasies. We have to try to intervene and help those people before violence occurs. So mental health has to be a part of this, but it's not the whole answer, because people with those kinds of proclivities, whether they are

violence-prone felons or people with dangerous mental health issues, we simply have to keep guns out of their hands. (C-SPAN, 2015f)

Gun control was regularly discussed, mentioned in 30% of my observations, and statistically significant and negatively related to the use of a treatment frame and statistically significant and positively related to the use of a danger frame. A frequent theme addressed was passing gun control measures, specifically background checks, "to keep firearms out of the hands of convicted felons and mentally unstable people" (C-SPAN, 2015g). Mentally ill people were equated with felons and criminals, all deemed too deviant and dangerous to have guns. Discussing the disenfranchisement of persons with mental illness in the 19th century and discourse among delegates at state constitutional conventions, Schriner (2005) writes, "the distinction between idiots and insane persons and criminals was not always so clear, suggesting that criminality and disability were somehow related in that both made a person an imbecile" (p. 66). The discourse among political elites today is not so clear either. Mentally ill people are framed as a group in need of treatment, but partially because they have violent and criminal proclivities, which treatment can help prevent from manifesting.

LIMITATIONS

There are a few limitations of my study, which future work could improve upon. First, my coding of adolescents includes both mentions of children and young adults. In future work, I would code young adults and children as separate variables, which may yield different findings than those of the present study. I expect that young adults would be statistically significant in Model 3 (danger-treatment), but children would not. Second, I clustered on speaker and not date, which would capture bias introduced by observations in the same congressional session or hearing. I ran separate models clustering on date, which yielded similar results as the three discussed above and so I did not display them in my results section or appendix. Future work could uncover an elegant way to cluster for both in the same model. Lastly, I would code for more nuance in the discussion of policies related to mental illness, such as increasing the capacity of law enforcement to involuntarily commit individuals with mental illness or increasing funding and resources for community mental health centers.

CONCLUSION

Through their discourse on mental illness, members of Congress contribute to the social construction of mental illness and mentally ill people. Rasinski, Viechnicki, and O'Muircheartaigh (2005) write, "The way in which mental illness is portrayed in public discourse is important to understanding the stigma associated with mental illness, and may suggest ways of alleviating that stigma" (p. 57). This chapter contributes to research seeking to understand the framing of mentally ill people in American culture and the stigma surrounding them by analyzing an understudied area of public discourse on mental illness and framing research: Congress.

I found that the treatment needs of mentally ill persons are discussed often. The treatment frame was employed in 63% of my cases. However, the treatment needs of subpopulations of the mentally ill populace were framed differently. Veterans were seen as deserving of treatment because of their service to our country, a service which in many cases resulted in PTSD and suicide. Nonveteran adults were often viewed as a population in need of treatment, not because they necessarily deserved it, but because treatment could prevent future acts of violence or violence from manifesting in the first place. The danger frame was employed in 43% of my observations, often accompanied with discussions of gun control and mass shootings, common topics in congressional discourse on mental illness. Discourse on mental illness, violence, and mass shootings is not only found in mass media sources, discussed above, but Congress as well, indicating that the stigma of mental illness and violence will continue to persist in the future.

ACKNOWLEDGMENTS

I am grateful for the support of the C-SPAN Archives, which allowed me to pursue this project. I would like to thank Robert Browning and Josh Tamlin for providing the data I analyzed, Christian Noah Clase for coding a sample of my data so I could conduct an inter-rater reliability test, and Rosalee Clawson for all her help along the way, including comments, suggestions, and editing on earlier drafts of this chapter. I would also like to thank Zoe Oxley, who gave me insightful feedback as a discussant at the 2017 C-SPAN conference, located at Purdue University.

NOTES

1. On the C-SPAN website, these short clips are known as "mentions."
2. There were two Independent members of Congress in my observations (Angus King and Bernie Sanders), but since they both caucus with Democrats, I included them in the Democratic category in the final analysis.

REFERENCES

Alexander, L., & Link, B. (2003). The impact of contact on stigmatizing attitudes toward people with mental illness. *Journal of Mental Health, 12*(3), 271–289.

Angermeyer, M., & Dietrich, S. (2006). Public beliefs about and attitudes towards people with mental illness: A review of population studies. *Acta Psychiatrica Scandinavica, 113*(3), 163–179.

Barry, C., McGinty, E., Vernick, J., & Webster, D. (2013). After Newtown—Public opinion on gun policy and mental illness. *New England Journal of Medicine, 368*(12), 1077–1081.

Baumgartner, F., & Jones, B. (2009). *Agendas and instability in American politics* (2nd ed.). Chicago: University of Chicago Press.

Beveridge, A. (1996). Images of madness in the films of Walt Disney. *Psychiatric Bulletin, 20*, 618–620.

Borinstein, A. (1992). Public attitudes toward persons with mental illness. *Health Affairs, 11*(3), 186–196.

Burstein, P. (2003). The impact of public opinion on public policy: A review and an agenda. *Political Research Quarterly, 56*(1), 29–40.

Callaghan, K., & Schnell, F. (2001). Assessing the democratic debate: How the news media frame elite policy discourse. *Political Communication, 18*, 183–213.

Cantor, A. (1996). Sample-size calculations for Cohen's kappa. *Psychological Methods, 1*(2), 150–153.

Chong, D., & Druckman, J. (2007). Framing theory. *Annual Review of Political Science, 10,* 103–26.

Cohen, A., Azrael, D., & Miller, M. (2014). Rate of mass shootings has tripled since 2011, Harvard research shows. Retrieved April 4, 2017, from http://www.motherjones.com/politics/2014/10/mass-shootings-increasing-harvard-research

Corrigan, P., Watson, A., Heyrman, M., Warpinski, A., Garcia, G., Slopen, N., & Hall, L. (2005). Structural stigma in state legislation. *Psychiatric Services, 56*(5), 557–563.

C-SPAN (Producer). (2013a, March 7). *Gun control legislation markup* [online video]. https://www.c-span.org/video/?311364-1/gun-control-legislation-markup

C-SPAN (Producer). (2013b, March 20). *Veterans' mental health care* [online video]. Available from https://www.c-span.org/video/?311617-1/veterans-admin-officials-questioned-mental-health-policies

C-SPAN (Producer). (2013c, May 20). *Immigration legislation markup, Day 4, Part 1* [online video]. https://www.c-span.org/video/?312843-1/senate-judiciary-cmte-immigration-legislation-markup-part-1

C-SPAN (Producer). (2014, June 10). *House session* [online video]. Available from https://www.c-span.org/video/?319861-2/us-house-general-speeches

C-SPAN (Producer). (2015a, July 14). *Senate session, Part 2* [online video]. Available from https://www.c-span.org/video/?327109-2/us-senate-debate-12-education

C-SPAN (Producer). (2015b, July 27). *Senators Cassidy and Vitter on Lafayette shootings* [online video]. Available from https://www.c-span.org/video/?327303-5/senators-cassidy-vitter-lafayette-shootings

C-SPAN (Producer). (2015c, September 24). *House session, Part 2* [online video]. Available from https://www.c-span.org/search/?searchtype=All&query=%22I+believe+we+owe+a+great+debt+to+those+war+fighters%22

C-SPAN (Producer). (2015d, September 24). *Senate session* [online video]. Available from https://www.c-span.org/search/?searchtype=All&query=%22There%E2%80%99s+no+inherent+connection+between+being+mentally+ill+and+being+violent%22

C-SPAN (Producer). (2015e, October 5). *Senate session* [online video]. Available from https://www.c-span.org/video/?328535-1/us-senate-executive-session

C-SPAN (Producer). (2015f, October 8). *Senate session* [online video]. Available from https://www.c-span.org/search/?searchtype=All&query=%22we+simply+have+to+keep+guns+out+of+their+hands%22

C-SPAN (Producer). (2015g, December 7). *Senate session* [online video]. Available from https://www.c-span.org/video/?401704-1/us-senate-morning-business

Day, D., & Page, S. (1986). Portrayal of mental illness in Canadian newspapers. *Canadian Journal of Psychiatry, 31*(9), 813–817.

Druckman, J. (2001). On the limits of framing effects: Who can frame? *Journal of Politics, 63*(4), 1041–1066.

Elbogen, E., & Johnson, S. (2009). The intricate link between violence and mental disorder. *Archives of General Psychiatry, 66*(2), 152–161.

Entman, R. (1993). Framing: Toward clarification of a fractured paradigm. *Journal of Communication, 43*(4), 51–58.

Foucault, M. (1965). *Madness and civilization: A history of insanity in the age of reason*. New York, NY: Pantheon Books.

Gamson, W., & Lasch, K. (1983). The political culture of social welfare policy. In S. Spiro & E. Yuchtman-Yaar (Eds.), *Evaluating the welfare state* (pp. 397–416). New York, NY: Academic Press.

Gamson, W., & Modigliani, A. (1989). Media discourse and public opinion on nuclear power: A constructionist approach. *American Journal of Sociology, 95*(1), 1–37.

Hemmens, C., Miller, M., Burton, V. S. J., & Milner, S. (2002). The consequences of official labels: An examination of the rights lost by the mentally ill and mentally incompetent ten years later. *Community Mental Health Journal, 38*(2), 129–140.

Hyler, S., Gabbard, G., & Schneider, I. (1991). Homicidal maniacs and narcissistic parasites: Stigmatization of mentally ill persons in the movies. *Hospital and Community Psychiatry, 42*(10), 1044–1048.

Iyengar, S. (1991). *Is anyone responsible? How television frames political issues*. Chicago, IL: University of Chicago Press.

Jensen, L. (2005). Constructing and entitling America's original veterans. In A. Schneider & H. Ingram (Eds.), *Deserving and entitled: Social constructions and public policy* (pp. 35–62). Albany, NY: State University of New York Press.

Kingdon, J. (2011). *Agendas, alternatives and public policies* (2nd ed.). Boston, MA: Longman.

Lombard, M., Snyder-Duch, J., & Bracken, C. C. (2002). Content analysis in mass communication: Assessment and reporting of intercoder reliability. *Human Communication Research, 28*(4), 587–604.

Lysiak, M. (2015). Charleston massacre: Mental illness common thread for mass shootings. Retrieved May 8, 2017, from http://www.newsweek.com/charleston-massacre-mental-illness-common-thread-mass-shootings-344789

McGinty, E., Kennedy-Hendricks, A., Choksy, S., & Barry, C. (2016). Trends in news media coverage of mental illness in the United States: 1995–2014. *Health Affairs, 35*(6), 1121–1129.

McGinty, E., Webster, D., Jarlenski, M., & Barry, C. (2014). News media framing of serious mental illness and gun violence in the United States, 1997–2012. *American Journal of Public Health, 104*(3), 406–413.

McHugh, M. (2012). Interrater reliability: The kappa statistic. *Biochemia Medica, 22*(3), 276–282.

McSween, J. (2002). The role of group interest, identity, and stigma in determining mental health policy preferences. *Journal of Health Politics, Policy and Law, 27*(5), 773–800.

Metzl, J., & Macleish, K. (2015). Mental illness, mass shootings, and the politics of American firearms. *American Journal of Public Health, 105*(2), 240–249.

Nelson, T., Bryner, S., & Carnahan, D. (2011). Media and politics. In J. Druckman, D. Green, J. Kuklinski, & A. Lupia (Eds.), *Cambridge handbook of experimental political science* (pp. 261–277). New York, NY: Cambridge University Press.

Nelson, T., & Kinder, D. (1996). Issue frames and group centrism in American public opinion. *Journal of Politics, 58*(4), 1055–1078.

Nelson, T., Oxley, Z., & Clawson, R. (1997). Toward a psychology of framing effects. *Political Behavior, 19*(3), 221–246.

Phelan, J., Link, B., Stueve, A., & Pescosolido, B. (2000). Public conceptions of mental illness in 1950 and 1996: What is mental illness and is it to be feared? *Journal of Health and Social Behavior, 41*(2), 188–207.

Rasinski, K., Viechnicki, P., & O'Muircheartaigh, C. (2005). Methods for studying stigma and mental illness. In P. Corrigan (Ed.), *On the stigma of mental illness: Practical strategies for research and social change* (pp. 46–65). Washington, DC: American Psychological Association.

Raymond, L. (2016). *Reclaiming the atmospheric commons: The regional greenhouse gas initiative and a new model of emissions trading.* Cambridge, MA: MIT Press.

Schneider, A., & Ingram, H. (1993). Social construction of target populations: Implications for politics and policy. *American Political Science Review, 87*(2), 334–347.

Schneider, A., & Ingram, H. (2005). *Deserving and entitled: Social construction and public policy.* Albany, NY: State University of New York Press.

Schriner, K. (2005). Constructing the democratic citizen: Idiocy and insanity in American suffrage law. In A. Schneider & H. Ingram (Eds.), *Deserving and Entitled: Social Constructions and Public Policy* (pp. 63–80). Albany, NY: State University of New York Press.

Seccombe, K., James, D., & Walters, K. B. (1998). "They think you ain't much of nothing": The social construction of the welfare mother. *Journal of Marriage and Family, 60*(4), 849–865.

Shain, R., & Phillips, J. (1991). The stigma of mental illness: Labeling and stereotyping in the news. In L. Wilkins & P. Patterson (Eds.), *Risky business: Communicating issues of science, risk, and public policy* (pp. 61–74). Westport, CT: Greenwood Press.

Wahl, O. (1992). Mass media images of mental illness: A review of the literature. *Journal of Community Psychology, 20,* 343–352.

Wahl, O. (1995). *Media madness: Public images of mental illness.* New Brunswick, NJ: Rutgers University Press.

Wahl, O., Hanrahan, E., Karl, K., Lasher, E., & Swaye, J. (2007). The depiction of mental illness in children's television programs. *Journal of Community Psychology, 35*(1), 121–133.

APPENDIX
Archives Search Terms and Inter-Rater Reliability Test

C-SPAN Archives Search Terms, 2013–2015

Search Term	No. of Cases
mental and emotional disorder	0
mental condition	0
mental defect	0
mental difficulties	0
emotional difficulties	0
mental disability	1
mental disorder	7
mental health challenge	3
mental health condition	4
mental health disorder	5
mental health issue	18
mental health problem	22
mental illness	177
mental instability	5
mental limitations	0
mental problems	4
mental stress	1
mentally ill	107
mentally impaired	0
mentally unstable	18
substance abuse disorder	4
emotional disorder	0
insane	50
insanity	66
mental and behavioral condition	0
mental and emotional difficulties	0
mental disease	6

Inter-Rater Reliability Test

	Agreement (%)	Expected Agreement (%)	Kappa	Std. Error	Z	Prob > Z
Treatment	93.85	50.58	0.8755	0.124	7.06	0.000
Danger	96.92	49.96	0.9385	0.1238	7.58	0.000
Adults	93.85	67.81	0.8088	0.1217	6.64	0.000
Vets	89.23	72.33	0.6108	0.1143	5.35	0.000
Adolescents	92.31	57.99	0.8169	0.124	6.59	0.000
Prisoners	100.00	64.50	1	0.124	8.06	0.000
Personal	96.92	88.40	0.7347	0.1196	6.14	0.000
Mass shooting	93.85	55.17	0.8627	0.1237	6.97	0.000
Gun control	92.31	61.82	0.7985	0.1215	6.57	0.000

CHAPTER 7

HEALTH AND POLITICS: PORTRAYAL OF HEALTH AND ITS NARRATIVES ON C-SPAN

Chervin Lam and Somrita Ganchoudhuri

A plethora of studies have explored the way health is portrayed in entertainment media (e.g., Arrington & Goodier, 2004; Blair, Yue, Singh, & Bernhardt, 2005; Cutcliffe & Hannigan, 2001; Diefenbach, 1997; Groesz, Levine, & Murnen, 2002; Smith, 2007; Stuart, 2006; Wahl, 2003; Zoller & Worrell, 2006). Such studies not only have helped to identify communication trends but, more crucially, have discovered how media can communicate ideas to the masses in subterfuge. For example, there is much research done in the area of entertainment media and thin models (e.g., Groesz et al., 2002; Thomsen, McCoy, Gustafson, & Williams, 2002); many scholars have opined that the unrealistically thin models in magazines may encourage eating disturbances among girls, with some connecting these portrayals to anorexic behaviors (see Inch & Merali, 2006). Other research work, such as studies on the media's role in stigmatization (Cutcliffe & Hannigan, 2001), media portrayal of drugs (Blair et al., 2005), and media messages on sex, alcohol, and tobacco (Bleakley, Romer, & Jamieson, 2014), also have contributed to our understanding of how media may—deliberately or not—convey pernicious messages to the masses. The contributions of these researchers notwithstanding, the current literature on how health is portrayed in media has been disproportionately focused on *entertainment* media. Thus, other forms of exclusive media, say, corporate media (e.g., health care industry websites), public relations media (e.g., fast-food social responsibility messages), or political media (e.g., C-SPAN), have not yet been thoroughly examined. This study addresses this gap by investigating how health is portrayed on political media, specifically C-SPAN, a cable network in the United States that covers politics and public affairs.

HEALTH PORTRAYAL IN MEDIA

Interest in health content in media began to proliferate in the early 1980s, and, by the 1990s, its popularity became evident in the increasing number of scholarly publications in edited volumes and textbooks (Kline, 2006). Scholars who study health portrayal in media examine how health issues are depicted via media, and if there are effects or consequences to such portrayals. According to Beullens and Schepers (2013), scholars have been increasingly concerned about the connection between how unhealthy behaviors are portrayed in media and the imitation of such behaviors (e.g., alcohol consumption). Scholars also look at issues such as inaccurate depictions of health portrayals in media, stigmatization due to how certain health issues are portrayed, and stereotyping as a result of consistent portrayals of how an individual with a certain health condition looks. For example, Gollust, Eboh, and Barry (2012) posit that health portrayal influences public attitudes such as reinforcing stereotypes of obese individuals; Smith (2007) contended that media depictions of individuals with HIV were associated with criminality; and mental health, perhaps the most maligned and inaccurately depicted health issue, has had a history of poor and stigmatizing portrayals (see Cutcliffe & Hannigan, 2001; Diefenbach, 1997; Smith, 2007; Stuart, 2006; Wahl, 2003; cf. Francis et al., 2004). Poor depictions that contribute to stigmatization are not only limited to mental health issues, but other health concerns as well; for example, Person and colleagues (2004) postulated that media coverage of the severe acute respiratory syndrome (SARS) outbreak was culpable for stigma against SARS patients and individuals traveling through Asia. Scholars, such as Smith (2007), contend that one must look at media portrayal to anticipate how audiences may view certain health issues. Given these considerations, therefore, the study of health portrayal in media is of significant import.

Seale (2003) posited four insights regarding how health may be portrayed or framed in media. First, a health issue may be portrayed as one of the dangers in modern life. Through focusing on and having repeated coverage of a health issue, the media may suggest to audiences what they should be concerned about (e.g., global warming, cancer). Second, certain individuals with health issues may be portrayed as "villains or freaks" (Seale, 2003, p. 521), depicting those who are, say, disabled or mentally unwell in unflattering ways (see Cutcliffe & Hannigan, 2001; Diefenbach, 1997; Smith, 2007; Stuart, 2006; Wahl, 2003; cf. Francis et al., 2004). Third, media may frame a particular demographic as victims; for example, the media may consistently relate obesity issues to children, thereby framing children as being highly susceptible to adiposity. Fourth, the media may have various depictions of how professionals or laypeople approach health issues; Seale (2003) postulated that media depictions of professionals' ethics and abilities in dealing with patients have been increasingly contentious. In the decades of research in how health is portrayed in media, many scholars have conducted their studies with a focus on entertainment media instead of other forms of media.

THE TRADITIONAL APPROACH TO STUDYING HEALTH PORTRAYAL IN MEDIA

Health portrayal has been traditionally studied in the purview of entertainment media, as opposed to other forms of media, such as political media. For example, Zoller and Worrell (2006) examined how multiple sclerosis was depicted on the television show *The West Wing*. There are multifarious examples of studies that examine health portrayal in the context of entertainment media; for example, Blair, Yue, Singh, and Bernhardt (2005) looked at depictions of substances in a reality television program, *The Osbournes;* Bleakley, Romer, and Jamieson (2014) examined the portrayal of alcohol-, sex-, and tobacco-related behaviors in movies; Arrington and Goodier (2004) explored the framing of prostate cancer in the prime-time series *NYPD Blue*; Groesz, Levine, and Murnen (2002) looked at female body image depictions in TV commercials and magazines; Pendo (2004) examined depictions of health insurance in the popular films *Critical Core, The Rainmaker,* and *John Q.* The amount of such research is expansive, and the proclivity toward studying health portrayal in the purview of entertainment media is still prevalent today; as an example, in a recent study, Jamieson and Romer (2014) investigated the portrayal of tobacco use in prime-time TV dramas, including police, detective, crime, medical, and legal shows from 1955 to 2010. Many studies that look at nondigital media nevertheless also look at entertainment media, such as magazines (see Groesz et al., 2002); for example, Smith (2007) examined how health issues were portrayed in various formats in magazines, brochures, and posters.

With the advent of new media—in particular, social media—investigations of health portrayal in media have often been entertainment-related, such as research on entertainment social media platforms YouTube and Facebook. As an example of such research in the context of social media, Beullens and Schepers (2013) investigated how alcohol use was visually and textually portrayed on Facebook and how friends responded to such postings. In a similar study, Moreno and colleagues (2010) analyzed how adolescents display alcohol use on the social networking platform MySpace. In another study, Morgan, Snelson, and Elison-Bowers (2010) examined how young adults posted images and videos of themselves related to alcohol, inebriated conduct, or marijuana use on social media platforms such as MySpace, Facebook, and YouTube. Health portrayal in the context of political media, on the other hand, has been largely relegated to the doldrums.

HEALTH PORTRAYAL IN POLITICAL MEDIA

"Health" as a concept is very much political (see Mattson & Lam, 2016; Navarro et al., 2006). Wallerstein (1992) argued that sociopolitical realities influence an individual's ability to access and maintain health; poverty predicaments, chronic stress from lack of social support, and lack of resources contribute to an individual's experiences with health. Similarly, Navarro and colleagues (2006) argued that political ideologies determine health policies, which, in turn, influence health outcomes for the population; for example, in their study, Social Democratic parties in countries such as Norway and Denmark provided universal health care coverage and social benefits to all citizens and have tended to implement policies that support women's health and well-being, such as home care services and paid maternity leave. On the other hand, liberal parties, such as those in the United Kingdom and United States, have not had a tradition of strong commitment to redistributive policies. On the farther end of the spectrum, countries that were governed by conservative dictatorships had poor public services, undeveloped welfare states, and very low public health care expenditure (4.8% of GDP). Navarro and colleagues (2006) contended that health outcomes such as infant mortality rate and, to a lesser extent, life expectancy are concomitant with politics and policies; Navarro and colleagues postulated that political parties with egalitarian ideologies tend to have redistributive policies, which seem to have more desirable indicators of health.

Therefore, "health" is very much a political concept. Yet, most studies that investigate health portrayals in media examine such depictions in the purview of entertainment media, as opposed to political media. Not only is this a gap in the literature, but such an ambit limits what we know and understand about "health portrayal in media," and much remains to be found. Gollust, Eboh, and Barry (2012)—as an example of the few scholars who investigate health portrayal in political media—found that news media coverage can influence how people view health-related issues (see also Saguy & Gruys, 2010). However, such studies involve static images (e.g., Gollust et al., 2012) or nondigital content (e.g., Saguy & Gruys, 2010). Furthermore, such studies are often limited to one specific health issue (e.g., obesity). Therefore, the current study attempts to address these gaps in the literature by investigating the portrayal of health issues in digitized media. C-SPAN, a U.S. cable network that began in March 19, 1979, holds a publicly accessible library archive of its recordings (Lamb, 2014). Leveraging this resource, this study examines the portrayal of health issues in C-SPAN videos (see Figures 7.1 and 7.2). Because the focus is on how health is portrayed, this study narrows its scope to a political event and period in which health was a major theme—namely, the 2016 coverage of then presidential candidates Donald Trump and Hillary Clinton, who espoused health care proposals and health care ideologies.

FIGURE 7.1 Donald Trump speaking at a campaign rally in Tampa, Florida.

FIGURE 7.2 Hillary Clinton speaking at a campaign rally in Greensboro, North Carolina.

Because "health" encompasses many issues, it will also be pertinent to investigate what health issues are prominently raised in C-SPAN videos. As previously mentioned, frequent coverage of a particular health issue may influence perspectives such as susceptibility (Seale, 2003) or stigmatization (Person et al., 2004). Therefore, finding what health issues are prominently raised may be useful for future studies on media influence. Also, it will be interesting to investigate what health issues are raised in the videos of the respective candidates. The following research questions are thus advanced:

> **RQ1:** What were the most prominent health issues raised in the 2016 C-SPAN reports on presidential candidates Donald Trump and Hillary Clinton?
>
> **RQ1a:** What were the most prominent health issues raised in the Donald Trump videos?
>
> **RQ1b:** What were the most prominent health issues raised in the Hillary Clinton videos?

In answering the above research questions, a general overview of how health is portrayed by the two presidential candidates may be gleaned. Therefore, the following research question is advanced:

> **RQ2:** How is health portrayed in the 2016 C-SPAN reports on presidential candidates Donald Trump and Hillary Clinton?

METHOD

This study examined health portrayal in C-SPAN reports. C-SPAN is a cable network organization that began in March 19, 1979, the sixth cable network launched in the United States (Lamb, 2014). A Hart Research survey in 2013 indicated that at least 47 million people tune in to C-SPAN at least once a week, with those who are 18–49 years old constituting the largest portion of the viewership (Eggerton, 2013). C-SPAN is an advertising-free network that gets six cents per subscriber and has an annual expenditure of $65 million (Lamb, 2014). The C-SPAN Archives' online Video Library holds more than 230,000 hours of programming and is the largest accessible political collection in the world (C-SPAN, n.d.). This study used content analysis and rhetoric/thematic analysis methods to analyze the C-SPAN reports. Content analysis involves defining search criteria that demarcate what data will be analyzed for its content. The scope of the study was limited to the most recent and prominent political news—the U.S. presidential election.

To that end, a search was conducted in the C-SPAN Archives using the search criterion "Donald Trump," and videos were filtered so that videos dating from June 16, 2015 to November 8, 2016 would remain; this was the period from his announcement of his candidacy to Election Day. The videos were further filtered with the additional search term "health." The tab "mentions" was chosen, so that videos of Donald Trump mentioning the term "health" would emerge. Eventually, this process resulted in 40 campaign videos. The same search and filtering process was conducted for the search criterion "Hillary Clinton," with the exception of the date filter; her announcement was April 12, 2015. This process resulted in 62 campaign videos. Coding was done using the transcripts provided by Federal News Service, therefore one Hillary Clinton video was omitted because it did not have transcripts available.

FINDINGS AND RESULTS

Results of RQ1, RQ1a, and RQ1b

RQ1 asked, "What were the most prominent health issues raised in the 2016 C-SPAN reports on presidential candidates Donald Trump and Hillary Clinton?" Table 7.1 provides a comprehensive listing of the health issues raised, the number of videos that mentioned a health issue (f), and the health issue's rate of appearance. As a note, frequency (f) counts the number of videos that mentioned a health issue, *not* the number of times a health issue was mentioned in videos. Therefore, whether a particular health issue was mentioned once in a video or multiple times in a video, they all count as 1. Also, the frequency total may not match the number of videos analyzed; some videos were omitted from the list because no specific health issue was raised. This was the case for some videos of Donald Trump, in which he just mentioned health in a generic way without specifying any health issue. Because frequency was counted as the number of videos that mentioned a health issue, the frequency total may sometimes be more than the number of videos analyzed. This is so because multiple health issues may have been mentioned in one video. This was the case particularly for videos of Hillary Clinton, in which she mentioned many health issues in a single event.

TABLE 7.1 *List of Health Issues Raised in Donald Trump and Hillary Clinton Videos, Frequency, and Rate of Appearance*

Health Issue	Frequency (f)	Rate of Appearance (%) (f/no. of videos)
Affordable Care Act (ACA)	30	29
Women's health	21	21
Children's Health Insurance Program	20	20
Mental health	19	19
Childcare (e.g., school-based health)	16	16
Planned Parenthood	15	15
Affordable health care	14	14
Drug issues (e.g., substance abuse, overdose)	13	13
Universal health care	7	7
Prescription drugs	6	6
Medicare	5	5
Veterans' health	5	5
Health care costs	4	4
Preexisting conditions	4	4
Access to health care	3	3
Health disparities	3	3
Medicaid	3	3
Building health centers	2	2
Cancer	2	2
Immigrant health (e.g., Latinas)	2	2
Children drinking and bathing in poisoned water	1	1
Chronic disease	1	1
Climate change	1	1
People waiting years for basic medication and wheelchairs	1	1

No. of videos analyzed = 102.

The Affordable Care Act was the most prominent issue, mentioned in 30 videos (29% of all 102 videos). Women's health was the second most prominent issue (21%). The Children's Health Insurance Program emerged as the third most prominent issue (20%). The issue of mental health was also rather prominent (19%). It should be stressed that the frequency of issues raised was not equal between Donald Trump and Hillary Clinton; for example, Hillary Clinton was the only one who raised the issue of the Children's Health Insurance Program on all 20 occasions. Tables 7.2 and 7.3 will shed more light on the differences between videos of Donald Trump and videos of Hillary Clinton. Nonetheless, it is interesting to see the prominence of certain health issues in this filtered list of C-SPAN videos.

In order to find out the differences in health issues raised between Donald Trump and Hillary Clinton videos, RQ1a asked, "What were the most prominent health issues raised in the Donald Trump videos?" and RQ1b asked, "What were the most prominent health issues raised in the Hillary Clinton videos?" Tables 7.2 and 7.3 show the list of health issues raised, the number of videos that mention a health issue, and the rate of appearance in response to RQ1a and RQ1b, respectively.

The most prominent health issue raised by the Donald Trump videos was the Affordable Care Act (14 videos; 35%). The most prominent health issues raised by the Hillary Clinton videos were the Children's Health Insurance Program (20 videos; 32%), women's health (18 videos; 29%), mental health

TABLE 7.2 List of Health Issues Raised in Donald Trump Videos, Frequency, and Rate of Appearance

Health Issue	Frequency (f)	Rate of Appearance (%) (f/no. of videos)
Affordable Care Act (ACA)	14	35
Women's health	3	8
Mental health	2	5
Veterans' health	2	5
Drug issues (substance abuse)	1	3
Health care costs	1	3
Planned Parenthood	1	3

No. of videos analyzed = 102.

TABLE 7.3 List of Health Issues Raised in Hillary Clinton Videos, Frequency, and Rate of Appearance

Health Issue	Frequency (f)	Rate of Appearance (%) (f/no. of videos)
Children's Health Insurance Program	20	32
Women's health	18	29
Mental health	17	27
Affordable Care Act (ACA)	16	26
Childcare (e.g., school-based health)	16	26
Planned Parenthood	14	23
Affordable health care	13	21
Drug issues (e.g., substance abuse, overdose)	12	19
Universal health care	7	11
Prescription drugs	6	10
Medicare	5	8
Preexisting conditions	4	6
Access to health care	3	5
Health care costs	3	5
Health disparities	3	5
Medicaid	3	5
Veterans' health	3	5
Building health centers	2	3
Cancer	2	3
Immigrant health (e.g., Latinas)	2	3
Children drinking and bathing in poisoned water	1	2
Chronic disease	1	2
Climate change	1	2
People waiting years for basic medication and wheelchairs	1	2

No. of videos analyzed = 62.

(17 videos; 27%), Affordable Care Act (16 videos; 26%), and childcare (e.g., school-based health) (16 videos; 26%).

DISCUSSION

The findings indicate an interesting difference between the candidates in terms of the number of health issues raised. Hillary Clinton raised vastly more health issues—24, as opposed to Donald Trump's 7. The quantity, of course, does not suggest that one had a qualitatively superior exposition of health issues than the other. A few of the issues that were most often raised by Hillary Clinton revolved around women and children, which is unsurprising given her campaign's focus on these two groups of people. She also consistently substantiated her credibility with the success of the Children's Health Insurance Program.

The one issue that was consistently brought up by both candidates was the Affordable Care Act. Although this is a common point, both approached the issue very differently. Donald Trump, being a candidate who was contesting against the current system, depicted the Affordable Care Act in lugubrious contexts—that the prevailing health care system is bad and the health care privateers are running amok. For example, during his campaign at Cleveland, Ohio, Donald Trump labeled the system as a "disaster" and a "horror show":

> We will also repeal and replace the total disaster known as Obamacare. Health insurance premiums are going through the roof, led by Obamacare. And companies are being driven out of business, they're leaving our country over the cost of health care. It is a total disaster. Many companies are being forced to flee. Fire everybody, flee, go to another country. We are going to stop it day one. And Hillary Clinton wants to double down and make Obamacare bigger and even worse. Just this month, the Democratic governor of Minnesota admitted the reality is the Affordable Care Act, he said, is no longer affordable. He said that. You probably saw last week Bill Clinton called Obamacare the craziest thing in the world.... Obamacare care is a disaster. Premiums are going up 60, 70, 80, 90%. Next year it's going to be worse. It is lousy health care. It is terrible. The deductibles

are so high, you don't want to use it anyway. If you need it you will never get to use it because the deductibles have gotten so high. It is our horror show. We are to repeal it and replace it. And, this is our chance to get rid of this law. We are going to approve and get something that is so much less expensive and so good. A great health care system, a system that you deserve. (C-SPAN, 2016b)

Ambiguity—such as the vagueness of the proposed "great health care system"—was a common feature in many of Donald Trump's speeches related to health. Perhaps Donald Trump's omission of a clear, issue-oriented blueprint was a reason for the low number of health issues he raised.

On the other hand, Hillary Clinton was supportive of the Affordable Care Act, which is expected given her affiliation as a Democrat. While she denounced health care privateers as well, she differed in focusing extensively on women's and children's health. For example, at the Minnesota Democratic-Farmer-Labor Party's fifth annual Humphrey-Mondale Dinner, Hillary Clinton said about the Affordable Care Act:

And it is helping so many people right now. We have 90% coverage; 10% short of universal coverage. No more denials because of pre-existing conditions. Young people up to the age of 26 can be on their parents' policies. Women no longer pay more for our insurance than men. And no more lifetime limits. (C-SPAN, 2016a)

Interestingly, health was often portrayed gloomily. Even the enthusiastic endorsements of the Affordable Care Act were done in the purview of problematic situations and an acknowledgment that the system needs revision and upgrading. Perhaps election candidates strategically and intentionally paint a gloomy picture so that their propositions—and effectively their role as president—may seem appealing and necessary. In any case, this form of negative portrayal is interestingly and markedly different from the health portrayals often found in entertainment media—desirable (e.g., Jamieson & Romer, 2014) or even fashionable (e.g., Veldhuis, Konijn, & Seidell, 2014).

Thus the findings help answer RQ2, which asked, "How is health portrayed in the 2016 C-SPAN reports on presidential candidates Donald Trump and Hillary Clinton?" Besides the gloomy portrayal of health, the findings indicate that the prominence of a health issue is largely dependent on who the politician is, as well as the strategy of the politician in campaigns. For example, because Hillary Clinton is a proponent for women's and children's health, it is unsurprising to see Planned Parenthood and children's health being prominently featured in the Hillary Clinton videos. One common thread between the Donald Trump and Hillary Clinton videos is the prominence of Affordable Care Act and insurance issues. The prominence may be owing to a shoot-and-retaliate pattern between the two candidates; each time Donald Trump attacks the Affordable Care Act, Hillary Clinton retaliates and defends the system. This back-and-forth pattern thus may have accumulated and burgeoned superfluously issues of the Affordable Care Act and insurance. Whereas entertainment media may feature health-related depictions or topics depending on, say, profitability for an organization to do so (e.g., tobacco companies promoting that smoking is cool), political media may feature health-related topics depending on political agenda, with a shoot-and-retaliate pattern beckoning from each agenda.

This study began by positing a gap in literature in which health portrayal is mostly studied in the purview of entertainment media instead of other forms of media such as political media. This study narrowed the gap by finding several key points that advance the latter scholarship. First, in political media, health is often narrated by politicians with public support as the main objective, as opposed to entertainment media in which companies narrate health with sales and consumption as the main objective. Because of such disparate objectives, the former narrates health in problem-solution terms (e.g., prescription drug prices are high, therefore support the Affordable Care Act), whereas the latter may avoid problematizing health in order to advance a product, show, or idea (e.g., Blair et al., 2005). Second, in political media, politicians focus on health matters that their affiliated parties prioritize, and thus politicians with the same objective (e.g., winning the presidential election) may focus on different health issues. For example, Donald Trump focused on the Affordable Care Act whereas Hillary Clinton focused more on children's and women's health. In contrast, in entertainment media, companies with similar objectives (e.g., increase cigarette sales) may sometimes focus on the same topic (e.g., cigarettes). Third, in political media, the way a health topic is framed is dependent on the political party's agenda. For example, both Donald Trump and Hillary Clinton discussed the Affordable Care Act, but the former framed it as a problematic system (see C-SPAN, 2016b) whereas the latter framed it as a system that works (see C-SPAN, 2016a). In contrast, in entertainment media, a topic (e.g., cigarette smoking) is often portrayed consistently among companies (e.g., smoking is cool).

This study had several limitations. First, the transcripts contained errors and omissions; however, these were not significant to the extent of compromising the study. Nonetheless, potential implications should be considered. Second, "health" is a complex concept that may include holistic elements; for example, poverty may be a precursor of and strong factor in poor health. However, this study did not code terms such as "poverty," because such in-depth and contextual analysis is beyond the ambit of the study. Third, this study limited the search criteria to mentions of "health," but Donald Trump or Hillary Clinton may have elaborated on health-related issues at other events without specifically mentioning the term "health." Such events, if any, would have been omitted in the analysis because of the search criteria. Fourth, the study focused on coding the number of videos that mentioned a health issue; therefore, the study does not say anything about the quality of explication of a health issue. For example, a candidate may have mentioned, say, health care costs much more often than the other candidate, but the latter may have provided greater exposition on the issue. In any case, quality of explication is also beyond the ambit of this study.

CONCLUSION

This study addressed a gap in the literature by analyzing how health is portrayed in political media. Previous literature tended to focus on health portrayal in entertainment media, such as magazines and movies. This study found that health was depicted gloomily during the campaigns leading to Election Day and postulated that politicians may portray health in this manner in order to enhance the appeal and necessity of their propositions. This study also found that health portrayal in political media may be predicated on political agenda and exacerbated by the shoot-and-retaliate nature of politicking. The study also found three characteristics of political media that makes its portrayal of health different from entertainment media: (1) health is often narrated by politicians with public support as the main objective, (2) politicians focus on health matters that their affiliated parties prioritize, and (3) the way a health topic is framed is dependent on the political party's agenda. There is much to explore in future studies, such as health portrayal beyond the ambit of elections, comparative studies between entertainment media and political media, and the relation between the prominence of health issues raised and political position.

REFERENCES

Arrington, M. I., & Goodier, B. C. (2004). Prostration before the law: Representations of illness, interaction, and intimacy in the *NYPD Blue* prostate cancer narrative. *Popular Communication, 2*(2), 67–84. https://doi.org/10.1207/s15405710pc0202_1

Beullens, K., & Schepers, A. (2013). Display of alcohol use on Facebook: A content analysis. *Cyberpsychology, Behavior, and Social Networking, 16*(7), 497–503. https://doi.org/10.1089/cyber.2013.0044

Blair, N. A., Yue, S. K., Singh, R., & Bernhardt, J. M. (2005). Depictions of substance use in reality television: A content analysis of *The Osbournes. BMJ, 331*(7531), 1517–1519. https://doi.org/10.1136/bmj.331.7531.1517

Bleakley, A., Romer, D., & Jamieson, P. E. (2014). Violent film characters' portrayal of alcohol, sex, and tobacco-related behaviors. *Pediatrics, 133*(1), 71–77. https://doi.org/10.1542/peds.2013-1922

C-SPAN. (n.d.). C-SPAN through the years.... Retrieved from https://www.c-span.org/about/milestones/

C-SPAN (Producer). (2016a, February 12). *2016 Humphrey-Mondale dinner* [online video]. Available from https://www.c-span.org/video/?404629-1/2016-humphrey mondale-dinner&start=3749

C-SPAN (Producer). (2016b, October 22). *Donald Trump campaign rally in Cleveland, Ohio* [online video]. Available from https://www.c-span.org/video/?417332-1/republican-ticket-campaigns-cleveland-ohio

Cutcliffe, J. R., & Hannigan, B. (2001). Mass media, "monsters" and mental health clients: The need for increased lobbying. *Journal of Psychiatric and Mental Health Nursing, 8*(4), 315–321. https://doi.org/10.1046/j.1365-2850.2001.00394.x

Diefenbach, D. L. (1997). The portrayal of mental illness on prime-time television. *Journal of Community Psychology, 25*(3), 289–302. https://doi.org/10.1002/(SICI)1520-6629(199705)25:3<289::AID-JCOP5>3.0.CO;2-R

Eggerton, J. (2013). *Exclusive: C-SPAN study finds almost quarter of cable/satellite subs watch weekly*. Retrieved from http://www.broadcastingcable.com/news

/programming/exclusive-c-span-study-finds-almost-quarter-cablesatellite-subs-watch-weekly/65409

Francis, C., Pirkis, J., Blood, R. W., Dunt, D., Burgess, P., Morley, B., ... & Putnis, P. (2004). The portrayal of mental health and illness in Australian non-fiction media. *Australian and New Zealand Journal of Psychiatry, 38*(7), 541–546. https://doi.org/10.1111/j.1440-1614.2004.01407.x

Gollust, S. E., Eboh, I., & Barry, C. L. (2012). Picturing obesity: Analyzing the social epidemiology of obesity conveyed through US news media images. *Social Science & Medicine, 74*(10), 1544–1551. https://doi.org/10.1016/j.socscimed.2012.01.021

Groesz, L. M., Levine, M. P., & Murnen, S. K. (2002). The effect of experimental presentation of thin media images on body satisfaction: A meta-analytic review. *International Journal of Eating Disorders, 31*(1), 1–16. https://doi.org/10.1002/eat.10005

Inch, R., & Merali, N. (2006). A content analysis of popular magazine articles on eating disorders. *Eating Disorders, 14*(2), 109–120. https://doi.org/10.1080/10640260500536250

Jamieson, P. E., & Romer, D. (2014). Portrayal of tobacco use in prime-time TV dramas: Trends and associations with adult cigarette consumption—USA, 1955-2010. *Tobacco Control, 24,* 243–248. https://doi.org/10.1136/tobaccocontrol-2012-050896

Kline, K. N. (2006). A decade of research on health content in the media: The focus on health challenges and sociocultural context and attendant informational and ideological problems. *Journal of Health Communication, 11*(1), 43–59. https://doi.org/10.1080/10810730500461067

Lamb, B. (2014). C-SPAN's origins and place in history: Personal commentary. In R. X. Browning (Ed.), *The C-SPAN Archives: An interdisciplinary resource for discovery, learning, and engagement* (pp. 15–26). West Lafayette, IN: Purdue University Press.

Mattson, M., & Lam, C. (2016). *Health advocacy: A communication approach.* Manhattan, NY: Peter Lang.

Moreno, M. A., Briner, L. R., Williams, A., Brockman, L., Walker, L., & Christakis, D. A. (2010). A content analysis of displayed alcohol references on a social networking web site. *Journal of Adolescent Health, 47*(2), 168–175. https://doi.org/10.1016/j.jadohealth.2010.01.001

Morgan, E. M., Snelson, C., & Elison-Bowers, P. (2010). Image and video disclosure of substance use on social media websites. *Computers in Human Behavior, 26*(6), 1405–1411. https://doi.org/10.1016/j.chb.2010.04.017

Navarro, V., Muntaner, C., Borrell, C., Benach, J., Quiroga, Á., Rodríguez-Sanz, M., ... & Pasarín, M. I. (2006). Politics and health outcomes. *Lancet, 368*(9540), 1033–1037. https://doi.org/10.1016/S0140-6736(06)69341-0

Pendo, E. (2004). Images of health insurance in popular film: The dissolving critique. *Journal of Health Law, 37,* 267–315.

Person, B., Sy, F., Holton, K., Govert, B., Liang, A., & the NCID/SARS Community Outreach Team (2004). Fear and stigma: The epidemic within the SARS outbreak. *Emerging Infectious Diseases, 10*(2), 358–363. Retrieved from https://wwwnc.cdc.gov/eid/article/10/2/03-0750_article

Saguy, A. C., & Gruys, K. (2010). Morality and health: News media constructions of overweight and eating disorders. *Social Problems, 57*(2), 231–250. https://doi.org/10.1525/sp.2010.57.2.231

Seale, C. (2003). Health and media: An overview. *Sociology of Health & Illness, 25*(6), 513–531. https://doi.org/10.1111/1467-9566.t01-1-00356

Smith, R. (2007). Media depictions of health topics: Challenge and stigma formats. *Journal of Health Communication, 12*(3), 233–249. https://doi.org/10.1080/10810730701266273

Stuart, H. (2006). Media portrayal of mental illness and its treatments: What effect does it have on people with mental illness? *CNS Drugs, 20*(2), 99–106. https://doi.org/10.2165/00023210 200620020-00002

Thomsen, S. R., McCoy, J. K., Gustafson, R., & Williams, H. (2002). Motivations for reading beauty and fashion magazines and anorexic risk in college-age women. *Media Psychology, 4*(2), 113–135. https://doi.org/10.1207/S1532785XMEP0402_01

Veldhuis, J., Konijn, E. A., & Seidell, J. C. (2014). Counteracting media's thin-body ideal for adolescent girls: Informing is more effective than warning. *Media Psychology, 17*(2), 154–184. https://doi.org/10.1080/15213269.2013.788327

Wahl, O. (2003). Depictions of mental illnesses in children's media. *Journal of Mental Health, 12*(3), 249–258. https://doi.org/10.1080/0963823031000118230

Wallerstein, N. (1992). Powerlessness, empowerment, and health: Implications for health promotion programs. *American Journal of Health Promotion, 6*(3), 197–205.

Zoller, H. M., & Worrell, T. (2006). Television illness depictions, identity, and social experience: Responses to multiple sclerosis on *The West Wing* among people with MS. *Health Communication, 20*(1), 69–79. https://doi.org/10.1207/s15327027hc2001_7

CHAPTER 8

PORTRAYALS OF PUBLIC POLICY DISCOURSE

Zoe M. Oxley

What is the nature of political discourse surrounding public policy discussions? What specific messages about policy issues do political elites communicate? Where do these messages originate? What messages reach the public? Which resonate with the public? To varying degrees, the prior three chapters in this volume address these questions, illuminating important features of public policy communication along the way. The benefits of using videos and transcripts from the C-SPAN Archives' online Video Library for scholarly research are also well on display in these chapters.

One rhetorical device used by policy advocates is issue framing. Framing is "the process by which a communication source ... defines and constructs a political issue or public controversy" (Nelson, Clawson, & Oxley, 1997, p. 567). The framing of an issue places attention on specific features of that issue and (often implicitly) away from other relevant features, which in turn can influence whether the recipient of the communication supports or opposes the issue at hand. Indeed, this is typically the goal of advocates, to frame an issue in a certain way in order to gain support for the advocates' preferred policy outcome. Examples of issue framing appear in all three of the previous chapters, especially so in Elizabeth Wulbrecht's research. Wulbrecht explores the framing of mental illness among members of Congress. She is particularly interested in the occurrence of two specific frames: a treatment frame that highlights the need to treat mental health needs and a danger frame that emphasizes dangers posed by those with mental illness. More fully capturing the nature of congressional discourse pertaining to mental health, however, required Wulbrecht to expand her conceptual lens beyond framing. Drawing upon Anne Schneider and Helen Ingram's (1993) important work on the social construction of groups who are the focus of policy discussions, Wulbrecht concludes that the framing of mental illness differs by target group. Members of Congress were more likely to use the treatment than the danger frame, for example, when discussing mental illness among military veterans. Both frames were present in discourse surrounding adolescents, especially young men. Wulbrecht draws upon textual evidence from member speeches to demonstrate that this group was viewed as needing mental health treatment precisely because they are a danger to themselves and to society.

We see examples of elite issue framing in Nancy Brown's work as well as the chapter by Chervin Lam and Somrita Ganchoudhuri. During the 1980s, the AIDS epidemic was framed by some as a public health crisis whereas others framed AIDS as a disease afflicting only intravenous drug users and gay men (Brown). The Affordable Care Act (also known as Obamacare) has been framed by critics as failing to keep the cost of insurance premiums as well as health care from rising and by supporters as successful in insuring many previously uninsured Americans (Lam and Ganchoudhuri). While these examples were identified by the authors in their research, neither of these projects were intended to be framing studies per se. Instead, both projects set out to conduct different types of analyses of elite policy communication. In particular, Lam and Ganchoudhuri examine how health was portrayed on the campaign trail during the 2016 U.S. presidential election. Anyone who followed the election happenings that year will know that Donald Trump devoted significant attention to criticizing Obamacare, while Hillary Clinton defended this policy, all the while pointing out where it could be improved. Clinton also frequently discussed the health care needs of women and children, certainly more than her opponent did. Lam and Ganchoudhuri also uncover some trends that many observers of the election might have missed.

Their analysis, for example, reveals large discrepancies in the number and range of health-related topics mentioned by the two candidates.

In her analysis of policy discussion surrounding HIV/AIDS during the 1980s, Brown is most interested in exploring whether messages that originated with gay and lesbian rights organizations became prominent in public discussions of this issue. She provides examples of subcommittee chairs in the both the U.S. House and the U.S. Senate discussing AIDS as a public health concern, much as activist groups had advocated. The presence of leaders in the gay and lesbian rights movement testifying at legislative hearings is also evidence, Brown argues, of the group's successful communication strategies. Yet, Brown also demonstrates that many messages counter to these activists' goals were present in the national discussion of HIV/AIDS. National lawmakers warned against the dangers of a too powerful homosexual rights lobby, differentiated between sympathetic AIDS patients versus the unsympathetic groups of drug users and gay men, or questioned whether gays and lesbians could undergo treatment to "make them normal." Public fears about and misinformation regarding the transmission of AIDS were also on display, as evidenced by the content of comments people made during call-in programs on C-SPAN. Ultimately, Brown paints a nuanced picture of HIV/AIDS policy discussion during this time period, capturing a multiplicity of views emanating from many different political actors.

Brown ends her chapter with a list of reasons why historians would benefit from using C-SPAN videos in their scholarship. Scholars from other disciplines who are interested in policy discourse should also heed Brown's advice. I wish to highlight in particular her point regarding the diversity of C-SPAN programming that is available for study. She examined, among others, congressional hearings, public call-in shows (which feature invited guests such as journalists, public officials, or activists), coverage of panels organized by professional organizations and interest groups, and campaign events. This variety was ideal for her research goals, allowing Brown to present a broad, contextualized analysis of the national conversation regarding HIV/AIDS during the early years of public attention to this issue. Many other public policy matters could be similarly explored via C-SPAN videos, whether in pursuit of addressing the questions I posed at the beginning of this chapter or others related to the nature, spread, and influence of public policy messages.

REFERENCES

Nelson, T. E., Clawson, R. A., & Oxley, Z. M. (1997). Media framing of a civil liberties conflict and its effect on tolerance. *American Political Science Review, 91,* 567–583.

Schneider, A., & Ingram, H. (1993). Social construction of target populations: Implications for politics and policy. *American Political Science Review, 87,* 334–347.

CHAPTER 9

DONALD TRUMP MEETS THE UBIQUITOUS PRESIDENCY

Delaney Harness and Joshua M. Scacco

President Donald Trump and the social media platform Twitter are intricately tied. Shortly after Trump's surprising victory in the 2016 presidential election, NPR White House correspondent Tamara Keith dubbed the president-elect "Commander-in-Tweet" (Keith, 2016). The moniker popped up again 50 days into his presidency when NBC News ran a story about "50 Days of @RealDonaldTrump" (Brand, Petulla, & Dann, 2017). For all the focus on Twitter, the president also has used other media to disseminate his administration's message. From more traditional venues, like his address to a joint session of Congress or the Saturday YouTube address, to softer, emergent venues like *Fox & Friends,* President Trump communicates from a variety of settings with a multitude of purposes. This chapter looks at Trump's communication during the first 30 days of his presidency, comparing his much-talked-about tweets to his more traditional communicative actions as documented by the C-SPAN Archives' online Video Library.

The first 30 days of a presidential administration present a critical time to examine executive communication. An administration is in flux—establishing an aggressive agenda, staffing agencies and government posts—while still needing to convey forward motion. Communication is critical to this endeavor. During this time, a president must position his administration as institutionally capable of working with Congress while also focusing on altering and defining parameters of public debate on agenda items. Again, communication is critical (Campbell & Jamieson, 2008; Hart, 2008). All of these actions occur under the news media's microscope, a difficult endeavor under the most standard of circumstances.

How Donald Trump communicatively took on the mantle of the presidency is the focus of this chapter. Yet the broader story we tell is how the new president faced and, in many ways, adopted a discursive style that emerged during the Clinton years: ubiquitous communicative outreach (see Scacco & Coe, 2016). This sense of "everywhereness" is critical to the power of a modern presidential institution jousting for public attention amid an endless stream of social, cultural, and political information. To tell this story, we review the state of contemporary presidential communication and the modern emergence of a ubiquitous presidency, including its main tenets of accessibility, personality, and pluralism. Our analysis then zeroes in on Trump's language in his speeches and tweets to document the ways in which Trump met, extended, and challenged the practices of presidential ubiquity. Trump arguably expands communicative outreach by looking beyond traditional communication platforms and news outlets to reach his supporters. To capture Trump's approach, this chapter expands the scope of inquiry to examine a unique data set including his traditional communications and tweets. By analyzing a diverse set of Trump's discourse, we visualize the ways Trump communicatively adopted, strained, and rejected modes of contemporary outreach.

PREVIOUS RESEARCH

Presidential Ubiquity

Contemporary presidential communication, particularly in the Obama and Trump administrations, has not only sparked popular press attention, but also academic interest as well (DiIulio, 2012; Herbst, 2012; Mercieca & Vaughn, 2009; Scacco & Coe, 2016; Stuckey, 2010). Scholarly inquiries have focused on how traditional modes of presidential rhetoric—mass appeals, the construction of arguments, traditional settings—have evolved with changing media and audiences. One of the original theorists on the rhetorical presidency, Tulis (2012), has called on scholars to take into account how rhetorical postmodernization changes the means, content, and purposes of presidential appeals (for the original conception of the rhetorical presidency, see Tulis, 1987). The ubiquitous presidency framework responds to scholarship and popular observations highlighting the fracturing of traditional modes of presidential communication (Scacco & Coe, 2016).

Presidential ubiquity is built on the premise that "modern presidents cultivate a highly visible and nearly constant presence in both political and nonpolitical arenas of American life via engagement in a fragmented media environment" (Scacco & Coe, 2016, p. 2015). The fragmentation of media, diversification of the American audience, and increased hybrid nature of communicative political content present a challenging environment for presidential influence. Contemporary presidents must now find audiences in the basketball section of ESPN.com or the clustered echo chambers of Twitter. As Hart (1987) remarked in the era of a rhetorical presidency, executive communication constitutes official governance when the materials of traditional governance—legislation and congressional negotiation—are in progress or stalled. It is precisely these perspectives that make examining the first month of a new presidential administration so important.

The first 30 days of a new administration present opportunities to examine how the president relates to others, talks about himself and his administration, and constitutes the American public through communication. With the possibility that many legislative actions will be "in progress" during this time, the president must put some wins on the board to illustrate forward motion. Indeed, President Franklin Roosevelt's first 100 days' legislative juggernaut established in the depths of the Great Depression weighs as a metric on his successors (Scacco, 2011). Official communications can paint the picture of progress. For the contemporary ubiquitous president, this means tying a sense of accessibility, personality, and pluralism to agenda movement.

Accessibility

The contemporary media environment, a fragmented mix of established and emergent digital platforms for conveying all kinds of information, demands that the president be venue agnostic and present a sense of interactivity with the public. Whether the president appears on late-night comedy programs or daytime talk shows, the venues for communication and opportunities for interaction have expanded the possibilities for official pronouncements. Scacco & Coe (2016) recognized this trait of contemporary presidential communication by examining the White House website and news media associations of the president with modes of executive address, including "speech" and "interview." Their findings build on research in political science and communication, including the importance of accessibility and narrowcasting to presidential agenda advocacy (Jacobs, 2005; Stuckey, 2010). This diversification and engagement approach appears to pay some dividends for the president. Eshbaugh-Soha (2016) finds that presidents can be successful agenda setters for their priorities when appearing in nontraditional venues.

The early presidency of Donald Trump has crafted digital-based accessibility via the social media platform Twitter. Specifically, as a candidate and later as president, Trump has used Twitter to present his policy positions and reactions to events in a simple manner. He also has used the platform to harass political opponents and bully journalists and individual citizens (Hardy, Phillips, & LaMarre, 2017; Scacco, Coe, & Harness, forthcoming). In an analysis of the first 100 days of the president's tweets, Hardy and colleagues (2017) find that Trump engaged in a sustained attack on news outlets. During this time, the president tweeted, on average, slightly less than five times per day on topics related to "fake news," the "failing *New York Times*," and "fake media." The president's use of Twitter also has an important participatory dimension for his supporters by fueling political engagement (Scacco, Coe, & Harness, forthcoming).

Comparing the president's more traditional offline communications to his outreach on Twitter will illustrate potentially different ways in which Donald Trump paints a portrait of accessibility for the public. In general, candidates and elected officials are reticent to engage transactionally with the public (Chadwick, 2013; Owen & Davis, 2008; Stromer-Galley, 2014). Yet, there may be other means by which Trump gave the illusion of accessibility during his first month in office. Populist-based movements in the United States and internationally have found needed adrenaline from social and digital media technologies (Engesser, Ernst, Esser, & Büchel, 2017; Groshek & Engelbert, 2013), a point not lost on the Trump team's messaging of "America First" and "Make America Great Again." Populist appeals thrive on demonization of opponents and calls to action (Jagers & Walgrave, 2007; Kazin, 1995). Building on the work of Hardy and colleagues (2017), how did the president discuss the media, press, and social media with regard to his administration's accessibility? How might the president have encouraged forms of interactive engagement with the administration's agenda?

Personality

The extent to which a president conveys informality and disclosiveness in his communication has been an understudied area of presidential discourse. The first scholarly recognition of a rhetorical presidency was wedded to a warning of the connection between personality and demagoguery (Ceaser, Thurow, Tulis, & Bessette, 1981). Yet, modern technology helped feed the management of political personality nonetheless. Political communication scholarship in the mass media golden age emphasized how radio and television created a more intimate presidential style (Hart, 1999; Jamieson, 1988) while placing image management at the center of modern communication (see Edelman, 1985). More recent work has tied media development to a more simple, illogical, and emotional presidential discourse style (Lim, 2008). Indeed, this "postrhetorical presidency" can use personality, in part, to frustrate and even confuse citizens (Hartnett & Mercieca, 2007). This drive for a more personable chief executive bumps up against established public expectations of more dignified, professional presidential communication (Scacco & Coe, 2017a).

Contemporary digital and social media technologies are inherently personal (McGregor, Lawrence, & Cardona, 2016), placing an emphasis on informality and disclosure critical to communicating in a myriad of settings (Scacco & Coe, 2016). Political campaigns, in America and internationally, take great care to market the affective, personality-based components of candidacies online and offline (Davis & Owen, 1998; Hermans & Vergeer, 2013; Stromer-Galley, 2014). The emotional tie to or "buy in" for candidates can create affective solidarity among supporters or opponents, an important component of message contagion and viral adaption on social media (see Papacharissi, 2015). These principles also apply to contemporary presidential communication.

President Trump's official communications during his first month in office may evince elements of personality characteristic of modern discursive ubiquity. Scacco and Coe (2016) in their original conceptualization of the ubiquitous presidency looked to Twitter biographies of cabinet officers in the Obama administration as well as mentions of the president with family in press accounts to illustrate the growing personalization of the presidency. We extend this work. Specifically, Donald Trump may convey informality by using emotionally laden language so as to establish affective ties with his base of supporters (Papacharissi, 2015). The president may have offered elements of disclosure by how he discussed his family members in official communications. We investigate these possibilities and compare their occurrences between traditional and Twitter communications.

Pluralism

The complexities of American life greet every occupant of the Oval Office. How the president speaks to these complexities, particularly within the body politic, has evolved. Traditionally, presidents have attempted to communicatively construct a whole public via mass communication technologies and in the process gloss over the ever-present pluralism in American political life (see Dahl, 1961; Schattschneider, 1975). The segmentation of media audiences, diversification of the national population, and diffusion of digital technologies has highlighted the nature of coalitional politics and led the president to respond to these changes in official communications (Papacharissi, 2015; Scacco & Coe, 2016; Stuckey, 2010).

In grappling with audience complexities, the contemporary ubiquitous presidency may adopt a more positive or negative communicative stance toward American pluralism. For instance, Scacco and Coe (2016) find that presidents since Bill Clinton increasingly emphasize diverse gallery guests during the State of the Union addresses—a means of highlighting American pluralism. Moreover, compared to their predecessors, Presidents Bush and Obama were increasingly associated in news accounts with historically sidelined groups in the United States: Hispanics, gays, and members of non–Judeo-Christian faiths.

Strikingly, Donald Trump—as candidate and as president—plays the politics of antipluralism (Scacco & Coe, 2017b). During the 2016 presidential campaign, Trump was associated more with Latinos and non–Judeo-Christian religions in major news publications compared to Hillary Clinton. The Republican candidate's calls for a border wall and a ban on Muslim immigration into the United States surely contributed to these mentions, instances of Trump addressing the pluralism inherent in American political life by explicitly resisting it. We extend these observations into the first 30 days of the Trump presidency. If Trump continued on this trajectory, we should expect to see him communicatively embrace national homogeneity ("we," "us," "our") within his construction of the American public and discursively separate himself and his voter base from elements of pluralism ("they," "them," "other").

METHODOLOGY

To examine the first 30 days of Donald Trump's presidential communication, we turn to computational methodologies designed to analyze large amounts of text for relationships. Semantic network analysis, a type of text mining, is a research approach that creates coreference pairs of words and word phrases (i.e., two words that are next to each other in text) from a text corpus, or body of text, to identify patterns in textual data that are too large to be coded by hand. The words are represented in a networked format by nodes and the relationships between words by a line between nodes, referred to as an edge (Brandes & Erlebach, 2005; Newman, 2003; Newman, Barabasi & Watts, 2011; Sowa, 1991). In a coreferencing semantic network, words that are close to each other in a text corpus are considered linked in the data (coreference pairs), and, within these linkages, meanings and concepts can be uncovered (Lambert, 2017). Semantic networks then visualize and categorize data to illustrate a concept network of the data set (Doerfel, 1998). The researcher then interprets the meaning of the semantic network.

Data Collection

We collected tweets and speeches of Donald Trump during the first 30 days of his presidency from January 20, 2017 to February 20, 2017. Tweets were collected using RStudio and transcripts of speeches and press conferences were provided by the C-SPAN Video Library. Transcripts of speeches and press conferences included any remarks made by the president within the transcript, whether they were prepared remarks or answers to questions from the press. A total of 192 tweets and 49 speech transcripts were collected.

Speeches and tweets were then put into separate text corpora that correspond with the collection of Twitter data or speech data. We then created a semantic network for each text corpus of all the tweets or transcripts collected, and they were then used as a comparison between the two message platforms.

Preprocessing Data

Based on the data collected, a text corpus was created for Trump tweets and Trump speeches and imported into AutoMap. AutoMap is a program that cleans text through a process called preprocessing, and then develops a list of coreference words that become the semantic list for a semantic network (Carley, 2001). Each text corpus was preprocessed to remove high-frequency and noise words that did not enrich the data (e.g., and, that, this, the, but); misspelled words were fixed; contractions and punctuation were removed. Word capitalization was removed to account for differences in transcripts.

Analyzing Networks

After preprocessing, AutoMap was used to generate a coreference semantic list. A total of 19,518 coreferences were generated from the speech transcripts text corpus and 1,814 coreferences were generated from the Twitter text corpus. The coreference list was then imported into NodeXL, an extension file of Excel spreadsheets, to create a semantic network from each text corpus (Smith et al., 2010). Nodes (words) in these semantic networks develop relationships with other nodes (words) and with the structure itself that can be explained with centralities: link frequency, degree centrality, betweenness centrality, and eigenvector centrality. These semantic networks were then used to interpret Trump's speeches, press conferences, and tweets through the lens of the ubiquitous presidency.

Link frequency can be interpreted as how often two words appear together in a text. The thicker the edge (line) between two words, the more often they occur together. For example, in Figure 9.1 the line between "join" and "me" is noticeably thicker than other lines in the network, indicating a greater link frequency.

Degree centrality can be thought of as the popularity of a word as it explains how often a word is connected to other words in a text. The degree centrality of the node "tremendous" in Figure 9.4 is relatively high for that network because it has many edges connecting it to other words.

Betweenness centrality measures the shortest distance between the farthest nodes in a network, and certain nodes act as bridges between parts of the network. Within these structures, words with high betweenness centralities are nodes that bridge ideas and concepts in the overall network. Often, without these words, the network would separate ideas or concepts. These words essentially broker what ideas are connected to other ideas. For example, the word "our" in Figure 9.3 acts as a connection between "news" and "media" to bridge concepts that are generated from each of these micro-networks.

Eigenvector centrality accounts for the power and influence of a node in a network and measures the relative connection of a node to other nodes within a network. Higher centrality is assigned to nodes connected to other more influential nodes. This measure ascertains the most important words or concepts in the network that dictate the key ideas and concepts within a text. In the Trump networks (for example, see Figures 9.6 and 9.7), "us" and "we" have high eigenvector scores that help shape how Trump constructs the American public.

FINDINGS AND DISCUSSION

To assess the extent to which President Trump adopted a ubiquitous communication style during his first 30 days in office, we look at the accessibility, personality, and pluralism displayed in his tweets and more traditional presidential communications.

Accessibility

We examined how the president conveys accessibility by how he encouraged individuals to interact or engage with his administration and how he talked about the multiple media platforms that carry his messages.

Interactivity
Looking first at how the president encouraged (or did not encourage) interaction with his administration reveals important differences between how

Trump communicates on Twitter compared to more traditional settings. One common way that the president advances his message on Twitter is through sharing news stories, videos, and photographs (see Figure 9.1). For example, on February 10, 2017, Trump tweeted a photo with the caption "Heading to Joint Base Andrews on #MarineOne with Prime Minister Shinzo earlier today. https://t.co/4JFhyYdeHO." Trump also encourages "click" engagement to advance his administration's central arguments and to lead traffic back to traditional speeches on the White House website or news associated with favorable media outlets. "Join"–"me"–"video_clip" are tied prominently within Figure 9.1 with a thicker edge between them than other words in the network, indicating a high link frequency. During this 30-day period, the president shared videos and news stories 38 times via Twitter, an average of more than one audiovisual share per day during this time. Not only do these audiovisual elements serve as invitations for his followers to view his speeches or particular news stories, but they also act as a selectivity cue for the president to direct particular types of media consumption. These aims extend and enhance individuals' general tendencies to view news information compatible with their own political leanings (Stroud, 2011).

President Trump's more traditional communications, including public speeches and press conferences, do not encourage the same level of

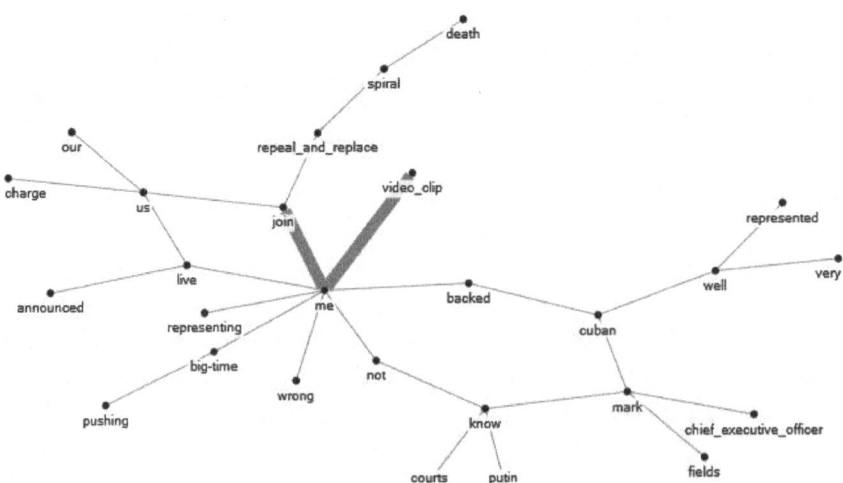

FIGURE 9.1 Interactivity network—Twitter communications. (Created with NodeXL Pro [http://nodexl.codeplex.com] from the Social Media Research Foundation [http://www.smrfoundation.org].)

interactivity, a potential direct consequence of the technological affordances of the Twitter platform. Trump develops interactivity on Twitter by sharing video clips and news stories, and inviting participation. His use of "join"-"me" and "join"-"us" in Figure 9.1 create at least the impression of interactivity. However, in speeches and press conferences, interactivity is limited to nonexistent. Trump never explicitly invites participation or shares news stories in any of his speeches or press conferences. Relegating interactivity to Twitter may assist the goals of reaching journalists while also engendering affective cohesion among supportive individuals.

Platform

The general image of a contemporary president is created when the president must communicate across multiple types of media platforms. For this reason, as well as journalists' perceived negativity toward his administration, President Trump is enamored with discussing "media." In both his traditional communications as well as tweets, Trump frequently discusses news, media, and the press. As Figures 9.2 and 9.3 show, Trump often mentions "foxandfriends," "abc," "abc2020," "cnn," "cbs," "foxnews," and the "failing"-"new_york_times."

For example, Trump tweeted "The FAKE NEWS media (failing @nytimes, @NBCNews, @ABC, @CBS, @CNN) is not my enemy, it is the enemy of the American People!" on February 17, 2017. In contrast he tweeted in January 2017, "Congratulations to @FoxNews for being number one in inauguration ratings. They were many times higher than FAKE NEWS @CNN - public is smart!"

In each of the networks (Figures 9.2 and 9.3), "news" and "media" both have high degree centrality and betweenness centrality, meaning these words are popular within Trump's communications and act as important bridges between the positive and negative dichotomies of the press. Yet, an important difference emerges in how Trump uses "news" between his traditional communications and tweets. "News" has a medium eigenvector centrality in the Twitter network, but no eigenvector centrality in the speech network. This means that while "news" is relatively influential in its position within the Twitter network as an important topic, it does not connect with powerful words in the traditional communication network and is a relative outlier. Trump appears to focus more on specific news outlet in his Twitter feed and prefers to generalize "news" in his traditional communications. "Press" and "media" have low eigenvector centrality for both networks, suggesting that Trump uses his communications to either target his supporters to attend to particular news or target news outlets for praise or scorn.

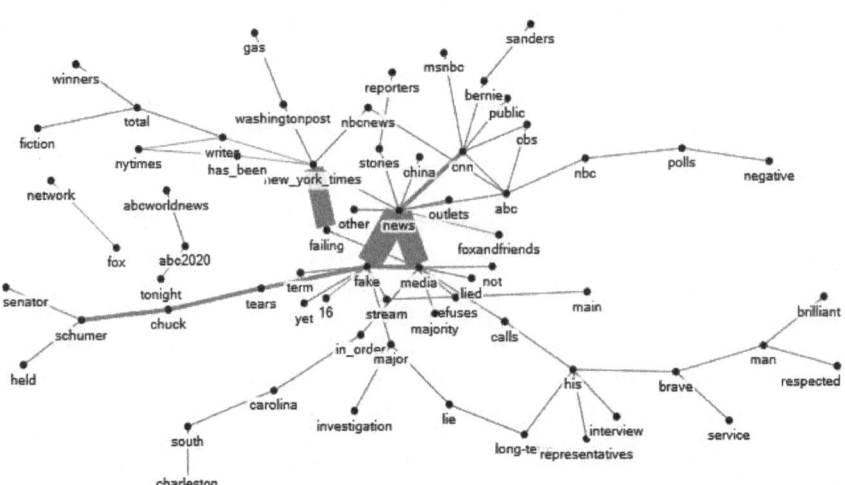

FIGURE 9.2 Space between Twitter communications. (Created with NodeXL Pro [http://nodexl.codeplex.com] from the Social Media Research Foundation [http://www.smrfoundation.org].)

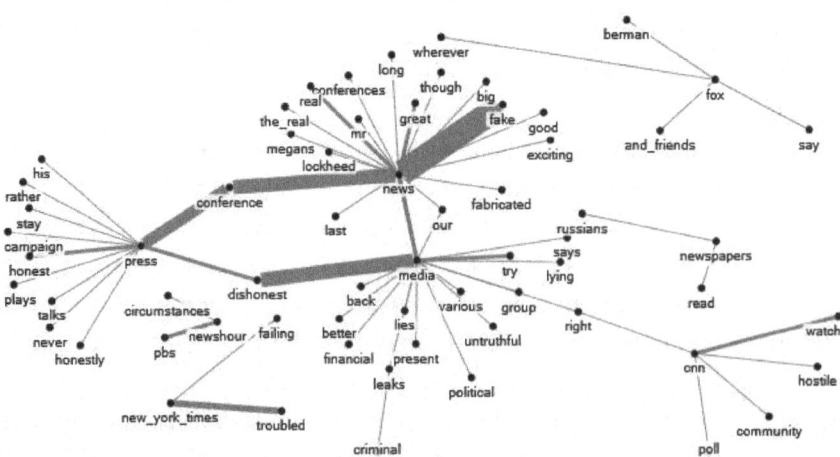

FIGURE 9.3 Space between traditional communications. (Created with NodeXL Pro [http://nodexl.codeplex.com] from the Social Media Research Foundation [http://www.smrfoundation.org].)

When we qualitatively examine the valence associated with the president's mentions of media, an interesting trend emerges. Some of the media mentions are relatively positive and encourage Trump's followers to watch or read a particular story (an extension of interactivity), as when the president tweeted about his sit-down interview on ABC News in late January. On January 25, 2017, he tweeted, "I will be interviewed by @DavidMuir tonight at 10 o'clock on @ABC. Will be my first interview from the White House.... https://t.co/4zuOrRdcoc." Large portions of the media mentions, however, are quite negative. Trump is consistently derogatory of traditional media in speeches and tweets. "Fake"-"news" has high link frequencies (i.e., the thick line connecting the words) in both the Twitter and speeches networks (see Figures 9.2 and 9.3) and "failing"-"ny times" has high link frequencies in the Twitter network (see Figure 9.2). These high link frequencies indicate the words are highly correlated with the other. Media outlets are linked to "lying" and "leaks" and "untruthful" in the traditional communications network (see Figure 9.3). The use of pejorative language communicatively casts news media as an opponent of the Trump administration. By engaging in these pointed attacks on news media outlets, Trump is rubbing salt in the distrustful wounds of conservatives who lack faith in mainstream news outlets (see Barthel & Mitchell, 2017). Moreover, Trump's jabs serve to build up outlets supportive of his administration—another means of encouraging selectivity processes and inoculation against perceived administrative countermessaging.

Assessing how the nascent Trump administration navigates the accessibility of the ubiquitous presidency reveals three interesting trends. First, the president's communications are adapted to the appropriate venue when we examine interactivity. The technological affordances of Twitter make particular engagement calls ("join" and "watch") appropriate for his followers compared to the broader reach of his more traditional speeches. This Twitter tact allows him to expand his messaging reach in a fragmented media environment. Second, Trump's communications reveal an early presidency straining against the demands of a fragmented media ecosystem. It is quite apparent that the president does not think too highly of news media outlets. Indeed, every presidency struggles with the demands and styles of journalists (Kernell, 2007; Kumar, 2007). Yet the prominence of the public attacks across his tweets and more traditional communications bears the hallmarks of a sustained strategy by his administration. Third, the administration's seeming struggles with multiple news media outlets, as well as their prominence in his communication, illustrates the modern demands of the presidency. Presidents must cooperate (begrudgingly) with a multitude of information sources if they are to have some messaging successes. The poisoning of this well may leave the president with only friendly platforms directly in his sphere of influence for messaging (e.g., Fox News, Twitter).

Personality

We considered the president's personality through his use of emotional language and the disclosure of personal information. To appear in a variety of communicative formats, the president crafts a variety of personality facets. The combination of informality and disclosure helps develop the front-stage persona the president presents to the public.

Informality

Trump's emotionally laden language in tweets, speeches, and press conferences creates an appealing conversational style for supporters. According to linguist Jennifer Sclafani, Trump's conversational style "may come off as incoherent and unintelligible ... or as authentic, relatable, and trustworthy" (Hines, 2016). This conversational tone is projected partly through emotional words such as "great" and "tremendous." Within the traditional communication network (see Figure 9.4), "tremendous" is used quite often and holds a central position in relation to other nodes in the larger speech network (i.e., high degree, betweenness, and eigenvector centrality). "Tremendous" becomes a hub of sorts within the network that bridges concepts like support and success with security and respect. Furthermore, "tremendous" holds a degree of power that connects it to other influential nodes and makes it a prominent word in the traditional communication network, which becomes a signature of sorts in Trump's communication. Using the ego network of "tremendous," a network with a single central point, we can note the wide array of words that are connected to the node (Figure 9.4).

Interestingly, we see the emergence of associated emotions as well as self-references in the ego network—a point of validation that these terms of interest connect with notions of personality. Words such as "love," "passion,"

Donald Trump Meets the Ubiquitous Presidency 159

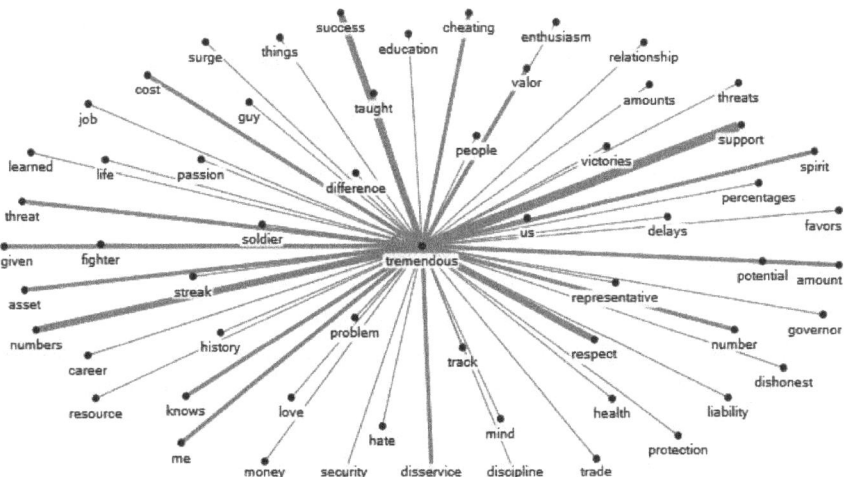

FIGURE 9.4 Informality network — traditional communications. (Created with NodeXL Pro [http://nodexl.code plex.com] from the Social Media Research Foundation [http://www.smrfoundation.org].)

and "enthusiasm" represent visible connections in the network (Figure 9.4). Trump not only connects his emotionally laden qualifier "tremendous" to traditional policy areas ("job," "education," "health"), but also to affective-based cues as well. During a roundtable with the National Sheriffs' Association on February 7, 2017, Trump said, "But there's tremendous, tremendous dishonest—pure, outright dishonesty from the media." The attack made here personally implicates the general character of media and journalists. Moreover, Trump makes a reoccurring connection between "tremendous" and himself (e.g., the thicker line connection to "me") compared to constructing a broader public (e.g., the thinner line connection to "us"). The use of emotional language thus is not just an end in itself, but also a means by which Trump communicatively packages himself in his traditional communication.

Although "tremendous" does not appear within the Twitter network, "great" has a broad presence including high centralities and connection to multiple clusters (Figure 9.5). In effect, it mirrors the use of the word "tremendous" in Trump's traditional communication network.

Of the 197 tweets within the first 30 days, "great" was tweeted 32 times—an average of more than once a day. For example, on January 22, 2017, Trump tweeted, "Had a great meeting at CIA Headquarters yesterday,

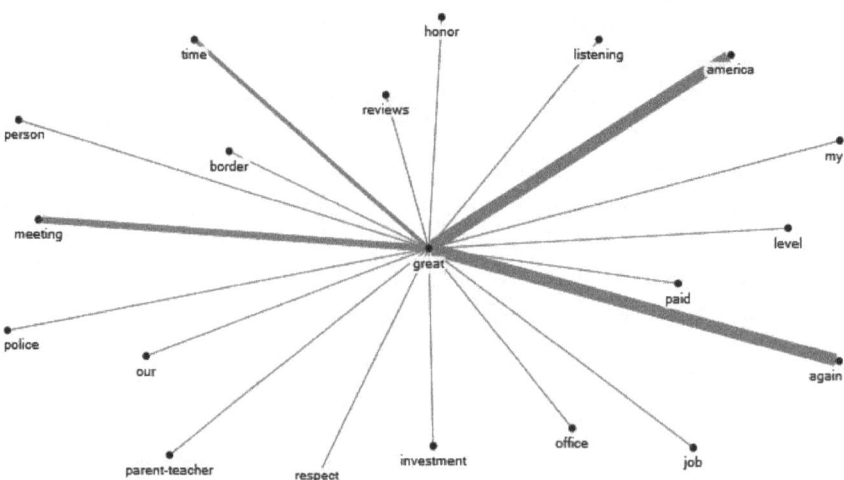

FIGURE 9.5 Informality network — Twitter communications. (Created with NodeXL Pro [http://nodexl.codeplex.com] from the Social Media Research Foundation [http://www.smrfoundation.org].)

packed house, paid great respect to Wall, long standing ovations, amazing people. WIN!" Although the network reveals the prominent linkages between "America," "great," and "again"—a direct result of Trump's repetition of his campaign slogan—we also find the connection of self ("my") and inclusive ("our") references to this emotionally infused language (Figure 9.5). Just as observed in the traditional communications, Trump continues a trend of self-reference to these emotional qualifiers. As a Trump tweet is worth 28,550 retweets on average (Scherer, 2017), the president can seek to tie his personality and agenda to positive linguistic qualifiers to increase support and the general appeal of his messages. Even an opponent counterarguing Trump's emotional language nonetheless spreads his positive messaging around himself and his policies on the Twitter platform.

Disclosure

The drive for a personable commander in chief has shaped how and when the president discusses family members. President Obama often told anecdotes of his wife and children during interviews. President Trump is not as disclosive with personal information, a counterpoint to his seeming informality. Across the first 30 days, the president discussed family in defense of his daughter Ivanka and to discuss his wife's hosting duties. "Ivanka" has a low degree centrality and is situated on the fringes in both the traditional communication and Twitter networks, effectively giving her no influence in regard to his communicative style. She is only mentioned in response to boycotts of her clothing and household lines. On February 11, 2017, Trump tweeted, "I am so proud of my daughter Ivanka. To be abused and treated so badly by the media, and to still hold her head so high, is truly wonderful!" Similarly, "Melania" (the president's wife and first lady) has slightly more prominence in the speech network (a degree centrality of four) and is only mentioned once in the Twitter network. On February 11, 2017, the president tweeted, "Melania and I are hosting Japanese Prime Minister Shinzo Abe and Mrs. Abe at Mar-a-Lago in Palm Beach, Fla. They are a wonderful couple!" No other family members are mentioned. Communicatively, Trump's lack of familial disclosure appears to clash with the informal brashness of his public persona.

Investigating Trump's informality and disclosure illustrates how the president foregrounds aspects of his personality, including emotionally laden language and its connection to himself. While the president has created this informal speaking style, he backgrounds information about his family. Refusing to discuss family could demonstrate President Trump's attempt to establish some public-private barriers characteristic of the presidency at many points in American history. This tact seems uncharacteristically cautious for an individual who can get quite personal with his political opponents. This contradiction between informality and disclosure colors the personality of Trump, leaving him somewhere between the personable and professional president.

Pluralism

Recent presidents, including Bill Clinton, George W. Bush, and Barack Obama, have spoken to the increasing diversity of American life in their public communication—often in a positive manner. President Trump acknowledges this complexity in his communications, though he reconstitutes pluralism based on the diversity of his own supporters while resisting traditional elements of pluralism associated with gender, race, ethnicity, and religion (Scacco & Coe, 2017b). We look further at how he constitutes this "in-group" versus "out-group" in his discourse.

In-Group

Trump positions himself and his supporters as members of the in-group through antipluralist messaging (i.e., "we," "our," and "us"). Although the pronoun "we" can indicate a collective that excludes the president in some instances (see Pennebaker, 2011), the construction serves as a proxy for understanding how Trump communicatively positions himself and his supporters vis-à-vis opposing forces. Within both the traditional communication and Twitter networks, "we" and "our" act as central nodes of the network, largely indicated through their positioning and high centrality scores (i.e., degree, betweenness, and eigenvector). "We" and "our" become central hubs, connecting with most concepts and ideas. This, in effect, promotes the immense influence and power these nodes have in constructing Trump's views of the American public. Moreover, both "we and "our," as central nodes, connect with most clusters across the networks, illustrating Trump's construction of an in-group to express an antipluralist message.

Within this antipluralist messaging, Trump connects "our" with other nodes to build a broader American identity (see Figures 9.6 and 9.7). "Our" is linked to "country," "citizens," and "government," implying and constituting Americans as the "in-group"—critical for the formation and continuity of a national identity (Anderson, 2006, Beasley, 2004). "Our"-"dreams," "heroes," "control," "success," "borders," "factories," "country," and "traditions" appear to place onus on the in-group to develop change and success in the country (Figures 9.6 and 9.7). From day one of his presidency, Trump's inaugural address immediately framed a communicative focus on nationalism: "We will bring back our jobs. We will bring back our borders. We will bring back our wealth. And we will bring back our dreams." These associations treat the nation as a closed entity, again important for constituting national identification.

Looking to the fringes of both "our" networks reveals some clues about who is placed in opposition to the nation and Americans. In the Twitter network (Figure 9.7), "Islamic" and "terrorism" are connected yet semantically separated from the collective. Similarly, "party" and "opposition" also are separated. Linguistically separating these identities establishes a rhetorical barrier between the in-group and out-group. Invoking terrorism, while discussing the national collective, may serve to create an affective front for supporters and the nation in general by reinforcing the concerns of his base of supporters.

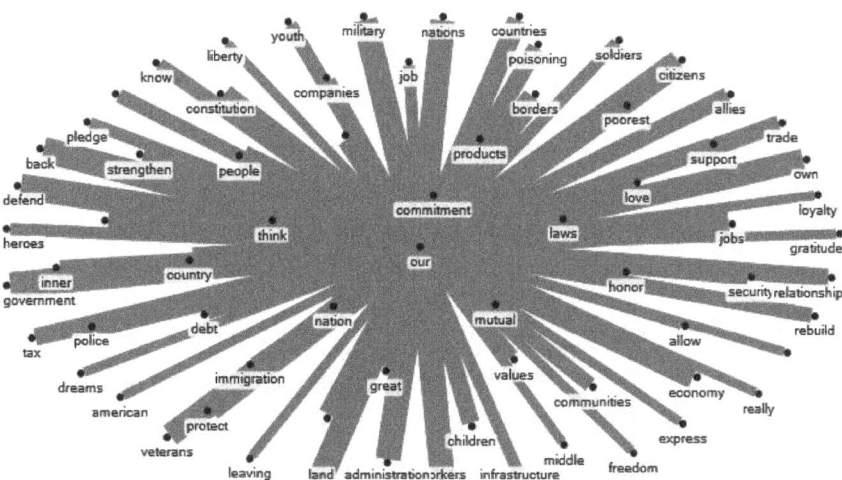

FIGURE 9.6 Pluralism network — traditional communications. (Created with NodeXL Pro [http://nodexl.codeplex.com] from the Social Media Research Foundation [http://www.smrfoundation.org].)

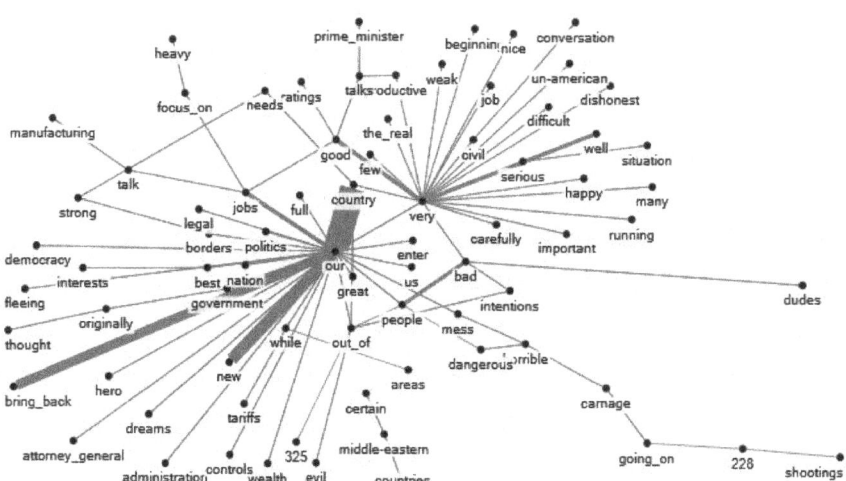

FIGURE 9.7 Pluralism network — Twitter communications. (Created with NodeXL Pro [http://nodexl.codeplex.com] from the Social Media Research Foundation [http://www.smrfoundation.org].)

Out-Group

Whereas Trump constructs an in-group based on national identification, the president may rhetorically exclude individuals, events, and ideas based on words like "them," "they," and "other." For example, "them" has medium centralities in the traditional communication network, meaning that it produces enough relationships between other words to shape Trump's discourse on pluralism. In contrast, "them" has low centralities in the Twitter network, effectively positioning itself with no power and on the fringes of the network. "Them" most often is used to represent some opposing force, often in the form of international entities like China. Trump's use of "other" blatantly casts the out-group as international. In linking "other" with "countries," "nations," "governments," "leaders," "international," "powers," and "Japanese" (see Figure 9.8), Trump may aim to convey nationalistic sentiment to complement his "America First" platform. Trump appears more likely to refer to the out-group in traditional communication settings rather than Twitter, potentially significant for the various audiences he must reach. These differences warrant additional investigation and offer an important

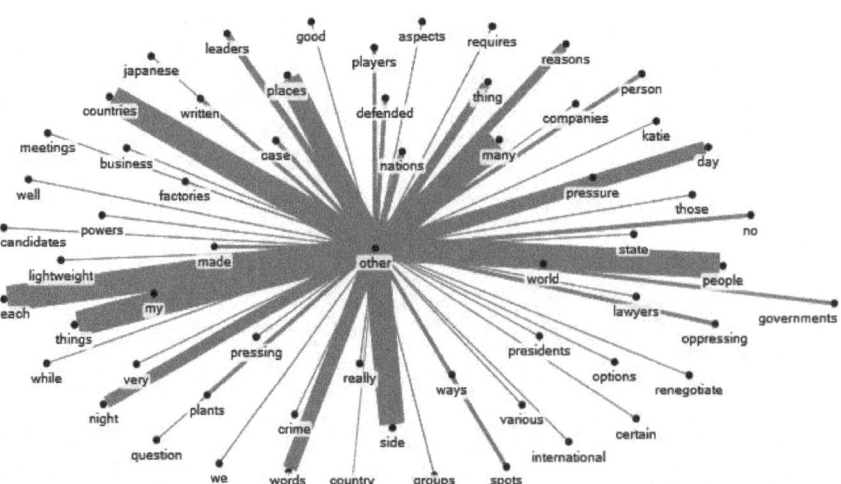

FIGURE 9.8 Pluralism out-group network — traditional communications. (Created with NodeXL Pro [http://nodexl.codeplex.com] from the Social Media Research Foundation [http://www.smrfoundation.org].)

finding about the increasing divergence between Trump's traditional and Twitter communications.

When we look domestically at how Trump uses "other" in relation to American referents, a clear messaging trend emerges that dovetails on the president's advocacy of "Law and Order." "Other" also is connected to "drugs," "dealers," and "gangs" within the Twitter network. On February 12, 2017, Trump tweeted, "The crackdown on illegal criminals is merely the keeping of my campaign promise. Gang members, drug dealers & others are being removed." Words like "gang" and "drugs" can act as racially implicit coded appeals to sway political judgments in some cases, particularly among more conservative individuals (Hurwitz & Peffley, 2005). In addition to weaving a thread with his anti-immigrant language used during the campaign, the president's language—by covertly racializing out-groups—serves to reconstitute law-abiding individuals (his supporters) against the perceived lawlessness of groups that form traditional conceptions of a pluralistic America.

Across different types of communication, President Trump consistently constructs nationalistic messages that separate America from the rest of the world and law-abiding citizens from the imagined threats of "lawless" individuals. This language has two implications. First, by constructing a nationalistic identity, Donald Trump rejects a broader international community that the modern presidency has had to engage with and account for in negotiating plural politics (Scacco & Coe, 2016). In place of a physical wall, the president erects a rhetorical one between an international "out-group" and an American "in-group." Second, by invoking implicitly racialized code words to associate domestic individuals with lawlessness, the president continues a series of questionable communicative choices toward historically marginalized individuals in the United States. Indeed, Trump's discourse as a presidential candidate negatively targeted non-White Americans (Scacco & Coe, 2017b). His language as president reflects this campaign practice and potentially appeals to a group of Americans whose support of Trump has been linked to racial bias and racial isolation (Rothwell & Diego-Rosell, 2016; Wood, 2017). If this communicative approach is indeed strategic, it is by design a means of keeping Trump's base of support intact.

CONCLUSION

Donald Trump's communication during the first 30 days of his presidency illustrates the initial stages of his adaptation to and adoption of contemporary communication practices. His traditional communications and tweets demonstrate how he uses the fragmentation of media and the changing norms of presidential communication to construct particular messages and reach target audiences. As presidential discourse evolves from rhetorical toward more ubiquitous approaches, this hybrid nature of political communication across platforms becomes increasingly critical to document.

Exploring President Trump's traditional communications and use of Twitter reveals that he differentiates his discourse in three distinct ways. First, Twitter becomes a place for the president to inoculate his supporters against oppositional communication and ideas. Second, Trump creates pseudo-interactivity between himself and his supporters through Twitter while distancing himself from more traditional news outlets. Finally, Trump uses Twitter to circumvent news media outlets and direct his message to supporters. Traditional communication is still viewed as wide-reaching, but Twitter becomes a route of direct access.

Donald Trump is by no means the first president to use more modern approaches to convey communicative accessibility, personality, and pluralism to the public—nor will he be the last (Scacco & Coe, 2016). His use of Twitter creates the appearance of interactive accessibility through sharing news content and videos. Yet, the president also heavily criticizes the news platforms he needs to expand the reach of his arguments beyond his base. These attacks may fuel political engagement and affective attachment to the president while instigating hostilities with journalists. The attacks nonetheless support the general premise of the ubiquitous presidency that the modern chief executive must negotiate messaging through multiple media platforms while constructing a seemingly transactional relationship with audiences. Gleaning the first 30 days of his communication, we find that President Trump faces rocky ongoing negotiations with the press.

The president also leans heavily on aspects of his personality, including informal, emotionally laden language in official communications and tweets, while refraining from the familial disclosures that were characteristic of the

Obama presidency. Recent scholarship has emphasized a simpler and more emotional presidential discourse style (Lim, 2008). Trump's communication reflects this development, but with considerable nuance. Although Trump is known for his brash demeanor, he is equally enigmatic in discussing his family. The president's informal speaking style subverts the wall Trump has built for his private life, leaving him with a personality that may complicate his ubiquitous appeal in less formal media settings.

Finally, the president's discourse style complicates the pluralism at the heart of American political life and the contemporary presidency. Trump's construction of a nationalistic identity while eschewing international commitments seemingly halts the global turn of American commitments post–World War II. Presidents have responded to this turn in their communications (Scacco & Coe, 2016). Yet, Donald Trump's language positions the international community, as well as imagined lawless domestic entities, opposite American nationals. A complicated geopolitical landscape and a diverse populace become opponents to be overcome. Although integral for constructing national identity under a Trump administration, the president's communication may simplify too much the contours of American life in the 21st century—a risk that may eventually cut against the grain of messy and complex executive decisions to come in the Trump administration.

This chapter is a snapshot of the first 30 days of a presidency that few political elites predicted would come to pass. In the traditional communications and tweets of Donald Trump, we see the outline of his presidency come into focus: modern on the surface, constantly on the political mind, but deviating from the practices of his immediate predecessor. Trump has staked his presidency and his personal brand on a communication style that is brash and disruptive, seemingly challenging the traditional presidential persona. However, his communication style, while visceral and nationalistic, uses many of the same techniques we have seen from previous presidents. Trump's traditional communication and tweets are often minimized for their potential impacts, but our results illustrate that his tweets should be taken seriously. Although some aspects of Trump's style are unique, he all too often finds himself in the company of his forebears in ways he would find utterly tweet-worthy.

REFERENCES

Anderson, B. (2006). *Imagined communities*. New York, NY: Verso.

Barthel, M., & Mitchell, A. (2017, May 10). Americans' attitudes about the news media deeply divided along partisan lines. Pew Research Center. Retrieved from http://www.journalism.org/2017/05/10/americansattitudes-about-the-news-media-deeply-divided-along-partisan-lines/

Beasley, V. B. (2004). *You, the people: American national identity in presidential rhetoric*. College Station, TX: Texas A&M University Press.

Brand, A., Petulla, S., & Dann, C. (2017, March 10). Commander-in-Tweet: 50 days of @RealDonaldTrump. NBC News. Retrieved from https://www.nbcnews.com/politics/donald-trump-commander-tweet-here-s-what-50-days-realdonaldtrump-looks-n731496

Brandes, U., & Erlebach, T. (2005). *Network analysis: methodological foundations*. Berlin, Germany: Springer Science & Business Media.

Campbell, K. K., & Jamieson, K. H. (2008). *Presidents creating the presidency: Deeds done in words*. Chicago, IL: University of Chicago Press.

Carley, K. (2001). AutoMap (version 3.0.10.41) [Computer software]. Pittsburgh, PA: CASOS, Carnegie Mellon University. Available from http://www.casos.cs.cmu.edu/projects/automap/index.php

Ceaser, J. W., Thurow, G. E., Tulis, J., & Bessette, J. M. (1981). The rise of the rhetorical presidency. *Presidential Studies Quarterly, 11*, 158–171.

Chadwick, A. (2013). *The hybrid media system: Politics and power*. New York, NY: Oxford University Press.

Dahl, R. A. (1961). *Who governs? Democracy and power in an American city*. New Haven, CT: Yale University Press.

Davis, R., & Owen, D. M. (1998). *New media and American politics*. Oxford, NY: Oxford University Press.

DiIulio, J. J., Jr. (2012). The hyper-rhetorical presidency. In J. Friedman & S. Friedman (Eds.), *Rethinking the rhetorical presidency* (pp. 106–115). New York, NY: Routledge.

Doerfel, M. L. (1998). What constitutes semantic network analysis? A comparison of research and methodologies. *Connections, 21*(2), 16–26.

Edelman, M. (1985). *The symbolic uses of politics*. Champaign, IL: University of Illinois Press.

Engesser, S., Ernst, N., Esser, F., & Büchel, F. (2017). Populism and social media:

How politicians spread a fragmented ideology. *Information, Communication & Society, 20*(8), 1109–1126. https://doi.org/10.1080/1369118X.2016.1207697

Eshbaugh-Soha, M. (2016). Presidential agenda-setting of traditional and nontraditional news media. *Political Communication, 33,* 1–20. https://doi.org/10.1080/10584609.2014.958261

Groshek, J., & Engelbert, J. (2013). Double differentiation in a cross-national comparison of populist political movements and online media uses in the United States and the Netherlands. *New Media & Society, 15*(2), 183–202. https://doi.org/10.1177/1461444812450685

Hardy, B. W., Phillips, C. L. D., & LaMarre, H. L. (2017, May 1). 100 days of @realDonaldTrump tweets: Trump's war on news. Temple University Communication, Politics, & Science. Retrieved from https://sites.temple.edu/commps/2017/05/01/100-days-of-realdonaldtrump-tweets-trumps-war-on-news/

Hart, R. P. (1987). *The sound of leadership: Presidential communication in the modern age.* Chicago, IL: University of Chicago Press.

Hart, R. P. (1999). *Seducing America: How television charms the modern voter* (rev. ed.). Thousand Oaks, CA: Sage.

Hart, R. P. (2008). Thinking harder about presidential discourse: The question of efficacy. In J. A. Aune & M. J. Medhurst (Eds.), *The prospect of presidential rhetoric* (pp. 238–248). College Station, TX: Texas A&M University Press.

Hartnett, S. J., & Mercieca, J. R. (2007). "A discovered dissembler can achieve nothing great"; Or, four theses on the death of presidential rhetoric in an age of empire. *Presidential Studies Quarterly, 37,* 599–621. https://doi.org/10.1111/j.17415705.2007.02616.x

Herbst, S. (2012). The rhetorical presidency and the contemporary media environment. In J. Friedman & S. Friedman (Eds.), *Rethinking the rhetorical presidency* (pp. 126–134). New York, NY: Routledge.

Hermans, L., & Vergeer, M. (2013). Personalization in e-campaigning: A cross-national comparison of personalization strategies used on candidate websites of 17 countries in EP elections 2009. *New Media & Society, 15*(1), 72–92. https://doi.org/10.1177/1461444812457333

Hines, A. (2016). Why Donald Trump's language is so tremendous. *Newsweek.* Retrieved from http://www.newsweek.com/donald-trump-speech-language-metaphor-odd-effective-truth-486701

Hurwitz J., & Peffley, M. (2005). Playing the race card in the post–Willie Horton era: The impact of racialized code words on support for punitive crime policy.

Public Opinion Quarterly, 69(1), 99–112. https://doi.org/10.1093/poq/nfi004

Jacobs, L. R. (2005). Communicating from the White House: Presidential narrowcasting and the national interest. In J. D. Aberbach & M. A. Peterson (Eds.), *Institutions of American democracy: The executive branch* (pp. 174–217). New York, NY: Oxford University Press.

Jagers, J., & Walgrave, S. (2007). Populism as political communication style: An empirical study of political parties' discourse in Belgium. *European Journal of Political Research, 46*(3), 319–345. https://doi.org/10.1111/j.1475-6765.2006.00690.x

Jamieson, K. H. (1988). *Eloquence in an electronic age: The transformation of political speechmaking.* New York, NY: Oxford University Press.

Kazin, M. (1995). *The populist persuasion: An American history.* Ithaca, NY: Cornell University Press.

Keith, T. (2016, November 18). Commander-in-tweet: Trump's social media use and presidential media avoidance. *NPR Politics Podcast.* Retrieved from http://www.npr.org/2016/11/18/502306687/commander-in-tweet-trumps-social-media-use-and-presidential-media-avoidance

Kernell, S. (2007). *Going public: New strategies of presidential leadership* (4th ed.). Washington, DC: CQ Press.

Kumar, M. J. (2007). *Managing the president's message: The White House communications operation.* Baltimore, MD: Johns Hopkins University Press.

Lambert, N. J. (2017). Text mining tutorial. In A. Pilny & M. S. Poole (Eds.), *Group processes: Computational and data driven approaches* (pp. 93–117). New York, NY: Springer Press.

Lim, E. T. (2008). *The anti-intellectual presidency: The decline of presidential rhetoric from George Washington to George W. Bush.* New York, NY: Oxford University Press.

McGregor, S. C., Lawrence, R. G., & Cardona, A. (2016). Personalization, gender, and social media: Gubernatorial candidates' social media strategies. *Information, Communication & Society.* Advance online publication. https://doi.org/10.1080/1369118X.2016.1167228

Mercieca, J. R., & Vaughn, J. S. (2009). The post-rhetorical legacy of George W. Bush. In M. O. Grossman & R. E. Matthews Jr. (Eds.), *Perspectives on the legacy of George W. Bush* (pp. 31–52). Newcastle, England: Cambridge Scholars Publishing.

Newman, M. E. (2003). The structure and function of complex networks. *SIAM Review, 45*(2), 167–256. https://doi.org/10.1137/S003614450342480

Newman, M., Barabasi, A. L., & Watts, D. J. (2011). *The structure and dynamics of networks*. Princeton, NJ: Princeton University Press.

Owen, D., & Davis, R. (2008). Presidential communication in the Internet era. *Presidential Studies Quarterly, 38*, 658–673. https://doi.org/10.1111/j.1741-5705.2008.02669.x

Papacharissi, Z. (2015). *Affective publics: Sentiment, technology, and politics*. Oxford, UK: Oxford University Press.

Pennebaker, J. W. (2011). *The secret life of pronouns: What our words say about us*. New York, NY: Bloomsbury Press.

Rothwell, J. T., & Diego-Rosell, P. (2016). Explaining nationalist political views: The case of Donald Trump. *Social Science Research Network*. Retrieved from https://papers.ssrn.com/sol3/papers.cfm?abstract_id=2822059

Scacco, J. M. (2011). A weekend routine: The functions of the weekly presidential address from Bill Clinton to Barack Obama. *Electronic Media & Politics, 1*(4), 66–88.

Scacco, J. M., & Coe, K. (2016). The ubiquitous presidency: Toward a new paradigm for studying presidential communication. *International Journal of Communication, 10*, 2014–2037.

Scacco, J. M., & Coe, K. (2017a). Talk this way: The ubiquitous presidency and expectations of presidential communication. *American Behavioral Scientist, 61*(3), 298–314. https://doi.org/10.1177/0002764217704321

Scacco, J. M., & Coe, K. (2017b). Acting "presidential": The modern campaign meets the ubiquitous presidency. In R. E. Denton Jr. (Ed.), *Political campaign communication: Theory, method and practice* (pp. 303–326). New York, NY: Lexington Books.

Scacco, J. M., Coe, K., & Harness, D. (forthcoming). From interactivity to incitement: Ubiquitous communication and elite calls for participatory action. In B. R. Warner, D. G. Bystrom, M. S. McKinney, & M. C. Banwart (Eds.), *An unprecedented election: Campaign coverage, communication, and citizens divided*. New York, NY: Praeger.

Schattschneider, E. E. (1975). *The semisovereign people: A realist's view of democracy in America*. Boston, MA: Wadsworth.

Scherer, M. (2017, March 23). Can Trump handle the truth? *Time*. Retrieved from http://time.com/4710614/donald-trump-fbi-surveillance-house-intelligence-committee

Smith, M., Ceni A., Milic-Frayling, N., Shneiderman, B., Mendes Rodrigues, E.,

Leskovec, J., & Dunne, C. (2010). NodeXL: A free and open network overview, discovery and exploration add-in for Excel 2007/2010/2013/2016. Available from http://nodexl.codeplex.com/

Sowa, J. F. (1991). Towards the expressive power of natural language. In J. F. Sowa (Ed.), *Principles of semantic networks: Exploration in the representation of knowledge* (pp. 157–191). San Mateo, CA: Morgan Kaufman.

Stromer-Galley, J. (2014). *Presidential campaigning in the Internet age*. New York, NY: Oxford University Press.

Stroud, N. J. (2011). *Niche news: The politics of news choice*. Oxford, NY: Oxford University Press.

Stuckey, M. E. (2010). Rethinking the rhetorical presidency and presidential rhetoric. *Review of Communication, 10,* 38–52. https://doi.org/10.1080/15358590903248744

Tulis, J. K. (1987). *The rhetorical presidency*. Princeton, NJ: Princeton University Press.

Tulis, J. K. (2012). The rhetorical presidency in retrospect. In J. Friedman & S. Friedman (Eds.), *Rethinking the rhetorical presidency* (pp. 266–284). New York, NY: Routledge.

Wood, T. (2017, April 17). Racism motivated Trump voters more than authoritarianism. *Washington Post*. Retrieved from https://www.washingtonpost.com/news/monkey-cage/wp/2017/04/17/racism-motivated-trump-voters-more-than-authoritarianism-or-income-inequality/?utm_term=.d0b668e2ecbd

CHAPTER 10

C-SPAN AND JOURNALISM

Michael Buozis, Shannon Rooney, and Brian Creech

It is often taken for granted that journalism plays many foundational roles in American public life: creating the shared basis of facts upon which democratic deliberation depends, providing watchdog oversight of elected leaders, and offering various actors the means to engage with and shape public opinion (Dewey, 1927; Lippmann, 1922; Overholser & Jamieson, 2005; Patterson, 2013). And yet, as contemporary debates about a crisis in journalistic authority and business models show, the press itself is heterogeneous and in constant flux (Alexander, Breese, & Luengo, 2016; Zelizer, 2015). This contingent and fluid character is an important aspect of journalism's relationship to other democratic institutions. When faced with shifting conditions, news organizations and actors often protect their authority over the truth and the public sphere by deploying discursive strategies rooted in appeals to common norms, such as objectivity, transparency, and a sense of public service (Carlson, 2017). However, philosophies and normative developments in journalism are held up as romanticized ideals and not often addressed from a critical point of view. By looking at the values and norms that guide the press as the product of certain historically situated conditions, which are often debated and articulated in very public forums, scholars can come to understand how journalism exists as not only an institution constituted in and through discourse, but also how these discourses allow for both institutional stability and adaptation. As Michael Schudson (2013) argues, "the news media have grown as institutional stewards of democratic citizenship by adapting: they were once organizations of elites speaking to elites, and then became for a long time political parties speaking through the newspapers to their own troops, and then emerged in an original blend of commercial organization and professional pride" (p. 174).

As with other democratic institutions, public discourses work as a kind of reflexive knowledge production, often revealing the ideas that guide the practice of journalism as well as responses to changing conditions (Levi-Faur, 2005; Schmidt, 2008). Recent years have seen Carlson's (2016) term "metajournalistic discourse" taken up as a useful analytic for understanding the boundary-making strategies and self-justifications journalists and news organizations use to legitimate their work and value in the public sphere. However, finding these discourses, discovering where they emanate from, and showing how they provide a normative bond across many disparate news organizations has proved a particular methodological difficulty for scholars of journalism. Furthermore, given journalism's myriad contemporary challenges, scholars have also tended to focus on the disruptions of the digital era, as opposed to the kind of discursive work that provided normative reinforcement during eras of relative institutional and financial stability.

It is these moments of relative stability, though, that provide the discursive tools that help make our current conditions sensible, the same tools we have at hand when crisis comes to our doorstep. To uncover the development, circulation, and contestation of these discourses, the C-SPAN Archives' online Video Library offers a wealth of materials. In conferences and panels documented throughout the Video Library, news executives and leading practitioners come together to define, debate, and articulate many aspects of journalism to the public. The people in these videos represent prominent regional and national news organizations, standard bearers who exemplify best practices and are celebrated for embodying journalism's highest ideals. Though journalism and journalism organizations are an overlooked part of the Video Library for those coming to these materials with a more overt focus on American politics and political institutions, they provide a useful window into the norms and values that guide the organizations charged with making issues and events sensible and consequential to government leaders and the public. Of particular use in this regard are video records of meetings held by four prominent journalism organizations: the American Society of Newspaper Editors, the Society of Professional Journalists, the National Press Club, and the Freedom Forum. To make sense of this wealth of materials, this chapter offers context for understanding them as part of journalism's broader normative discourses as well as practical advice and analytic considerations for using journalism-related videos in the C-SPAN Video Library for critical and interpretive research.

THEORETICAL CONTEXT: METAJOURNALISTIC DISCOURSE AND JOURNALISM'S PUBLIC AUTHORITY

In order to understand the usefulness of journalism-related materials in the C-SPAN Video Library for scholarly research, it is important to first establish the theoretical and normative conditions under which these materials operate and circulate. Most obviously, they constitute a style of "metajournalistic discourse," that is, discourses about journalism, articulated to both those in the press and the public at large, that operate across a wide collection of reasonably public venues. An analytic concept from Matt Carlson's (2015, 2016, 2017) recent works, metajournalistic discourses establish the power of ideas and public debates to both shape and reveal the philosophies that guide journalism and establish "symbolic boundaries" between it, other kinds of cultural practice, and other institutions that guide American public life. Metajournalistic discourses must be understood as productive in their own right, structuring the ideational and boundary-making work that sustain an institution's sense of autonomy and coherence amid changing conditions and outside threats (Carlson, 2015).

As such, it is important to consider these archival materials as both revealing and constituting journalism's shifting discourses at different historical moments and amid various challenges to the press's financial viability and public credibility. As Ryfe (2017) argues, the prevailing normative work of these discourses occurs in a "conditional voice" which both constructs certain norms as contingent, but also provides a conceptual index for what *should* be done (p. 107). The kinds of normative and institutional discourses found in the C-SPAN Video Library provide evidence of how journalism "holds together not because journalists agree but because they share an understanding of how to disagree, and which disagreements matter," especially as these discourses reveal qualifications, refutations, and shifting opinions in the face of change over time (p. 65). Schudson (1982) has drawn attention to the ways in which informal processes of "consensus-formation" allow journalists and news organizations to build trust in each other, as well as to "trust also the very forms of discourse around which their work is oriented and their gossip centered. These forms, which they must control if they are to be respected professionals, have an extraordinary power to control the journalists themselves and, through them, their readers" (pp. 110–111).

The norms and philosophies that constitute journalism's prevailing values and structure its relationship to other institutions, then, are constituted by conceptual and rhetorical techniques deployed to help perceive changing conditions and navigate them. As Deuze (2005) writes, "journalism continuously reinvents itself—regularly revisiting similar debates (for example on commercialization, bureaucratization, 'new' media technologies, seeking audiences, concentration of ownership) where ideological values can be deployed to sustain operational closure, keeping outside forces at bay" (p. 447). In this way, journalists act as what Zelizer (1993) has called "interpretive communities," constantly negotiating the rules, practices, and modes of representation that come to define what counts as journalism. It is this rearticulation of common values and definitions that provides stability and practical coherence over time. Journalism, then, is an unstable and precarious institution constructed through stable and persistent—even nostalgic—discourses that articulate how and why certain enduring values, economic models, and institutional relationships matter (van Dijk, 1990).

Journalism is discursively constituted by not only internal negotiations of what it means to be a professional journalist (Meyers & Davidson, 2016) but also public exhortations that attempt to legitimate journalism's authority to represent the social world (Waisbord, 2013). Institutional discourses draw out "[t]he way journalists define their relationship with society," which "helps them give meaning to their work and enables them to justify and emphasize the importance of their work to themselves and others" (Hanitzsch

& Vos, 2017, p. 1). Historical memory is an important, yet subtle aspect of this discursive work, as legacy organizations, in particular, often "[s]take a claim to 'history,' to provide authoritative explanations of the passage of time ... as they construct repositories and communities of memory for the future" (Kitch, 2014, p. 239).

Discursive understandings of journalism, then, are an important means for showing not only how it coheres as a field, but also how it interacts and overlaps with other public and private institutions. Pierre Bourdieu's (1993) articulation of field theory as a way of understanding how domains of cultural practice and production, like journalism, interact with the fields of politics and the economy has recently provided scholars a means to show how journalism possesses a particular kind of power ossified in the institutional relations that undergird liberal democracy (Benson & Neveu, 2005). As Ryfe (2017) argues, journalism's form in any social context emerges in the tensions between the market, politics, and the general structures of civil society: tensions that are given intelligible form, usually via discourse. Field relations are ultimately power relations, but conceived of in a way that pushes against traditional structure/agency dichotomies and privileges institutional autonomy and cultural capital as central analytics (Vos, 2016). As such, journalists embody a particular "habitus," or the seemingly commonsensical practices, norms, and values that allow them to navigate the particular relations that constitute their field (Bourdieu, 1977). Therefore, it is through tracing the discourses and practices that comprise journalistic institutions that we can begin to understand journalism's particular power vis-à-vis other institutions, and postulate how "journalism has been complicit in some of the transformational changes that have faced our world" (Vos, 2016, p. 394).

Yet, journalism is not a singular field; it is made up of a wide variety of organizations serving various and overlapping publics, with competing actors vying for symbolic and financial resources at different periods of time (Carlson, 2015). Furthermore, it has been particularly tricky for journalism studies scholars to show how the relationship between journalism organizations, governmental institutions, market forces, and the public manifests over time. As Nadler (2016) shows, predominant managerial techniques and discourses within journalism often obscure implicit values and assumptions about audiences and have given rise to an institutional arrangement that privileges a market-oriented understanding of the press, as opposed to a more publicly centered vision. For much of journalism history, these relations were presented as natural extensions of American political culture, rarely contested beyond specialized scholarly circles (McChesney, 1999; Nerone, 2015; Schudson, 1978).

However, the decisions, debates, techniques, and discourses that comprise journalism's normative development and institutional composition are historically contingent, imbued with the relations they emerged from. The perspective of history, and in particular a genealogical history indebted to the methods of Foucault (1969) and reliant upon a rigorously verifiable record, can be useful for showing how these various modes of normative development are always in formulation (Roessner, Popp, Creech, & Blevens, 2013). Foucault's (2000) understanding of discourse requires the researcher not only to operate under the assumption that publicly circulating words and ideas possess a productive power, but to see certain values and normative claims as occupying a specific position, reflective of context, by tracing discourses across various forms and venues. For the study of institutions such as journalism, this means that

> rather than using history to uncover eternal journalistic beliefs or epistemological commitments, research along genealogical lines is more likely to argue that the connections we see in our current era and the past are either the working out of particular power relations, or the temporary alignment of fragile, provisional values. (Anderson, 2017, p. 78)

Accounting for normative development within the field of journalism, while also attending to changing material arrangements outside of it, requires contending with the institutions that have the financial and discursive capital necessary to make changes in the field. This work benefits from a corpus that shows journalistic actors and institutions wrestling with these same issues in a highly public form, which is why the C-SPAN Video Library is such a particularly useful resource for strands of research that seek to substantiate the values undergirding journalism practice and critically engage with the processes that bring them into being.

JOURNALISM ORGANIZATIONS IN THE C-SPAN VIDEO LIBRARY

Key to exploring the research potential for journalism-related videos in the C-SPAN Video Library is an understanding of how each journalism organization produces modes of discourse that emanate into the public and governmental spheres. Researchers must draw upon contextual materials outside of the C-SPAN Video Library in order to understand not only the organization's stated mission and membership composition, but also its political and economic relationships to the broader journalism industry. This context reveals the ideological commitments that color and characterize the statements and debates recorded in these videos. Furthermore, as the literature indicates, the professional norms and philosophies that constitute the institution of American journalism do not just emanate from the ether, fully formed. Instead, they are formulated and debated by formal and informal groups with agendas, sometimes stated and sometimes tacit. Elaborating the institutional context surrounding each of these groups is essential to understanding how they may shape those norms and philosophies through the discourses captured in the Video Library.

Using this theoretical perspective, the remainder of this chapter provides important context for four organizations that have hosted a significant number of events found in the Video Library: the American Society of Newspaper Editors, the Society of Professional Journalists, the National Press Club, and the Freedom Forum. These four organizations vary in their composition and relationships to media ownership, the managerial class, editors, news producers, and political and cultural elites. Though other journalism-related organizations have hosted events recorded by C-SPAN, these four organizations represent an array of ideological commitments, an understanding of which is essential for researchers interested in tapping this rich resource of discursive material. To that end, the organizational context is followed by a brief overview of the academic research addressing each organization with the aim of identifying gaps in the scholarship that can be filled using videos in the Video Library. A summary of the Video Library's holdings for each organization and a few suggestions for preliminary research round out each section.

American Society of Newspaper Editors

Founded in 1922 "to defend the profession from unjust assault" (Hayt, 2016), the American Society of Newspaper Editors (ASNE) stood out among existing press organizations like the American Newspaper Publishers and Southern Newspaper Publishers Association for representing individuals rather than publications. It was different, too, from the Society of Professional Journalists, which invited journalists working in any capacity to join. Membership in ASNE is limited to a managerial class of editors and other newsroom leadership and has since expanded to include deans and journalism school faculty as well as heads of other journalism-adjacent agencies like foundations and training organizations. Since its first convention in 1923, the group has met every year except 1945 and 2009, often hosting U.S. presidents and government officials (History, n.d.). Today most of these meetings—their panels and community discussions—have been archived after airing on C-SPAN. As it is the oldest organization of editors and other journalism leadership, records of ASNE's annual conventions provide a unique opportunity to witness the evolution of norms related to journalists' identities, the business models in the industry, and its professional values over nearly a century. ASNE has published proceedings from its annual meetings going back to its first convention in 1923, and C-SPAN videos offer a useful supplement to these records by showing how these discourses are often embodied (see Figure 10.1).

Scholarly inquiry has only glanced at ASNE, and much of that research has referenced the organization's founding principles and subsequent meetings as they relate to credibility (Romero-Rodríguez & Aguaded, 2016) and ethics (Rodgers, 2007; Wilkins & Brennan, 2004) or simply to reference regular presidential speeches at the annual convention (Kennedy, 1961). Scholars have made the most significant use of ASNE archival materials to examine the dominance of white men in the newsroom—and hence among ASNE's membership of the managerial class (Mellinger, 2003, 2008; Pratte, 1994, 2001; Uriarte & Valgeirsson, 2014). The variety of recordings available in the C-SPAN Video Library presents researchers with numerous opportunities to further extend the limited work that has been conducted or to engage with the materials in entirely new ways.

The video recordings of ASNE meetings found in the C-SPAN Video Library predate even the founding of the network, and begin with President

FIGURE 10.1 C-SPAN televises a speech by the Newspaper Editors.

John F. Kennedy's address to the group in 1961 regarding the Bay of Pigs invasion (Kennedy, 1961). The Video Library includes panel discussions, presidential addresses, speeches made by presidential candidates and other politicians, and interviews with ASNE leadership from 1986 through the present day. The panel discussions held during the association's annual meetings provide particular insight into the crises that have preoccupied newspaper management in the period immediately preceding and following the advent of the digital age. Editors can be seen wrestling in real time with questions of who should be allowed to be called a journalist, how to attract and retain diverse talent in the newsroom, and what kinds of ethical considerations should be deployed in war-torn regions. Discussions largely focus on threats to the financial viability of the news business, the makeup of the newsroom and its management, a growing incursion by television entertainment—and later the Internet—into the sanctum of news, and critical self-examinations of news content. The breadth of the video collection offers journalism researchers, in particular, a tremendous opportunity to witness discourses about norms and practices of the field unfold.

While some researchers (Mellinger, 2003, 2008; Pratte, 1994, 2001; Uriarte & Valgeirsson, 2014) have already established a foundation for citing ASNE meetings in examinations of diversity in the newsroom, much work remains to be done. The association has returned several times to the Kerner Report and its indictment of the field and its homogeneity since its release in 1968. The preponderance of such materials would seem to indicate the fruitful nature of a future study examining the ways in which newsroom diversity has grown and changed since Kerner and the parallel ways in which editors and newsroom leadership address—or don't—the necessity of those changes. Several panel discussions in the pre-Internet era also address the role of entertainment or titillation in news as television talk shows grew in popularity. Because ASNE represents journalism's managerial class, there are many opportunities to understand how news leaders came to understand and articulate various threats to journalism over time, as well as the conceptual and discursive tools deployed to articulate stability in the face of change. A future study could use the Video Library to compare discourses surrounding television talk shows in the 1980s and 1990s with similar panel discussions addressing social networking sites more recently. Temporal qualities of the Video Library will allow future researchers the chance to chart the ways in which discussions of Internet related disruption has itself disrupted formerly stable discourses of what constituted crisis in the field.

Society of Professional Journalists

Founded in 1909 as the Sigma Delta Chi fraternity at DePauw University, the Society of Professional Journalists (SPJ) wasn't officially renamed until 1988. Today the society touts itself as the nation's most broad-based journalism organization (Society of Professional Journalists, 2017); membership is open to a variety of individuals, ranging from students to part- and full-time journalists practicing in any medium to journalism educators worldwide. Members may participate in regional and state-based chapters that are themselves divided into student and professional components. Members are also invited to join SPJ communities, which are arranged according to interests such as freelancing, digital journalism, and community journalism. Perhaps given the breadth of its membership base, the society's resources and advocacy issues are also quite broad and geared toward rank-and-file members of the newsroom, focusing largely on professional development and a variety of national and regional awards. The society attends particularly to issues related to the First Amendment, and its motto is "Improving and protecting journalism since 1909" (Society of Professional Journalists, 2017).

What little scholarship does exist related to SPJ is divided almost exclusively between references to the group's role as publisher of the professional code of ethics found in many American newsrooms and critical inquiries into the norms, boundaries, and authority that belong to *professional* journalists. Particular attention has been paid to the evolution of the society's code, with researchers wrestling with its broader social and moral implications (Hickey, 2003); exploring the ways in which ethics are considered differently by sports reporters (Hardin & Zhong, 2010) and photo editors (Dahmen, 2016); interrogating the ethics of anonymous sourcing (Kimball, 2011); and even examining the morality of revisions to the code itself (Slattery, 2016). In particular, critical scholar Jane Singer (1998, 2003, 2006, 2007) has attended extensively to the role the society's code of ethics plays in discursively creating norms and a sense of identity and authority in the field. Zelizer (1993) also cited the society specifically in her theory of the profession as an interpretive community.

Videos of SPJ events or discussions are relatively sparse in comparison to the other organizations discussed in this chapter, but the 34 available span more than 30 years and a wide variety of topics. Most relate to ethics (C-SPAN, 1989a, 1995, 2005a), the First Amendment and confidential sourcing (C-SPAN, 1989b, 1989c, 2005b), and access (C-SPAN, 1990, 1992, 1994a, 2016). A handful of others focus on the White House press corps and journalists' performance covering particular stories, and several others include keynote addresses. Among the most popular in the archive is a 1985 roast of Walter Cronkite.

Because many SPJ videos available in the C-SPAN Video Library relate to elections and the White House (C-SPAN, 1991a, 2007a, 2007b), future studies could easily examine the norms and professional responses to political coverage as articulated among the arbiters of what makes journalists *professionals*. In the current era when popular press attention is increasingly focused on the norms and roles of reporters in the White House press corps, the panels related to those journalists specifically invite close textual analysis. Such investigation may shed light on how the unwritten rules of the press corps have ossified the body's relationship to the White House, particularly in televised press briefings. Several other recordings capture journalists in moments of critical self-reflection, either assessing journalists' lived experiences (C-SPAN, 1994b, 2006) or rendering judgment on the quality of the reporting on a specific, recent topic (C-SPAN, 1990b, 1991b). By looking more closely at the examples in which journalists are debating which kinds of journalistic responses are professionally correct, and comparing claims made in SPJ videos to the actual journalistic texts under review, we may better understand how certain kinds of metajournalistic discourses work to define the boundaries of professionalism and proper practice.

The National Press Club

In the early years after its founding in 1908, the National Press Club served as a venue for Washington journalists to socialize with each other and with their cultural and political sources, from Hollywood celebrities to railroad barons to presidents of the United States and foreign dignitaries (National Press Club, 2017). This close relationship with political elites has continued to this day. In 1950, the club hosted Secretary of State Dean Acheson, who delivered a speech that historians, and many South Koreans, believed was instrumental in initiating the Korean War (Matray, 2002). More recently, presidential candidates have used the club as a forum for announcing their campaigns and, once elected, to set their policy agendas in front of high-profile journalists (Reagan, 1981). The club also maintains an important physical presence in Washington, occupying the top two floors of the National Press Building since 1927, where the organization has hosted "scores of influential persons involved in the political, cultural or societal news of the day" just blocks away from the White House (Murray, 2011, para. 2). In the mid-1990s, the club began producing *The Kalb Report*, a television, radio, and now online series devoted to "the vital role of the press in our democracy and the transformation of journalism in the 21st century" (GW Global Media Institute, n.d., para. 1). Slow to change its policies, at least in its early years, the club excluded women from membership into the 1970s, reflecting its alignment with an old-guard political power structure and its facilitation of the political and social status quo (Washington Press Club Foundation, 2011).

Perhaps emblematic of the National Press Club's proximity to power and to official discourses, many transcripts of club speeches made by domestic and international policy actors have been published in peer-reviewed academic journals in disciplines as diverse as criminal justice (e.g., Holder, 2015), diplomacy (e.g., Hanley, 2002), business (e.g., Zoellick, 2008), and political history (Nelson, 2016). The rare critical work on the club has started to address gender (Voss & Speere, 2014) and racial (Pease, 2009) discrimination in the organization's early decades. However, with the exception of a study by Beasley (1988), this research has only scratched the surface. Though running for more than 20 years, *The Kalb Report* has attracted no discernible scholarly interest. For an organization with such close ties to those in power, which hosts speeches that are often published verbatim in academic journals, the National Press Club has received remarkably little critical attention from scholars of any discipline, let alone scholars of journalism.

Though the C-SPAN Video Library is not comprehensive in its capture of the first eight years of the network's programming, from 1979 to 1986 when the Video Library began to save all C-SPAN programs, many speeches hosted by the National Press Club in this earlier period have been archived. Nearly 2,700 videos of club events from 1982 to June 2017 are available in the Video Library, with more videos added nearly every month. By far the largest proportion of these videos show speeches made to the club by American political elites, including sitting presidents, cabinet members, House majority leaders, governors, and others. Many talks also feature military officials, prominent cultural and business figures, and thought leaders. Remarkably, far fewer videos in which the topic of conversation is journalism or the national press are available in the Video Library. However, the Video Library contains a rich enough assortment of prominent journalists, historians, and other pundits discussing the role of journalism in American democracy to offer many research opportunities in this domain.

The earlier sections of the National Press Club archive, in which the press is discussed more frequently, offer substantial material for scholars interested in understanding how elite political journalists discursively construct the challenges and triumphs of mainstream American political journalism. These rich discourses include the valorization of journalists who cover the federal government (e.g., C-SPAN, 1985a), the mortal dangers of conflict reporting (e.g., C-SPAN, 1985b), and the financial success of *USA Today*, which represented a new brand of newspaper for the television age (e.g., C-SPAN, 1984). Many of these themes persist through the club's videos, particularly the focus on protecting press freedom when the federal government appears to be pushing back against press privileges, as when the Department of Justice under President Obama seized Associated Press phone records in 2013 (e.g., C-SPAN, 2013c). Taken along with *The Kalb Report*—videos of which are also available online[1]—these videos can help scholars understand how discourses facilitated by the club, ostensibly to cast a critical eye at the national press corps, often merely reiterate standard notions of what types of journalism and journalists are important and worthy of protection. Working to the Video Library's strengths, however, scholars can find opportunities to interrogate how the club works as a quasi-journalistic forum for the legitimation of the ideologies of political and cultural elites who espouse neoliberal business practices (e.g., C-SPAN, 2013a), military expansion (e.g., C-SPAN, 2012), and environmental protection (e.g., C-SPAN, 1988), just to name a few examples from across the political spectrum. Members of the club are often allowed to ask questions of these speakers, demonstrating the discourses that structure the relationship between the press and other democratic institutions and political actors.

The Freedom Forum

Founded in 1991 by former Gannett Company executive Al Neuharth, the Freedom Forum, according to its website, is no longer officially affiliated with Gannett, which has owned dozens of American newspapers, including *USA Today*, for decades (Newseum Institute, n.d.). However, the foundation has persisted as an ideological extension of the mainstream newspaper business through its continued association with former Gannett executives and Neuharth's family (Hopkins, 2011). At its founding, the forum's stated mission was to promote "a free press, free speech and other democratic ideals both in the United States and abroad" (Elliot, 1991). In more recent years, the foundation has endowed media programs at universities, scholarships for minority journalism students, and two think tanks devoted to the First Amendment (Newseum Institute, n.d.). In 2001, the Freedom Forum downsized its staff, closed nearly all of its offices, and invested in an expensive new building in Washington, DC for a museum it funds, the Newseum (Heyboer,

2001). Celebrating journalism of the past and present, the Newseum soon became the foundation's primary venture. In 2015, the forum and museum board faced a financial crisis, coming under scrutiny for a string of risky investments and excessive executive salaries (McGlone & Brittain, 2015).

Perhaps because the efforts of the Freedom Forum's think tanks are somewhat amorphous, the academic literature has neglected the foundation in general as a topic for study, instead focusing on how the Newseum shapes public understanding of the relationship between mainstream journalism and democracy. Scholars have recognized the institutional bias of the Newseum, which presents a heroic American news media, critiquing the museum's exhibits for being "unresponsive to real criticism of the press" (Gans, 2002, p. 370) and for "deploy[ing] interactive technologies in order to subtly educate its visitors on the primacy of a distinctly U.S.-centered and staunchly patriotic view of what journalism is meant to do" (Palmer, 2017, p. 337). Others have praised the museum's educational and experiential value, but even these scholars argue that the Newseum "avoids problematizing the role of journalism in American democracy and instead trumpets only its successful intervention in historical movements" (Teresa, 2015, p. 382), charging its curators with "misplaced emphasis and potential misrepresentation" (Streitmatter, 1997, p. 92).

The video recordings of events hosted or co-hosted by the Freedom Forum and the Newseum, available in the C-SPAN Video Library, cover the period from the founding of the forum up to the present. Videos from the 1990s, which tend to be cohosted by the forum and various universities, largely focus on conflicts in journalism values brought on by contemporary domestic and geopolitical issues, such as the war in the Middle East and the end of apartheid in South Africa. As the bulk of the videos shifted over to the Newseum, in the early 2000s, the discussions begin to celebrate journalists as key actors in important moments of American history, such as World War II, the civil rights movement, and 9/11. These videos offer an opportunity for expanding on the still nascent critical work on how the foundation and museum shape the public face of contemporary and historical American journalism. More importantly, however, the videos offer opportunities for new avenues in the discursive study of the institution of American journalism.

For example, a close textual study of the two sets of videos—those hosted by the forum and those hosted by the Newseum—would offer insight into how the discourse produced by a single organization can lead to decidedly different representations of the democratic functions of American journalism as the mission and financial considerations of that institution shift over time. Many of the Newseum videos also offer an opportunity for more nuanced readings of how mainstream journalists and journalism institutions work together to construct collective memories of their own role in important moments in history. These videos often occur on the anniversaries of those moments, and thus over time, the role of journalism in certain events, such as the Watergate scandal (e.g., C-SPAN, 1997, 2014), the Vietnam War (e.g., C-SPAN, 2001, 2015), and the assassination of John F. Kennedy (e.g., C-SPAN, 2003, 2013b), will be reiterated, reshaped, and remembered differently for each contemporary moment. The Video Library's temporal dimension allows researchers to study how the discourses of institutional memory change over time.

CONCLUSION

As the conditions surrounding journalism shift, so too do the discourses that structure journalism's relationship to other institutions of liberal democracy. The uptake of digital technologies poses myriad challenges to journalism, but as Brüggemann, Humprecht, Nielsen, Cornia, and Esser (2016) show, existing normative languages and concepts offer journalistic actors a means to frame these challenges in ways that are commensurate with existing practice, providing the kinds of discursive continuity that privilege existing organizations and institutional arrangements. Furthermore, Nielsen (2017) notes, as democracy faces populist challenges globally, there is a particular need to understand the means by which journalistic norms develop in the context of broader political and social realities, with an eye to the practical consequences of these developments. The C-SPAN Video Library provides one such opportunity to uncover how journalists and news organizations make sense of the realities they are immersed within and articulate norms and practices that respond to those realities.

So far, we have laid out an agenda for studying single organizations and understanding the discourses they mobilize, as contextualized by their ideological commitments. Just a few examples of specific research opportunities made possible by the Video Library have been elaborated above, such as a comparative study of the discourses surrounding the threats to print newspapers posed by television news in the 1980s and social networks in the 2000s found in the ASNE archive; an analysis of the discourses of professional legitimation among White House correspondents found in the SPJ archive; an examination of how quasi-journalistic organizations, like the National Press Club, can serve to reiterate and legitimize the discourses of power produced by other institutions and private corporations in a democratic society; or a study of how journalists and the curators of the Newseum work to produce an institutional collective memory of important moments in American journalism history. These research opportunities, and the others hinted at above, represent only a fraction of the paths available for researchers accessing each of these organizations' materials in the C-SPAN Video Library as discrete archives.

However, getting one's arms around journalism as a broader, heterogeneous field requires a more comprehensive and comparative perspective. In addition to focusing on discussions hosted by a single journalism-related organization, researchers should also conduct analyses across the different organizations in the Video Library, only four of which have been discussed here. This method of cross-institutional analysis will allow scholars to understand how specific, topical discourses are shaped by organizational commitments, historical contingencies, and ideological commitments that span the field. For instance, the discursive permutations of a specific journalism value, such as objectivity, or a challenge to the industry, such as technological change, can and should be traced across organizations and through time, both to reveal a diverse range of responses and to establish the discursive limits within which such values and challenges operate. The Video Library offers quite a broad array of mainstream, institutional discourses, which often dictate how day-to-day journalism practices and business decisions are made sensible to those within and outside of the industry, offering researchers the means to show how a range of articulations constitute the discourses that shape journalistic norms.

However, just as C-SPAN's valiant efforts to capture governmental proceedings by necessity miss discussions held behind closed doors or by state and local governments far from the hallowed halls of Washington, the Video Library is by no means representative of all journalism discourses in the

United States. The discourses of ASNE, SPJ, the National Press Club, or the Freedom Forum may represent the anxieties and commitments of a certain class of national political journalist, editor, and media owner, but they may be far removed from the anxieties and commitments, for example, of a journalist working for a Spanish-language newspaper in Philadelphia, or the editor of a tech blog in Silicon Valley, or the executive of a media cooperative covering news in the Rust Belt. Though the journalists in each of these examples may face similar economic conditions and possess common understandings of journalistic norms and values, the organizational structures, story values, and public commitments of these various news outlets and producers differ drastically from those of the D.C. press corps. Surely some discourses will be shared by most in the journalism industry, but researchers should always acknowledge that the most elite mainstream voices cannot be taken as representative of all voices. That said, these videos do enable an understanding of journalism's institutional character, and as such, rich discursive engagement with this part of the C-SPAN Video Library can contribute to a broader understanding of American journalism as a heterogenous institution maintaining a variety of relationships with the workings of political power.

NOTE

1. http://www.press.org/news-multimedia/video/kalb.

REFERENCES

Alexander, J., Breese, E. B., & Luengo, M. (Eds.). (2016). *The crisis of journalism reconsidered: Democratic cultures, professional codes, digital future.* Cambridge, UK: Cambridge University Press.

Anderson, C. W. (2017). Newsroom ethnography and historical context. In C. W. Anderson & P. Boczkowski (Eds.), *Remaking the news: Essays on the future of journalism scholarship in the digital age* (pp. 61–79). Cambridge, MA: MIT Press.

Beasley, M. (1988). The Women's National Press Club: Case study of professional aspirations. *Journalism History, 15*(4), 112–121.

Benson, R., & Neveu, E. (Eds.). (2005). *Bourdieu and the journalistic field*. Malden, MA: Polity Press.

Bourdieu, P. (1977). *Outline of a theory of practice* (R. Nice, Trans.). Cambridge, UK: Cambridge University Press.

Bourdieu, P. (1993). *The field of cultural production: Essays on art and literature*. (R. Johnson, Ed.). New York, NY: Columbia University Press.

Brüggemann, M., Humprecht, E., Nielsen, R. K., Cornia, A., & Esser, F. (2016). Framing the newspaper crisis: How debates on the state of the press are shaped in Finland, France, Germany, United Kingdom and United States. *Journalism Studies, 17*(5), 533–551. https://doi.org/10.1080/1461670X.2015.1006871.

Carlson, M. (2015). Introduction: The many boundaries of journalism. In M. Carlson & S. C. Lewis (Eds.), *Boundaries of journalism: Professionalism, practices and participation* (pp. 1–18). New York, NY: Routledge.

Carlson, M. (2016). Metajournalistic discourse and the meanings of journalism: Definitional control, boundary work, and legitimation. *Communication Theory 26*(4), 349–368.

Carlson, M. (2017). *Journalistic authority: Legitimating news in the digital era*. New York, NY: Columbia University Press.

C-SPAN (Producer). (1984, September 20). *USA Today* [online video]. Available from https://www.c-span.org/video/?124661-1/usa-today

C-SPAN (Producer). (1985a, September 28). *A free press: Endangered or dangerous* [online video]. Available from https://www.c-span.org/video/?125699-1/free-press-endangered-dangerous

C-SPAN (Producer). (1985b, October 28). *Memorial ceremony for journalists killed* [online video]. Available from https://www.c-span.org/video/?125759-1/memorial-ceremony-journalists-killed

C-SPAN (Producer). (1988, December 22). *Nuclear weapons industry and nuclear pollution* [online video]. Available from https://www.c-span.org/video/?5496-1/nuclear-weapons-industry-nuclear-pollution

C-SPAN (Producer). (1989a, May 8). *A question of ethics: Press disclosure* [online video]. Available from https://www.c-span.org/video/?7562-1/question-ethics-press-disclosure

C-SPAN (Producer). (1989b, October 20). *Confidential sources: Uses or abuses?* [online video]. Available from https://www.c-span.org/video/?10029-1/confidential-sources-uses-abuses

C-SPAN (Producer). (1989c, October 20). *The Supreme Court and the First Amendment: What the future holds for the press* [online video]. Available from https://www.c-span.org/video/?9963-1/supreme-court-first-amendment

C-SPAN (Producer). (1990a, April 25). *Keeping secrets: Justice on trial* [online video]. Available from https://www.c-span.org/video/?15829-1/keeping-secrets-justice-trial

C-SPAN (Producer). (1990b, October 29). *Who is minding the store?* [online video]. Available from https://www.c-span.org/video/?14825-1/minding-store

C-SPAN (Producer). (1991a, April 24). *Ways to energize the Washington press corps* [online video]. Available from https://www.c-span.org/video/?17691-1/ways-energize-washington-press-corps

C-SPAN (Producer). (1991b, November 5). *Media coverage of the Thomas hearings* [online video]. Available from https://www.c-span.org/video/?22509-1/media-coverage-thomas-hearings

C-SPAN (Producer). (1992, March 27). *Keeping secrets: Justice on trial* [online video]. Available from https://www.c-span.org/video/?25247-1/keeping-secrets-justice-trial

C-SPAN (Producer). (1994a, September 16). *Campus courts: Public Arts, private justice* [online video]. Available from https://www.c-span.org/video/?60224-1/campus-courts-public-acts-private-justice

C-SPAN (Producer). (1994b, September 16). *Journalism career* [online video]. Available from https://www.c-span.org/video/?60223-1/journalism-career

C-SPAN (Producer). (1995, November 10). *Pulliam Editorial Fellowship Award* [online video]. Available from https://www.c-span.org/video/?68260-1/pulliam-editorial-fellowship-award

C-SPAN (Producer). (1997, June 12). *Breaking the Watergate story* [online video]. Available from https://www.c-span.org/video/?87494-1/breaking-watergate-story

C-SPAN (Producer). (2001, July 15). *Covering the Vietnam War* [online video]. Available from https://www.c-span.org/video/?165185-1/covering-vietnam-war

C-SPAN (Producer). (2003, November 18). *Kennedy assassination anniversary* [online video]. Available from https://www.c-span.org/video/?179166-1/kennedy-assassination-anniversary

C-SPAN (Producer). (2005a, October 18). *Ethical case studies in investigative journalism* [online video]. Available from https://www.c-span.org/video/?189398-2/ethical-case-studies-investigative-journalism

C-SPAN (Producer). (2005b, October 18). *The reporter's privilege under siege* [online video]. Available from https://www.c-span.org/video/?189398-1/reporters-privilege-siege

C-SPAN (Producer). (2006, October 26). *Working for the* New York Times [online video]. Available from https://www.c-span.org/video/?195117-1/working-new-york-times

C-SPAN (Producer). (2007a, October 5). *White House press corps* [online video]. Available from https://www.c-span.org/video/?201380-1/white-house-press-corps

C-SPAN (Producer). (2007b, October 15). *White House press secretaries* [online video]. Available from https://www.c-span.org/video/?201380-2/white-house-press-secretaries

C-SPAN (Producer). (2012, November 16). *State of the navy and strategy* [online video]. Available from https://www.c-span.org/video/?309492-1/state-navy-strategy

C-SPAN (Producer). (2013a, April 3). *Ninja innovations* [online video]. Available from https://www.c-span.org/video/?311896-1/ninja-innovation

C-SPAN (Producer). (2013b, May 1). *JFK remembered by veteran broadcasters* [online video]. Available from https://www.c-span.org/video/?312462-1/jfk-remembered-veteran-broadcasters

C-SPAN (Producer). (2013c, June 19). *Protection of newsgathering practices* [online video]. Available from https://www.c-span.org/video/?313450-1/ap-responds-doj-phone-record-seizure

C-SPAN (Producer). (2014, October 30). *Tom Brokaw on his career* [online video]. Available from https://www.c-span.org/video/?322328-1/tom-brokaw-career

C-SPAN (Producer). (2015, July 27). *Women reporters in Vietnam* [online video]. Available from https://www.c-span.org/video/?327343-1/discussion-women-reporters-vietnam

C-SPAN (Producer). (2016, April 27). *Access to government records* [online video]. Available from https://www.c-span.org/video/?408749-1/investigative-reporters-discuss-access-government-records

Dahmen, N. S. (2016). "Moving" the pyramids of Giza: Measuring the effects of ethics education in a visual communication curriculum. *Visual Communication Quarterly, 23*(1), 26–38. https://doi.org/10.1080/15551393.2015.1128334

Deuze, M. (2005). What is journalism for? Professional identity and ideology of journalists reconsidered. *Journalism 6*(4), 442–464.

Dewey, J. (1927). *The public and its problems.* New York, NY: Henry Holt.

Elliot, S. (1991). Neuharth and Lois are a team again. *New York Times,* July 3, 1991.

Foucault, M. (1969). *The archaeology of knowledge* (A. M. Sheridan Smith, Trans.). New York, NY: Routledge.

Foucault, M. (2000). Interview with Michel Foucault. In J. D. Faubion (Ed.), *Power: The essential works of Foucault 1954–1984* (pp. 239–299). New York, NY: Penguin.

Gans, R. M. (2002). The Newseum and collective memory: Narrowed choices, limited voices, and rhetoric of freedom. *Journal of Communication Inquiry, 26*(4), 370–390. https://doi.org/10.1177/019685902236897

GW Global Media Institute. (n.d.). About the Kalb Report. https://research.gwu.edu/about-kalb-report

Hanitzsch, T., & Vos, T. P. (2017). Journalistic roles and the struggle over institutional identity: The discursive constitution of journalism: Journalistic roles and institutional identity. *Communication Theory*, published online ahead of print January 10, 2017. https://doi.org/10.1111/comt.12112

Hanley, D. C. (2002). Palestinian representative speaks to National Press Club. *Washington Report on Middle East Affairs, 21*(5), 96–97.

Hardin, M., & Zhong, B. (2010). Sports reporters' attitudes about ethics vary based on beat. *Newspaper Research Journal, 31*(2), 6–19. https://doi.org/10.1177/073953291003100202

Hayt, T. (2016). Why join ASNE? Retrieved April 08, 2017, from http://asne.org/content.asp?contentid=122

Heyboer, K. (2001, November). The Freedom Forum's shrinking endowment. *American Journalism Review.* http://ajrarchive.org/Article.asp?id=2414

Hickey, T. W. (2003). A masochist's teapot: Where to put the handle in media ethics. *Journal of Mass Media Ethics, 18*(1), 44–67. https://doi.org/10.1207/s15327728jmme1801_05

History. (n.d.). Retrieved April 8, 2017, from http://asne.org/content.asp?contentid=83

Holder, E. (2015). Remarks at the National Press Club. *Federal Sentencing Reporter, 27*(5), 297–299. https://doi.org/10.1525/fsr.2015.27.5.297

Hopkins, J. (2011). Freedom Forum's new chair has a familiar name; quiet board reshuffle keeps a Neuharth in control. *Gannett Blog*, December 8, 2011. http://gannettblog.blogspot.com/2011/12/freedom-forums-new-chair-has-familiar.html

Kennedy, J. (1961). *President John F. Kennedy on "Bay of Pigs"* [online video]. Available from https://www.c-span.org/video/?192032-1/bay-pigs-invasion

Kimball, M. B. (2011). Granting sources anonymity requires complex process. *Newspaper Research Journal, 32*(2), 36–49.

Kitch, C. (2014). Historical authority and the "potent journalistic reputation":

A longer view of legacy-making in American news media In B. Zelizer and K. Tenenboim-Weinblatt (Eds.), *Journalism and memory* (pp. 227–241). Houndmills, Basingstoke, Hampshire: Palgrave Macmillan.

Levi-Faur, D. (2005). "Agents of knowledge" and the convergence on a "New World Order": A review article. *Journal of European Public Policy, 12*(5), 954–965.

Lippmann, W. (1922). *Public opinion*. New York, NY: Harcourt, Brace.

Matray, J. (2002). Dean Acheson's press club speech reexamined. *Journal of Conflict Studies, 22*(1). Retrieved from https://journals.lib.unb.ca/index.php/JCS/article/view/366/578

McChesney, R. (1999). *Rich media, poor democracy: Communication politics in dubious times*. New York, NY: New Press.

McGlone, P., & Brittain, A. (2015, July 1). Heavily in debt, Newseum considered risky strategy to improve finances. *Washington Post.* https://www.washingtonpost.com/lifestyle/style/heavily-in-debt-newseum-considered-risky-strategy-to-improve-finances/2015/07/01/b5e94286-19e7-11e5-bd7f-4611a60dd8e5_story.html?utm_term=.16c88fa3d8cb

Mellinger, G. (2003). Counting color: Ambivalence and contradiction in the American Society of Newspaper Editors' discourse of diversity. *Journal of Communication Inquiry, 27*(2), 129–151. https://doi.org/10.1177/0196859902250862

Mellinger, G. (2008). The ASNE and desegregation: Maintaining the white prerogative in the face of change. *Journalism History, 34*(3), 135–144.

Meyers, O., & Davidson, R. (2016). Conceptualizing journalistic careers: Between interpretive community and tribes of professionalism. *Sociology Compass, 10*(6), 419–431.

Murray, B. (2011, June 28). D.C.'s iconic National Press Building trades for $167.5M. *Commercial Property Executive.* https://www.cpexecutive.com/post/d-c-s-iconic-national-press-building-trades-for-167-5m/

Nadler, A. (2016). *Making news popular: Mobilizing U.S. news audiences*. Urbana, IL: University of Illinois Press.

National Press Club. (2017). History. http://www.press.org/about/history

Nelson, D. D. (2016). BAAS keynote speech: A passion for democracy: Proximity to power and the sovereign immunity test. *Journal of American Studies, 50*(2), 279–303. https://doi.org.libproxy.temple.edu/10.1017/S0021875816000499

Nerone, J. (2015). *The media and public life: A history*. Malden, MA: Polity.

Newseum Institute. (n.d.). Freedom forum. http://www.newseuminstitute.org/freedom-forum/

Nielsen, R. K. (2017). The one thing journalism just might do for democracy:

Counterfactual idealism, liberal optimism, democratic realism. *Journalism Studies.* Advance online publication. https://doi.org/10.1080/1461670X.2017.1338152

Overholser, G., & Jamieson, K. H. (Eds.). (2005). *The press.* New York, NY: Oxford University Press.

Palmer, L. (2017). World news at the Newseum: Interactive imaginings of international news reporting. *International Journal of Cultural Studies, 20*(3), 321–340. https://doi.org/10.1177/1367877915617012

Patterson, T. (2013). *Informing the news: The need for knowledge-based journalism.* New York, NY: Vintage.

Pease, E. C. (2009). Reliable sources: 100 years at the National Press Club. *Journalism and Mass Communication Quarterly, 86*(2), 476–478.

Pratte, A. (1994). "A tortuous route growing up": The rise of women in the American Society of Newspaper Editors. *Journal of Women's History, 6*(1), 51–66. https://doi.org/10.1353/jowh.2010.0153

Pratte, A. (2001). "… But there are miles to go": Racial diversity and the American Society of Newspaper Editors, 1922–2000. *Journal of Negro History, 86*(2), 160–179. https://doi.org/10.2307/1350163

Reagan, R. (1981). Remarks to members of the National Press Club on arms reduction and nuclear weapons. Retrieved from http://www.presidency.ucsb.edu/ws/?pid=43264

Rodgers, R. R. (2007). "Journalism is a loose-jointed thing": A content analysis *of Editor & Publisher*'s discussion of journalistic conduct prior to the canons of journalism, 1901–1922. *Journal of Mass Media Ethics, 22*(1), 66–82. https://doi.org/10.1080/08900520701315277

Roessner, A., Popp, R., Creech, B., & Blevens, F. (2013). "A measure of theory?": Considering the role of theory in media history. *American Journalism, 30*(2), 260–278.

Romero-Rodríguez, L. M., & Aguaded, I. (2016). Toward a taxonomy of newspaper information quality: An experimental model and test applied to Venezuela dimensions found in information quality. *Journalism.* Advance online publication. https://doi.org/10.1177/1464884916663596

Ryfe, D. (2017). *Journalism and the public.* Malden, MA: Polity.

Schmidt, V. (2008). Discursive institutionalism: The explanatory power of ideas and discourse. *Annual Review of Political Science, 11*(2), 303–326.

Schudson, M. (1978). *Discovering the news: A social history of American newspapers.* New York, NY: Basic Books.

Schudson, M. (1982). The politics of narrative form: The emergence of news conventions in print and television. *Daedalus, 111*(4), 97–112.

Schudson, M. (2013). Reluctant stewards: Journalism in a democratic society. *Daedalus, 142*(2), 159–176. https://doi.org/10.1162/DAEDa00210.

Singer, J. B. (1998). Online journalists: Foundations for research into their changing roles. *Journal of Computer-Mediated Communication, 4*(1). https://doi.org/10.1111/j.1083-6101.1998.tb00088.x

Singer, J. B. (2003). Who are these guys? *Journalism, 4*(2), 139–163. https://doi.org/10.1177/146488490342001

Singer, J. B. (2006). The socially responsible existentialist. *Journalism Studies, 7*(1), 2–18. https://doi.org/10.1080/14616700500450277

Singer, J. B. (2007). Contested autonomy. *Journalism Studies, 8*(1), 79–95. https://doi.org/10.1080/14616700601056866

Slattery, K. L. (2016). The moral meaning of recent revisions to the SPJ code of ethics. *Journal of Media Ethics, 31*(1), 2–17. https://doi.org/10.1080/23736992.2015.1116393

Society of Professional Journalists. (2017). About. https://www.spj.org/aboutspj.asp

Streitmatter, R. (1997). Journalism history goes interactive at the Newseum. *American Journalism, 14*(1), 92–96. https://doi.org/10.1080/08821127.1997.10731884

Teresa, C. (2015). Newseum education. *American Journalism, 32*(3), 381–382. https://doi.org/10.1080/08821127.2015.1064704

Uriarte, C. B., & Valgeirsson, G. (2014). Institutional disconnects as obstacles to diversity in journalism in the United States. *Journalism Practice, 9*(3), 399–417. https://doi.org/10.1080/17512786.2014.963367

van Dijk, T. (1990). *News as discourse.* New York, NY: Routledge.

Vos, T. (2016). Journalistic fields. In T. Witschge, C. W. Anderson, D. Domingo, & A. Hermida (Eds.), *The SAGE handbook of digital journalism* (pp. 383–396). New York, NY: Sage.

Voss, K., & Speere, L. (2014). Taking chances and making changes: The career paths and pitfalls of pioneering women in newspaper management. *Journalism & Mass Communication Quarterly, 91*(2), 272–288. https://doi.org/10.1177/1077699014527453

Waisbord, S. (2013). *Reinventing professionalism: Journalism and news in global perspective.* Cambridge, UK: Polity Press.

Washington Press Club Foundation. (2011). History of the WPCF. http://wpcf.org/history-of-the-wpcf/#1980s

Wilkins, L., & Brennen, B. (2004). Conflicted interests, contested terrain: Journalism ethics codes then and now. *Journalism Studies, 5*(3), 297–309. https://doi.org/10.1080/1461670042000246061

Zelizer, B. (1993). Journalists as interpretive communities. *Critical Studies in Mass Communication, 10*(3), 219–237.

Zelizer, B. (2015). Terms of choice: Uncertainty, journalism, and crisis. *Journal of Communication, 65*(5), 888–908.

Zoellick, R. B. (2008). Speech at the National Press Club, Washington, DC. *Law and Business Review of the Americas, 14*(2), 243–254.

CHAPTER **11**

NOBODY SAW THIS COMING? SUPPORT FOR HILLARY CLINTON AND DONALD TRUMP THROUGH AUDIENCE REACTIONS DURING THE 2016 PRESIDENTIAL DEBATES

Austin D. Eubanks, Patrick A. Stewart, and Reagan G. Dye

The passionately involved electorate of the 2016 presidential election played a pivotal role in the unexpected victory of novice political outsider and long-shot Republican Party candidate Donald Trump over Democratic Party mainstay and electoral favorite Hillary Clinton. The results defied early predictions and many citizens, pundits, and political operatives alike found themselves saying, "Nobody saw this coming." They would argue there was no way to anticipate the intensity of support Trump would amass, especially in comparison with the more traditional candidacy of Clinton. However, the presidential debates can be seen as providing early insights concerning the "enthusiasm gap" between the two candidates from the start of the primary season. When comparing each major party's respective initial primary election debates, Trump was met with raucous audience applause, laughter, and even booing to a greater extent than was Clinton. These collective audience responses may in turn be seen as valid and reliable indicators of the intensity of shared individual and emergent group attitudes toward the respective candidates (Stewart, 2012, 2015; Stewart, Eubanks, & Miller, 2016).

Though a great deal of debate-focused research to date has concentrated on the powerful role these electoral events play in influencing viewer response to candidates, the disentangling of the particulars of how the candidates and the media influence voters is largely in its infancy. This is mainly due to the great majority of existing research treating debates as a single and discrete event. While providing useful insights concerning the larger electoral process, these approaches do not take into consideration the uncontrolled and unpredictable aspects of debates during which candidate rhetorical approach (Benoit, 2013), nonverbal behavior, and media visual presentation style choices (Wicks, Eubanks, Dye, Stewart, & Eidelman, 2017) all play a role in viewer perceptions during the course of these events. This is before the influence of campaign pitch-and-spin and media coverage bias/slant (Clayman, 1995; Schroeder, 2016) is even considered. In other words, most research to date does not consider the process of change in viewer perceptions that might occur during debates by disentangling and identifying those defining moments that are critical for both candidates and viewers.

Recent research addressing this oversight by using continuous response measures (CRM), dial testing focus groups, and large-scale analysis of social media such as Twitter has provided insight concerning how audience members respond to candidates during presidential debates. These studies suggest that the nonverbal behavior of the candidates, even more so than their verbal acclaims, attacks, and defenses (Benoit, 2013), influences audience response. However, a major critique concerns these audience reactions being too cognitively complex to reflect the contemporaneous feelings of the audience (Bucy & Holbert, 2014; Hughes & Bucy, 2016; Reinemann & Maurer, 2005). Turning a CRM dial or composing a tweet are actions subject to cognitive control and thus may be too intrusive and prone to social conformity pressures to accurately reflect the emotions of viewers. Furthermore, by focusing on an individual's response to what may be considered the most primal of group activities, that of politics, such measures might be missing the highly important attribute of implicit sociality.

However, audience vocalizations such as applause, laughter, and booing may be seen as reflecting an almost automatic and highly contagious affective and behavioral response to the candidates (Hatfield, Bensman, Thornton, & Rapson, 2014; Hatfield, Cacioppo, & Rapson, 1994). As a result, these group vocalizations likely do a better job of identifying the defining moments that occur during a debate. This in turn provides insight into the type of relationship the audience members have with the candidates, and perhaps as important, the connection members have with each other in the room. Furthermore, insights concerning the developmental process of these bonds between the candidates, the audience, and fellow audience members can be explored in greater detail.[1]

This chapter seeks to understand the type of support for candidates during presidential debates by describing and analyzing collective audience utterances such as applause-cheering, laughter, booing-jeering, and combinations of these "vocalizations." Here we focus on the 2016 general election debates between Donald Trump and Hillary Clinton that were carried on C-SPAN. More specifically, this study considers patterns in audience response to Trump and Clinton during the three general election debates. We first review the ethological and psychological literature concerning the qualities of audible group response and those leaders who elicit these responses by dominating their attention to understand their value in social and political realms. We then analyze the three general election debates using ANVIL content analysis software to code candidate speaking turns and time, and more importantly for this chapter, the audience applause, laughter, and booing (or combinations thereof) that occurred during these debates and were evident to viewers watching. These group utterances will be considered in terms of the number of these vocalizations and their length. This allows us to consider each debate in turn before comparing them with each other. We conclude by considering the implications of our research.

INTRODUCTION

Dominance of Attention

It is a well-established finding that when dealing with social animals such as humans, one of the best (if not *the* best) indicators of leadership is dominance of group attention (Chance, 1967; Eibl-Eibesfeldt, 1989; Mazur, 2005; Salter, 2007). In other words, leaders may be defined as those who are either given more speaking time or are more successful at taking it by force through interrupting other individuals. Because media presentation of candidates, especially during debates, often places them virtually face-to-face with viewers in a manner that is artificially intimate, candidates with more speaking time (and hence camera time) have significant advantages through increased viewer preference and trust. This is especially the case when there is high perceived social connectedness between the viewer and the candidate, as exposure to the candidate on its own can lead viewers to be more likely to vote for that particular candidate (Verrier, 2012). Thus, speaking time—and with it camera time—primes the viewers to see candidates as particularly viable as possible leaders. As a result, we consider whether one candidate or the other dominated viewer attention through their aggregate speaking time, what types of strategies they engaged in through the number of speaking turns taken, and implicitly how many interruptions were attempted.

Audience Response to Political Figures

When evaluating audible audience response to speakers a key factor, if not the most important factor, is the reliability of such audience utterances in reflecting the audience's emotions and with it their behavioral intent. In this case, reliable indicators of emotion may be defined by two major characteristics. First, observers must be able to accurately recognize the emotional state of the communicator, and with it the resultant behavioral intent. Second, the signal should function as an index of the sender's underlying emotional state. This is done typically by being difficult to fake, or if the emotional state and behavioral intent is feigned, leading the individual posing the emotion to physiologically feel the emotional state.

Because of the social nature of group vocalizations, these utterances should be stereotyped and contagious. Stereotypic utterances are easier to mimic, allowing for the involvement of consenting individuals, whereas contagion provides for rapid coordination of social action. As stated by Hatfield and colleagues (1994), emotional contagion is "the tendency to automatically mimic and synchronize facial expressions, vocalizations, postures, and movements with those of another person's and, consequently, to converge emotionally" (p. 169).

Generally speaking, one can identify three general types of audible audience response, which in turn might be mixed depending on the makeup of the audience and the intensity of their response. Specifically, applause, laughter, and booing serve to signal shared audience response to political candidates and their willingness to support or oppose them. These group utterances can likewise be seen as a major means by which large groups of followers can provide their leaders signals concerning the level of their support and appreciation or opposition and approbation for different statements. As pointed out by West (1984, pp. 28–29), audible reactions by the audience provide immediate feedback enabling speaker evaluation of success, are unobtrusive, and provide a means of continuously monitoring the audience. Furthermore, group utterances in the forms of applause-cheering, laughter, and booing may be seen as accurately indicating coalition size and strength (Dunbar, 1993).

However, it should be noted that the acoustic qualities of a location may enhance or diminish the subjective emotional and physiological response of audience members. While these forms of group utterances function to bond groups together the larger they get, there is a point of diminishing returns the more dispersed the audience is as the strength of such utterances dissipates. This in turn is influenced by the size and acoustics of the locale where the debates are held, as well as how well microphones broadcasting these events capture audience response (Stewart, 2012). Thus, in addition to the type of audience "vocalization" and potential mixtures that might occur, the magnitude of audience response may be best characterized by utterance length.

However, it should be noted that the length of an utterance may be accentuated or attenuated premised upon its type. Here we note that at least three different types of group utterances are observed in political events such as those analyzed here, with each serving distinct communicative ends. Specifically, laughter, applause-cheering, and booing allow for audiences to communicate their support or disapproval for statements by leaders and putative leaders, with concomitant intensity and mixtures providing insight concerning intensity and unanimity in these positions.

Applause and Cheering
Of all the forms of audible group utterances, applause-cheering is perhaps most likely to be observed in settings such as political speeches and intra-party debates. As a result, applause-cheering has been appreciated for the role it plays in providing an important barometer of a politician's appeal to groups or in direct competition with other candidates during debates. On

the other hand, research suggests that due to applause and cheering likely not being as costly to produce physiologically and easier to inhibit than laughter (Stewart, 2015), it might not be as reliable a social signal. That does not mean that this activity is not stereotyped and easy to identify. Research concerning applause bouts in small groups (13–20) found that most involve only 9 to 15 claps per person, although some last over 30 claps. A study considering applause in larger groups suggests this activity typically begins with an uncoordinated loud burst of high-frequency clapping that then synchronizes through a form of social contagion and coordination. Thus, while the initial applause is louder, the synchronicity of audience response afterward suggests connection between audience members.

In the context of general election debates, and especially in comparison with the more partisan primary election debates, applause and cheering is quite rare. This is likely due to both moderator instructions to applaud the candidates only before and after the debate, as well as the norms of politeness and the nature of the audiences themselves (e.g., the 2012 Republican presidential primary, where moderator instruction diminished the total amount of applause that occurred; Stewart, 2015). Furthermore, the partisanship of general election audiences tends to be mixed, often selected by their candidates' campaigns based upon their higher status and seated in a manner that does not allow for social groupings to occur easily. In comparison, applause-cheering during primary debates is very much in evidence, especially in crowds not dominated by higher status partisans. Findings from the first two Republican Party debates during the 2016 presidential primaries are instructive with the nine times larger crowd for the FOX debate (4,500 in attendance) applauding much more than at smaller, more elite CNN Republican Party debate (500 attendees), despite the CNN event being an hour longer. However, due to the controllable nature of applause-cheering, these audience utterances do not necessarily reflect voter preferences, as Donald Trump was in the bottom half of both debates' candidates in terms of applause-cheering occurrences and total length.

Laughter
Vocalic utterances such as laughter are limited physiologically to a much greater extent than those created through rhythmic mechanical noisemaking such as applause, making it a potentially more reliable indicator of audience

members' emotional state. Extensive research suggests laughter by individuals may be seen as a costly signal by virtue of it being evoked in a manner that is difficult to control and that even when initially faked can lead to physiological change. Individual laughter likewise serves as a social lubricant by affecting a subject's mood states by decreasing negative affect, increasing positive affect and pain tolerance, while also increasing social cooperation and group identity (Van Vugt, Hardy, Stow, & Dunbar, 2014). With this latter exception, much of the extant research considers laughter from the lens of individual behavior with interpersonal implications; the emergent qualities of laughter as representing group preferences have only recently been explored in a tentative manner.

Laughter as a group vocalic utterance is much more stereotyped in length than applause-cheering, and likely booing (although the rarity of these types of group utterances makes strong assertions untenable). When humorous comments are savored to a great extent by a larger social group, applause-cheering prolongs the laughing utterance, likely due to the physiologically taxing demands of extended "laughing jags," which, while they do occur, are comparatively rare (Stewart, 2012; Stewart et al., 2016). This suggests that laughter is a highly important social signal with a good deal of reliability concerning behavioral intent.

The nature of this physiologically and emotionally costly signal was underscored during the 2016 presidential primary debates, especially regarding Donald Trump. Indeed, if there is one thing that set Trump apart from his fellow competitors during his initial primary debate performances, it was his ability to evoke laughter through his ridicule and insults of the other candidates, the opposition political party, and more generally, anyone who appeared to stand in opposition to him. This audience laughter, in conjunction with the media coverage given him—likely due to his arousing audiences—arguably catapulted him from reality television oddity to serious candidate.

Heckling and Booing

Much rarer than supportive in-person audience response through laughter and applause-cheering are those disaffiliative vocalizations of jeers and boos. While they have been observed in political events, boos and jeering are quite rare. Specifically, West (1984) in his analysis of 1980 campaign speeches found that Republican Party candidate Ronald Reagan elicited more than twice as many boos as both his Democratic Party competitor Jimmy Carter and independent John Anderson. While West found that being booed by the "right" crowd enhanced Anderson's electoral status by emphasizing his willingness to take an unpopular stand (for that audience), West's groundbreaking and exhaustive study did not systematically analyze the strategic nature of such boo elicitations. More recently, Bull and Miskinis (2015) found that affiliative booing—in other words, booing that is invited through attacks on out-groups and policy positions—occurred in roughly equal proportions for Republican candidate Mitt Romney and incumbent Barack Obama when they considered nearly two and a half hours of campaign speeches by each candidate.

When general election debate behavior is considered, the one published study suggests that like booing during political speeches, booing behavior in general election debates is a relatively rare event (Clayman, 1992). Specifically, in the two 1988 presidential and one vice-presidential debate, a total of only 8 instances of booing occurred out of 169 total events. Here, the audience members only appeared to boo in response to attacks by a candidate. In other words, booing was a defensive gesture employed by audience members in a politically mixed audience, as opposed to the politically homogenous audience of primary debates. Most recently, multiple incidents of booing, both alone and mixed with applause-cheering and laughter, were in evidence during the initial two 2016 Republican Party presidential primary debates (Stewart et al., 2016). Specifically, of the 343 audience events during the Fox News and CNN GOP debates, 17 involved booing. Here, 8 of these involved audience response to the divisive, yet ultimately successful populist outsider Donald Trump as he contravened GOP canon.

In summary, applause-cheering, laughter, and booing provide means by which the audience present with a politician can make their voices heard in distinctive ways. While preverbal, these utterances can be used successfully to strategically communicate factional preferences not just to the speaker, but also to other potential group members. As a result, there are social benefits and costs from joining or not joining in; indeed, audience members must consider if engaging in these forms of group utterances will be more socially costly to them for not joining in or joining in when candidates break norms of politeness and civility.

CONTENT ANALYZING THE 2016 PRESIDENTIAL DEBATES ON C-SPAN

The three-debate approach, with two podium-based events bookending a town hall meeting and covered by C-SPAN, has been enshrined as part of the presidential electoral process since 1992. However, while politicians of varying charisma and interpersonal skills have occupied center stage, the 2016 presidential debates were the first to see a reality-TV star and public figure such as Donald Trump contend for a position normally held by the most carefully vetted of political party selections. Indeed, given the circumstances, expectations for Donald Trump's successful performance in the debates were relatively low, especially as Hillary Clinton was a veteran of over 10 head-to-head debates, as well as an up-close and personal observer of her husband's presidential debates, including the first town hall debate held in 1992. However, it was noted in advance that Trump's "ability to read a room, to sense when he is losing an audience, and to try the theme or tone that will win them back" (Fallows, 2016, p. 73) might play a role in his being successful. Indeed, while general election debates are notable for being more respectful and polite than primary election debates, playing to the studio audience may in turn play to the audience at home. This, then, is the starting point for our analysis: Studio audience audible utterances both provide insight into candidate support intensity and may also influence the perceptions of those watching at home.

The first of three 90-minute general election debates between Democratic Party presidential nominee Hillary Clinton and Republican Party nominee Donald Trump occurred on Monday, September 26, 2016 and was hosted by Hofstra University just outside of New York City and moderated by NBC News's Lester Holt (see Figure 11.1). Though Clinton had maintained a lead in the polls coming into this initial meeting between the candidates, Trump had narrowed her lead from nearly 15 percentage points in the month prior to a 2.7-point gap.[2] While this likely reflected those on the political right coming to accept outsider Trump as their candidate rather than any serious missteps by Clinton or actions by Trump, the tightening of the polls reflected the competitive nature of this race. An estimated total of 84 million voters watched this debate on television, making it the most watched debate in U.S. history, and underscoring the importance and influence of this first head-to-head meeting between Trump and Clinton.[3]

FIGURE 11.1 C-SPAN televises 2016 debate between Donald Trump and Hillary Clinton at the University of Nevada, Las Vegas.

The second debate, hosted at Washington University in St. Louis, Missouri, was held on Sunday, October 9, 2016, and was moderated by CNN's Anderson Cooper and ABC's Martha Raddatz. Unlike the traditional debate format used in the first and third debates—indeed, the format used in nearly every debate since the 1960 Kennedy-Nixon debates, in which a moderator asks questions to the candidates one-on-one with rules regarding speaking time and rebuttals—the second debate featured a "town hall" style wherein half of the questions were posed by audience members (of uncommitted voters selected by the Gallup Organization).[4] Between the first and second debates, a slight uptick in Clinton's polling and decline in Trump's had the candidates coming into the second debate with only a 4.6 point difference in the polls. Despite viewership being less than for the first debate, the second debate saw an impressive 66.5 million viewers.

The third and final debate between Clinton and Trump, hosted by the University of Nevada, Las Vegas, took place on Wednesday, October 19, 2016, and was moderated by Fox News's Chris Wallace. The slow rise and decline of Clinton and Trump's poll numbers, respectively, continued after the second debate such that the candidates entered the final debate with a 6.5-point difference in the polls. This final debate had an increase in viewership from the second debate with 71.6 million viewers watching the broadcast.

METHOD

Candidate speaking time and audible audience reactions[5] (both duration and type: *applause, laughter, booing, applause and boos, applause and laughter, laughter and boos*) were coded using ANVIL annotation software (Kipp, 2010). This software allows for incredibly precise (down to the level of frame-by-frame) measurement of time. First, each of the debates was downloaded and split into shorter clips (generally < 10 min.) to accommodate file size restrictions of the software. The primary coder was trained on the coding scheme used in previous research regarding the primary debates (any identifiable utterance is coded as a speaking turn, and any audible audience reaction except for opening and concluding applause is coded as well; Stewart et al., 2016), and then coded 30 minutes' worth of video clips from those primary debates to assess intercoder reliability (ICR) against the published data. After initial training, the primary coder achieved acceptable ICR (Cohen's kappa, κ > .80). Then, to verify ICR for the current project, approximately 30 minutes of the clips from the first general election debate were randomly selected and coded by both the primary coder and the first author (κ > .92). Having far surpassed "acceptable" ICR, the primary coder coded all three debates, and the data were exported for analysis.

RESULTS

Debate 1

During the first debate (see Table 11.1), speaking time for the two candidates, when taking into account speech overlap and interruptions, indicated nearly 5 minutes more speaking time for Trump at 47 minutes (2,795 seconds) in comparison with Clinton's 42 minutes (2,492 seconds). This is likely due to Trump attempting to dominate speaking time through interruptions, as he had nearly twice as many speaking turns ($N = 80$) as Clinton ($N = 43$).

During this debate, the audience engaged in 31 audible vocalizations for a total of 94.09 seconds in response to either of the candidates' statements or retorts (see Table 11.2). A great majority of these group utterances were, as can be expected given their relatively irrepressible nature, laughter. Specifically, roughly two-thirds ($n = 21$; 52.12 s) of audience vocalizations involved laughter alone ($n = 19$; 38.94 s) or in combination with other utterances. There were 8 applause events for a total of 45.61 seconds, and only 2 booing events for a total of 3.03 seconds. Of these 31 audience responses, 18 were in response to Donald Trump (58.79 s), and 13 were in response to Clinton (35.30 s). As shown in Table 11.2, the largest difference in audience responses between Clinton and Trump was laughter, wherein Trump had 5 more occurrences ($n = 12$; 29.13 s) than Clinton, for a total of approximately 19 additional seconds of laughter over Clinton.

Debate 2

During the second debate, each candidate spoke for approximately 40 minutes, with Trump (2,444 seconds) speaking slightly longer than Clinton (2,376 seconds). Again, Trump's propensity for interruptions led to his having nearly

TABLE 11.1 *Candidate Speaking Time During the 2016 General Election Debates*

	N	M	SD	Sum
Debate 1				
Clinton	43	57.96	60.22	2,492.22
Trump	80	34.94	45.81	2,794.92
Total	123	42.98	52.24	5,287.14
Debate 2				
Clinton	28	84.85	51.09	2,375.84
Trump	52	47.00	49.69	2,443.95
Total	80	60.25	53.07	4,819.79
Debate 3				
Clinton	49	52.15	46.71	2,555.41
Trump	82	26.72	37.25	2,190.97
Total	131	36.23	42.70	4,746.38
All Debates				
Clinton	120	61.86	54.05	7,423.47
Trump	214	34.72	44.26	7,429.84
Total	334	**44.47**	**49.67**	**14,853.31**

TABLE 11.2 Audience Reactions to the Candidates for the 2016 General Election Debates

	Applause		Laughter		Booing		Applause & Laughter		Laughter & Booing		Total	
	N	Sum	N	Sum	N	Sum	N	Sum	N	Sum	N	Sum
Debate 1												
Clinton	4	19.82	7	9.81	1	1.33	1	4.34	–	–	13	35.30
Trump	4	25.79	12	29.13	1	1.7	–	–	1	2.17	18	58.79
Total	8	45.61	19	38.94	2	3.03	1	4.34	1	2.17	31	94.09
Debate 2												
Clinton	2	12.01	–	–	–	–	–	–	–	–	2	12.01
Trump	1	6.21	3	10.94	1	4.9	2	10.41	–	–	7	32.46
Total	3	18.22	3	10.94	1	4.9	2	10.41	–	–	9	44.47
Debate 3												
Clinton	1	5.01	2	7	–	–	–	–	1	3	4	15.01
Trump	1	4.3	6	22.53	–	–	–	–	–	–	7	26.83
Total	2	9.31	8	29.53	–	–	–	–	1	3	11	41.84
All Debates												
Clinton	7	36.84	9	16.81	1	1.33	1	4.34	1	3.00	19	62.32
Trump	6	36.30	21	62.60	2	6.60	2	10.41	1	2.17	32	118.08
Total	**13**	**73.14**	**30**	**79.41**	**3**	**7.93**	**3**	**14.75**	**2**	**5.17**	**51**	**180.40**

twice as many speaking turns ($N = 52$) as Clinton ($N = 28$), although he was not able to capitalize with more speaking time in this debate. This was likely due to stricter moderator control over the audience in response to the first debate's relatively unrestrained audience as well as the nature of the town hall audience, who were randomly chosen from the region based upon their being independent or undecided on their presidential vote.

With only nine audience responses (44.47 s) recorded, the second debate proved to be a much more placid event than the first. Of these responses, the largest portion was applause ($n = 3$; 18.22 s). Besides Clinton's two applause events (12.01 s), all other audience responses were for Trump. Trump's responses included three laughter events (10.94 s), one booing event (4.9 s), and two events of laughter followed by applause (10.41 s).

Debate 3

Finally, during the third debate, Clinton spoke for nearly 43 minutes (2,555 seconds) in comparison with Trump's 36.5 minutes (4,746 seconds). Though not quite nearly double as in the first and second debates, Trump had far more speaking turns ($N = 82$) than Clinton ($N = 49$).

Though the third debate had more audience response events than the second ($n = 11$), the responses were shorter, leaving cumulatively less response time (41.84 s). Much like the first debate, Clinton and Trump had roughly equal applause with one event each (5.01 and 4.30 s, respectively), but a sharp contrast existed vis-à-vis laughter where Trump's 6 events (22.53 s) dwarfed Clinton's 2 events (7.00 s). Finally, Clinton elicited one combined laughter and booing event, which lasted 3.00 seconds.

DISCUSSION

Though Trump dominated speaking time during the first debate, Clinton spoke more during the third debate and the candidates had roughly equal amounts of speaking time during the second debate. In total, Trump's and Clinton's speaking time across all three debates came within 7 seconds of each other (7,430 and 7,423 seconds, respectively). However, Trump had 214 speaking turns to Clinton's 120, which suggests that the two candidates were "playing by different rules" during the debates. Clinton acted like a more traditional front-running politician who valued politeness, whereas Trump's approach as the brash outsider led to him interrupting on a regular basis and the studio audience, as discussed below, reveling in that activity.

The candidates' ability to elicit audience responses throughout the debates reveals remarkable differences between the two. When considering the two most common audience responses, applause and laughter, both Trump and Clinton were able to invite nearly identical degrees of audience applause and cheering (only differing by 0.54 s cumulatively) through their utterances with 6 and 7 events, respectively; however, there was a very large disparity when it comes to laughter. Indeed, with 21 total laughter events to Clinton's 9, the duration of laughter Trump elicited (an impressive 62.60 seconds in total) was over 3.5 times longer than Clinton's cumulative laughter responses. Arguably, laughter-inducing impoliteness on the part of a candidate might be more likely to cause audience-member norm violations; in other words, if the audience is in a mirthful state of mind they might be more likely to audibly break with instructions given by the moderators to not respond, as was the case in the first debate. Here, Donald Trump's showmanship likely played a major role in emancipating the audience from their customary role as polite bystanders to one in which they were more aggressively vocal partisans. To the point, for the studio audiences at all three debates, Trump was funny; when critiquing government or other politicians, humor beats sanctimony for mobilizing emotions any day of the week (except maybe Sunday).

Though traditional measures of public opinion do a fair job of capturing patterns of support for candidates, and more recently the application of such technologies as continuous response measures (CRM) and large-scale analyses of online activity (e.g., Twitter and other forms of social media) effectively capture the dynamics of response to candidates during debates, these approaches are obtrusive and may miss highly important information altogether. Especially when it comes to analysis of online activity, many confounding variables may be in play. It could well be that what is published by any given user on social media isn't the most accurate reflection of that individual's true beliefs or ideals, but rather that of the online persona the user has created for him- or herself—a persona that may or may not even be linked with the individual (i.e., anonymous accounts).

In other words, these social media users have the luxury of conscientiously crafting their "response" (e.g., their tweet) before putting it on display for the world to see. Indeed, this contrast of cognitive control over response is what separates these responses from (automatic/relatively uncontrollable) laughter, and what makes laughter in particular such a "costly" signal. Most people do not have to think too hard to remember a time when they "couldn't help but laugh," even though laughing was highly ill advised or inappropriate given the particular situation at hand (e.g., at a funeral, during group prayer, during Marine Corps boot camp). As such, by its natural and unobtrusive nature, observational analysis of audience response in terms of applause-cheering, laughter, and booing is likely better able to reliably capture the intensity of studio audience response to the contenders as emergent phenomena.

At the same time, this response by the studio audience may be contagious for those watching at home. While much research is still needed to disentangle and characterize the effects of such audible audience response, producers and moderators of the presidential debates are intuitively aware of the effects such utterances have (or, perhaps, they merely believe them to be "distracting") as evidenced by giving and enforcing (with varying degrees of success) audience instructions to refrain from responding. Though one could argue that Clinton simply elicited less audience response because her supporters were "more well behaved" (i.e., followed these moderator instructions to a greater extent than did those who supported Donald Trump), the fact is that the audience at home was exposed to more people laughing for Trump, and "against the rules" or not, which could affect viewer perceptions of the candidates. Furthermore, a few overriding questions remain: Is the studio audience a conversational partner in these events? And if so, what right to speech—in the form of group vocalizations—do they have?

Finally, when so many people around the United States, and indeed around the world, exclaim, "Nobody saw this [Donald Trump's election victory] coming," we argue that perhaps "nobody" was looking in the right place. When you consider audience responses to Donald Trump and Hillary Clinton throughout the election, and specifically throughout the debates, the evidence of the "enthusiasm gap" that arguably led to Trump's election was present all along.

NOTES

1. Research has shown that CRM and Internet feedback, which are individual responses presented in the aggregate, can influence how viewers respond to the putative leaders, likely by appealing to the sociability and group interests humans have and utilize to survive and thrive. And just as television provides an analogous experience to that of face-to-face interactions with leaders, which in turn expedites a followership connection on a massive scale through evolved sensory adaptations, CRM and Internet feedback serve mainly to quantify grouped feedback in an interval manner.
2. All poll data from Real Clear Politics. http://www.realclearpolitics.com/epolls/2016/president/us/general_election_trump_vs_clinton-5491.html
3. All viewership data are from the Nielsen Company and do not include the millions to tens of millions of viewers who watched each debate online either simulcast or in the days following each debate.
4. From the Commission on Presidential Debates. http://www.debates.org/index.php?page=2016debates
5. The moderator (and for Debate 2, the audience members asking questions) was also coded, but is not considered to be of interest for the present study, and only Trump's and Clinton's data are discussed herein.

REFERENCES

Benoit, W. L. (2013). *Political election debates: Informing voters about policy and character.* Lanham, MD: Lexington Books.

Bucy, E. P., & Holbert, R. L. (2014). *Sourcebook for political communication research: Methods, measures, and analytical techniques.* New York, NY: Routledge.

Bull, P., & Miskinis, K. (2015). Whipping it up! An analysis of audience responses to political rhetoric in speeches from the 2012 American presidential elections. *Journal of Language and Social Psychology, 34*(5), 521–538. https://doi.org/10.1177/0261927X14564466

Chance, M. R. A. (1967). Attention structure as the basis of primate rank orders. *Man, 2*(4), 503–518. https://doi.org/10.2307/2799336

Clayman, S. E. (1992). Caveat orator: Audience disaffiliation in the 1988 presidential debates. *Quarterly Journal of Speech, 78*(1), 33–60.

Clayman, S. E. (1995). Defining moments, presidential debates, and the dynamics of quotability. *Journal of Communication, 45*(3), 118–147.

Dunbar, R. I. M. (1993). Co-evolution of neocortex size, group size and language in humans. *Behavioral and Brain Sciences, 16*(4), 681–735.

Eibl-Eibesfeldt, I. (1989). *Human ethology*. New York, NY: Aldine De Gruyter.

Fallows, J. (2016, October). Who will win? *The Atlantic, 318*(3), 64–79.

Hatfield, E., Bensman, L., Thornton, P. D., & Rapson, R. L. (2014). New perspectives on emotional contagion: A review of classic and recent research on facial mimicry and contagion. *Interpersona, 8*(2), 159.

Hatfield, E., Cacioppo, J. T., & Rapson, R. L. (1994). *Emotional contagion (Studies in emotion and social interaction)*. New York, NY: Cambridge University Press.

Hughes, S. R., & Bucy, E. P. (2016). Moments of partisan divergence in presidential debates: Indicators of verbal and nonverbal influence. In D. Schill, R. Kirk, & A. Jasperson (Eds.), *Political communication in real time: Theoretical and applied research approaches*. New York, NY: Routledge.

Kipp, M. (2010). Multimedia annotation, querying and analysis in ANVIL. In M. Maybury (Ed.), *Multimedia information extraction* (pp. 351–368). Hoboken, NJ: John Wiley & Sons.

Mazur, A. (2005). *Biosociology of dominance and deference*. Lanham, MD: Rowman & Littlefield.

Reinemann, C., & Maurer, M. (2005). Unifying or polarizing? Short-term effects and postdebate consequences of different rhetorical strategies in televised debates. *Journal of Communication, 55*(4), 775–794.

Salter, F. K. (2007). *Emotions in command: Biology, bureaucracy, and cultural evolution*. New Brunswick, NJ: Transaction.

Schroeder, A. (2016). *Presidential debates: 40 years of high-risk TV* (3rd ed.). New York, NY: Columbia University Press.

Stewart, P. A. (2012). *Debatable humor: Laughing matters on the 2008 presidential primary campaign*. Lanham, MD: Lexington Books.

Stewart, P. A. (2015). Polls and elections: Do the presidential primary debates matter? Measuring candidate speaking time and audience response during the 2012 primaries. *Presidential Studies Quarterly, 45*(2), 361–381. https://doi.org/10.1111/psq.12191

Stewart, P. A., Eubanks, A. D., & Miller, J. (2016). "Please clap": Applause, laughter, and booing during the 2016 GOP presidential primary debates. *PS: Political Science & Politics, 49*(4), 696–700. https://doi.org/10.1017/S1049096516001451

Van Vugt, M., Hardy, C., Stow, J., & Dunbar, R. (2014). Laughter as social lubricant: A biosocial hypothesis about the pro-social functions of laughter and humor. Centre for the Study of Group Processes Working Paper, University of Kent.

Verrier, D. (2012). Evidence for the influence of the mere-exposure effect on voting in the Eurovision song contest. *Judgement and Decision Making, 7*(5), 639–643.

West, D. M. (1984). Cheers and jeers: Candidate presentations and audience reactions in the 1980 presidential campaign. *American Politics Research, 12*(1), 23–50.

Wicks, R. H., Eubanks, A. D., Dye, R. G., Stewart, P. A., & Eidelman, S. (2017). Perceptions of Donald Trump and Hillary Clinton based on presentation style. In A. Cavari, R. J. Powell, & K. E. Mayer (Eds.), *The 2016 presidential election: The causes and consequences of a political earthquake* (pp. 43–57). Lanham, MD: Lexington Books.

CHAPTER **12**

SELECTING C-SPAN VIDEO CLIPS FOR CREATIVE COLLABORATIVE LEARNING

Pavla Hlozkova

When creative collaborative learning (CCL) started being used in economics classes at the New York Institute of Technology, the first classes were conducted with in-person professionals. However, this approach was not very efficient since it was very difficult to bring professionals to the classroom because of issues such as logistics, lack of resources, and the availability of a network of professionals over a limited time frame. The need for an alternative solution brought us to the C-SPAN Archives' online Video Library. After several experiments in which we used the C-SPAN Video Library for CCL, we realized very important findings. The method itself was very successful in most cases in terms of engaging students and bringing new ways of thinking. These methods opened students' minds and helped them understand international and domestic geopolitical issues affecting macroeconomics and world trade. However, there was one very significant difference between successful and less successful attempts when C-SPAN video clips were used for CCL. The difference resides in the selection of C-SPAN video clips, which is crucial to achieving success with the approach.

The CCL experience described in this chapter was designed specifically for an MBA classroom of international students studying in Canada. The approach is suitable for any subject matter where circumstances change such as macroeconomics, international trade, and politics. CCL is not suitable for disciplines in which a framework of knowledge has been well established for many years, such as training physicians (Lorne & Hlozkova, 2016).

CREATIVE COLLABORATIVE LEARNING

The idea of CCL comes from the idea of collaborative learning that is referenced and promoted in several publications (Barkley, Cross, & Major, 2005; Gokhale, 1995; Járay-Benn, 2013; Peppler & Solomou, 2011; Roberts, 2004; Thousand, Villa, & Nevin, 2002). It is student-centered learning, which differs from the traditional approach by involving students more, leaving more work up to them. It also changes the directive leadership style of teachers to a consultative one (McCarthy, 2015). CCL combines collaborative learning with a multimedia learning environment, which is considered an improvement in the learning process (Pobiner, 2006, Lorne, Jhan, Kumar, Singh, & Tuladhar, 2013).

CCL differs from traditional student-centered learning by involving three participants instead of two. The three participants are the student, the professional, and the instructor. Students learn directly from professionals through watching C-SPAN videos, and the instructor's role is to help with understanding the content and leading the discussion according to the curriculum at hand. Based on the CCL model, instructors and professionals do not absolutely define the acquired knowledge. The approach requires self-driven involvement by students and the desire to acquire knowledge led by their own interests and career preferences.

C-SPAN video clips bring indisputable advantages over printed reports. Printed reports provide facts and are generally suitable for teaching subject matter where conditions are unchangeable over time. On the other hand, by studying C-SPAN video clips, students experience learning with real professionals, and the video clips bring a visual aspect of learning, which makes the material easier to remember for students, who can easily recall the knowledge afterward. They can experience the "in the moment" learning that is not possible to experience by reading printed reports. Students can also recognize certain emotions and tactics of policymakers and national leaders, and ideally the process elevates students' thinking beyond the ordinary.

The application of CCL was tried in international MBA classrooms in Vancouver, Canada, where students come from countries all over the world to study. Their backgrounds vary from music to finance. The class usually holds between 10 and 18 students, and the duration of the course is approximately 15 weeks (Lorne & Hlozkova, 2015, 2016). This international student population values learning about the professional manners of public figures even more than Canadian and American students because public speaking styles differ from country to country based on cultural values (Galvin & Power, 1997). The advantage of learning how to deliver public speeches in a second language, such as English, goes hand in hand with the previous point about professional manners. MBA programs prepare students for management roles in which being able to articulate and defend ideas and decisions in front of business partners, colleagues, and subordinates is particularly important. Since it is expected that these international students will work in Canada after graduation, it is particularly important for them to learn how to deliver speeches in English effectively. C-SPAN video conferences enable students to virtually attend talks by important policymakers and enhance their professional English knowledge to prepare them for their future professional paths.

C-SPAN video clips enable students to be part of conferences and discussions with important policymakers without leaving the classroom. Although some might argue that real talks would be more suitable for a CCL approach, the C-SPAN video clips are more practical for learning purposes. An instructor can pause the speech and provide particular guidance to students. Speakers in C-SPAN video clips are very well prepared for speaking in public since the clips are recorded and posted on the Internet where they are viewed by thousands of people. It would be very difficult and expensive to bring the same speakers to a classroom. The instructor can prescreen conferences to ensure that the talks are valuable and worthwhile to view. This is more reliable and provides some guarantee of a speaker's performance, which is impossible in the classroom. C-SPAN video clips also allow students to stop the recording and play it over and over based on their needs and understanding. The transcript of talks provided by C-SPAN combines video with printed reports, thus making the learning process even more effective and efficient (Lorne & Hlozkova, 2016).

CCL could be probably conducted with other online video sources than just the C-SPAN Video Library. However, there are several advantages of using C-SPAN that can't be found at any other online video source. The C-SPAN Video Library provides records that are not edited and show the entire content of talks. C-SPAN provides an informational infrastructure of political, economic, and social discussions so students can witness decision making and policies being made on the spot. The presented data can be captured in clips based on learning purposes, and students can use other sharing and saving functions on the website (Browning, 2014).

C-SPAN CLIPS SELECTION, EVALUATION, AND EXAMPLES

The C-SPAN video library is a great tool that can serve as a vehicle for CCL; however, not every clip is appropriate for a CCL application. Some clips are better than others, and that is the reason why selection has to be made carefully.

Selected clips are evaluated based on following criteria:

1. Understanding of the issue discussed
2. Use of the English language and professional manners
3. "In the moment" expression
4. Elevation of thinking

The first two components are usually met by most of the clips. However, the last two areas bring challenges for students and for instructors. The following section shows clip selection criteria and illustrates three different examples: the first one is the most successful clip; the second can generate output, but the clip is particularly difficult for students for several reasons that will be described; and the third clip is an example of an unsuitable clip for CCL.

Although it might seem quite simple, the thing that needs to be taken into consideration is who should be the primary person appearing in a clip for CCL learning purposes. The article "Designing Creative Collaborative Learning (CCL) for Economics: Using Professionals and Video Clips in MBA Classroom" (Lorne & Hlozkova, 2015) demonstrated CCL using a C-SPAN recorded public speaking forum from May 6, 2015, with Christine Lagarde of the International Monetary Fund (IMF) and Janet Yellen of the U.S. Federal Reserve (C-SPAN, 2015). It satisfied all four evaluating areas mentioned above. The selected clip led students to generate valuable interactions after the clip was played in the MBA classroom. Students started asking the right questions and generated discussions within the classroom. The topic of the forum was related to the financial crisis in 2008, and this topic was relevant to the topic taught at a macro-economic course at New York Institute of Technology (NYIT) at that time. Janet Yellen, the chair of the Board of Governors of the Federal Reserve System, presented the idea of a well-functioning financial system and its ability to improve overall economic growth, promote innovation, and generate new jobs. Her speech was mostly prepared, and something similar could be found in some other sources. The speech by Christine Lagarde, the managing director of the International Monetary Fund, was very different in speaking style. She talked spontaneously, with no prepared speech, and included a quotation from Voltaire: "If you see a banker jump out of the window, follow him because there is certainly money to be made." It provoked questions and curiosity from students and extended their thinking beyond the conventional.

The questions discussed included the following:

- What did she mean by the window? Was it a suggestion of a subprime market loan?
- Did she want to separate the banking and nonbanking sectors by the window mentioned?

The conducted experiment pointed out a very important finding: namely, it is not particularly important what she meant by the quotation from Voltaire, but the important takeaway was how it generated questions and discussion within the classroom based on "in the moment" expression and the elevation of thinking in the audience.

The second example is a press conference between the new president of the United States and the prime minister of Japan during a formal visit at the White House on February 10, 2017 (C-SPAN, 2017, February 10). The clip was chosen for the purpose of using CCL in the World Trade class at NYIT during the 2017 spring semester. There were several reasons for selecting this clip over others. The 2016 U.S. presidential election brought significant changes in American and global politics. One of the changes, for instance, is the U.S. withdrawal from the Trans-Pacific Partnership (TPP). This change affects Japan greatly because Japan was one of the biggest players involved and TPP could have meant substantial growth for the country (Wakatable, 2017).

Despite that, the tone of the talk was very friendly, contained several personal remarks, and showed an understanding between two countries. The intention in selecting this clip was to illustrate an emerging international circle of influence that can be influenced by the relationship between country leaders rather than simply trade agreements between two countries. The clip initiated discussions about factors that contribute to an emerging circle of influence. After several rounds of discussion in the classroom, the professor, Frank Lorne, decided to intervene in the learning process by providing revised questions that should help students express their own opinions on the final exam at the end of the semester. This particular clip is very difficult in the topic itself. The fact that the speech of the prime minister of Japan is translated into English by his translator doesn't make it easier, and therefore the interpretation can be different and the audience doesn't necessarily get the same expression as if speakers were using English. The "in the moment" expressions and attitude of the speech can be lost in the translation and not recognized at all. However, as Professor Lorne stated in an email communication: "it is arguably suitable for CCL, as the paradigm of evaluation and the knowledge is still changing" (April 17, 2017).

The third clip demonstrates an unsuitable example of a video clip for CCL (C-SPAN, 2017, January 26). It is a video clip of a speech that was prepared, scripted, and recited by the British prime minister, Theresa May, speaking at the Republican congressional retreat on January 27, 2017. She used the usual diplomatic language that was very well written; however, since she only read the prepared transcript from top to bottom, the only point where this clip can satisfy the learning purposes of CCL is in understanding the issue that was being discussed. Successful clips require some spontaneity from the speaker.

Challenges and Difficulties Related to Clip Selection

Clip selection brings certain difficulties and challenges for students and instructors. On the instructor side, the most challenging fact that an instructor must face and overcome is probably the diverse background of students in the classroom and the willingness of students to actively participate in collaborative learning. MBA programs prepare students for management roles in several areas of business, and students join MBA programs from different fields of undergraduate studies. The instructor should be able to recognize whether there is a gap in students' knowledge and provide appropriate materials to prepare students for C-SPAN talks ahead of time. One of the reasons why CCL was designed was to bring something new to motivate students and increase their engagement in the classroom; however, active participation is purely up to the student.

Although it is expected, students who join MBA programs are adults who should be eager to gain new knowledge. Time is also a concern because every semester has a limited number of lectures and a final exam in which students' knowledge of a subject matter should be realized (Lorne & Hlozkova, 2016). On the other side, professors' expectations may bring difficulties for students. Since the professor is the one who designs objectives and questions before watching a clip with students, his or her different perceptions of reality can be influenced by experience, knowledge, or a generation gap that may lead to difficulties in executing CCL in the MBA classroom. The video clips are brought to the classroom through technology and to be able to play clips in the classroom, students and institutions need certain equipment. The process definitely has some limitations because it can't be done offline and without the equipment. However, many modern classrooms are equipped with computer displays and Internet access, so this may be diminishing as a concern. An instructor, however, must be willing to use the technology and the CCL approach.

Instructor's Intervention

One of the advantages of using C-SPAN video clips for CCL is allowing an instructor to intervene. The instructor plays a significant role in the CCL learning process and it can't be executed without intervention. An unconstrained CCL set up without instructor intervention is a sure recipe for failure, as students lack the background knowledge as well as a roadmap to probe the unknown. The instructor's intervention involves selecting suitable clips, recognizing gaps in students' knowledge, and overcoming that by identifying learning objectives. In addition, designing questions and exercises; tracking and requiring students' participation and effort; offering critical comments, exams, and quizzes; and finally, providing explanations are all necessary ingredients of success. CCL is always monitored by an instructor and each exercise needs to be evaluated on individual basis to make sure all members of the team participate in the exercise (Lorne & Hlozkova, 2016).

Selecting the suitable clips is the most important intervention of the instructor, which was shown in one of the experiments conducted at NYIT (Lorne & Hlozkova, 2015), where students picked clips based on their own preferences and interests. This experiment wasn't very effective and proved the necessity of the instructor's intervention in the CCL approach.

CONCLUSION

Using C SPAN video clips for CCL is certainly suitable for MBA students since it brings a virtual learning experience with important policymakers from recognized institutions and the real world. It also provides a visual aspect of learning, which helps students to recognize the particular institution associated with the speaker. The selection of the clips is crucial and the experience that students get from the whole learning process depends on it very much. Research and experiments conducted at NYIT have shown several very important findings, pointing out difficulties that must be considered to successfully apply the CCL approach. Clips where talks are prepared and recited are not very suitable for CCL purposes because they are too much like a printed format. Clips in which we can find spontaneous talks with "in the moment" expressions are arguably suitable for CCL because they lead students to ask the right questions, generate discussions, and collaborate in teams. It leads to an elevation in their thinking about a subject matter and, more importantly, prepares them for their future professional paths in real life where they have to be able to voice their opinions and form their thoughts into conversation. The approach of CCL brings a new way of learning that is full of opportunities. Of course, there are difficulties related to the learning process; however, as Harry S. Truman (U.S. president from 1945 to 1953) said, "A pessimist is one who makes difficulties of his opportunities and an optimist is one who makes opportunities of his difficulties."

ACKNOWLEDGMENTS

The research was supported by a grant from Purdue University. I would like to thank the C-SPAN Archives for the opportunity to participate in the C-SPAN research conference; my professor, Frank Lorne, for letting me be a part of the creative collaborative learning project; and Michael Andersen, Gordon Andersen, and Lee Harris for their help with editing and providing comments along the way on drafts of this chapter.

REFERENCES

Barkley, E. F., Cross, K. P., & Major, C. H. (2005). *Collaborative learning techniques: A handbook for college faculty.* San Francisco, CA: Jossey-Bass.

Browning, R. X. (Ed.). (2014). *The C-SPAN Archives: An interdisciplinary resource for discovery, learning, and engagement.* West Lafayette, IN: Purdue University Press.

C-SPAN (Producer). (2015, May 6). *Christine Lagarde and Janet Yellen on the financial crisis* [online video]. Available from https://www.c-span.org/video/?325849-1/christine-lagarde-janet-yellen-financial-crisis

C-SPAN (Producer). (2017, January 26). *Theresa May remarks at congressional Republican retreat* [online video]. Available from https://www.c-span.org/video/?422831-1/british-prime-minister-theresa-may-addresses-congressional-republicans

C-SPAN (Producer). (2017, February 10). *U.S.-Japan relations* [online video]. Retrieved from https://www.c-span.org/video/?423837-1/president-trump-says-doubt-courts-will-restore-us-travel-ban

Galwin, C., & Power, M. R. (1997). The culture of speeches: Public speaking across cultures. *Culture Mandala: Bulletin of the Centre for East-West Cultural and Economic Studies, 2*(2). Retrieved from http://epublications.bond.edu.au/cgi/viewcontent.cgi?article=1032&context=cm

Gokhale, A. A. (1995). Collaborative learning enhances critical thinking. *Journal of Technology Education, 7*(1). Retrieved from http://scholar.lib.vt.edu/ejournals/JTE/v7n1/gokhale.jtev7n1.html?ref=Sawos.Org

Járay-Benn, C. (2013). *Collaborative creative learning in professional training* [IATEFL Hungary Conference slide presentation]. Retrieved from https://www.slideshare.net/CsillaJB/collaborative-creative-learning-in-professional-training

Lorne, F., & Hlozkova, P. (2015). Designing creative collaborative learning (CCL) for economics: Using professionals and video clips in MBA classroom. *European Journal of Educational Sciences, 2*(4). Retrieved from http://ejes.eu/wp-content/uploads/2016/01/2-4-2.pdf

Lorne, F., & Hlozkova, P. (2016). Creative collaborative learning for macroeconomics: C-SPAN video clips in MBA classroom. *International Journal of Learning and Teaching, 8*(4), 215–223. Retrieved from https://www.researchgate.net/publication/310050295_Creative_Collaborative_Learning_for_Macroeconomics_C-SPAN_Video_Clips_in_MBA_Classroom

Lorne, F., Jhan, A., Kumar, A., Singh, B., & Tuladhar, E. (2013). Perception of reality via multimedia communication in MBA classrooms. *Journal of Arts & Humanities, 2*(4). Retrieved from https://theartsjournal.org/index.php/site/article/view/96

McCarthy, J. (2015, September 9). Student-centered learning: It starts with the teacher [Blog post]. Retrieved from https://www.edutopia.org/blog/student-centered-learning-starts-with-teacher-john-mccarthy

Peppler, K. A., & Solomou, M. (2011). Building creativity: Collaborative learning and creativity in social media environments. *On the Horizon, 19*(1), 13–23.

Pobiner, S. (2006). Collaborative multimedia learning environments. In *CHI '06 extended abstracts on human factors in computing systems.* https://doi.org/1125451.1125682

Roberts, T. S. (2004). *Online collaborative learning: Theory and practice.* Hershey, PA: Information Science Publishing.

Thousand, J. S., Villa, R. A., & Nevin, A. I. (Eds.). (2002). *Creativity and collaborative learning: The practical guide to empowering students, teachers, and families* (2nd ed.). Baltimore, MD: Paul H. Brookes.

Wakatable, M. (2017, January 30). Can Japan get a better deal than the TPP? *Forbes.* Retrieved from https://www.forbes.com/sites/mwakatabe/2017/01/30/can-japan-get-a-better-deal-than-the-tpp/#474195431964

CHAPTER 13

C-SPAN IN CHANGING SPACES OF POLITICAL COMMUNICATIONS

Terri L. Towner

When many people think of C-SPAN, they often think about television coverage of congressional hearings. As the previous chapters demonstrate, the C-SPAN Archives offers so much more. In addition to congressional floor action, the C-SPAN Archives' online Video Library includes White House press briefings, news conferences, State of the Union speeches, coverage of conference panels, presidential debates, videos of public policy seminars, speeches from notable experts, interviews with scholars, and event coverage. Despite this wealth of information, the C-SPAN Archives is underutilized by scholars, pundits, and teachers. In this book, the assembled authors have begun to address this oversight by using C-SPAN videos to examine presidential communications, audience response to presidential debates, and historical changes in professional journalism. In addition, one author demonstrates how best to use C-SPAN videos as an instructional tool. Below, I provide a summary of each chapter, focusing on critical takeaways. Building on these main points, I offer future directions for research utilizing the C-SPAN Archives.

230 CHAPTER 13

THE TWITTER PRESIDENT

In Chapter 9, Delaney Harness and Joshua Scacco examine President Trump's first 30 days of presidential communication. The authors make clear that "presidential communication" is no longer an official speech in the Rose Garden or a White House press conference. Instead, President Trump skips the traditional press and turns to Twitter. To examine how President Trump expanded his communication outreach, the authors systematically compared Trump's tweets to his speeches and press conferences during his first month in office. The textual analyses reveal several notable findings. Consistent with prior literature (e.g., Gainous & Wagner, 2013; Parmelee & Bichard, 2012; Towner, 2016), the Twitter platform allows President Trump to display more pseudo-interactivity on Twitter, such as invitations to participate, engage, and share, than in traditional communication. Trump employs Twitter, rather than filtered speeches, to speak directly to his supporters, further solidifying American identity and nationalism while eschewing international bodies. Overall, Harness and Scacco provide early evidence that Twitter is a unique extension to presidential communication, allowing the president to sidestep the mainstream media.

SHIFTS IN JOURNALISM

In Chapter 10, Michael Buozis, Shannon Rooney, and Brian Creech call for a historical examination of journalism as an institution. To understand journalism today, we must trace back to early changes in journalism. Between the 1960s and today, newspapers declined, cable television climbed, and online news boomed. The latter is what we know based on readily available subscription, viewer, and user data. Instead, shifts in journalism might be better understood by examining C-SPAN's archival video from four prominent journalism organizations, the American Society of Newspaper Editors, the Society of Professional Journalists, the National Press Club, and the Freedom Forum. The authors argue that historical footage of panels, speeches, and events—some dating back to the early 1980s—are an overlooked and untapped data source for mapping the changing discourses and practices that encompass journalism as a profession. The authors leave us wondering if we fully understand today's institution of journalism.

PRESIDENTIAL DEBATE RESPONSES

In Chapter 11, Austin Eubanks, Patrick Stewart, and Reagan Dye focus on audience responses to Hillary Clinton and Donald Trump's three general election debates. For decades, audience reactions have been used to measure the impact of presidential debates on candidate evaluations, political knowledge, and vote choice. Traditionally, audience reactions to debates are measured with dial-testing, traditional polling, focus group responses, and, more recently, smartphone applications and social media comments (e.g., Boydstun, Glazier, Pietryka, & Resnik, 2014; Gainous & Wagner, 2013). Eubanks, Stewart, and Dye offer new measurements for spectator reactions: applause, laughter, and booing. Unlike traditional measures, these audible measures require less cognitive control and perhaps are less susceptible to social pressures. For example, instead of thinking about turning a dial to 70 or 80, cheers, jeers, claps, boos, heckling, and hollering are more automatic and natural behavioral responses. These authors examine C-SPAN debate videos; their content analysis of the duration and type of audible audience responses show variation in some spectator responses to Clinton and Trump speaking. Interestingly, Trump and Clinton garnered the same amount of applause, but different amounts of laughter. As these authors report, Trump received more laughter than Clinton, and that laughter occurred for a longer duration. Hence, Trump was seen as funnier than Clinton. Did Trump laugh his way into the White House?

TEACHING WITH C-SPAN

In Chapter 12, Pavla Hlozkova puts "active learning" in the college classroom under the microscope, providing insights on how to incorporate C-SPAN videos into creative collaborative learning (CCL) classrooms. In a CCL environment, students are expected to be highly engaged in group tasks, discussing and debating issues, and making collaborative decisions. It is the instructor's role to provide interesting readings, stimulating hands-on activities, meaningful question-and-answer sessions, incredible multimedia demonstrations, and experiential learning events. To aid instructors, Hlozkova notes the advantages of using C-SPAN videos, particularly since digital video allows real professionals and experts to be inserted directly into the classroom at a low cost. In addition, instructors and students can pause and discuss, stop and rewind, and watch the entire video again for deeper understanding. An important disadvantage is that not all video segments—often long and unedited—are best for learning in a CCL classroom. To overcome this challenge, instructors should evaluate videos based on (1) understanding of the issue discussed, (2) language and professional skills, (3) "in the moment" expression, and (4) thinking enhancement. Most importantly, the author provides several "classroom-tested" examples, illustrating that some C-SPAN videos meet the criteria whereas other videos do not.

RESEARCH QUESTIONS AND FUTURE DIRECTIONS

The question then becomes. Where does research and teaching with C-SPAN videos go from here, and, more importantly, what kind of research questions will be central to employing C-SPAN videos as a data resource? Considering the previous chapters, many interesting questions remain. Harness and Scacco nod to the Twitter presidency, indicating that digital tools are an integral part of presidential communication in the digital era. Previous presidents used Rose Garden speeches or Oval Office addresses to communicate with citizens about critical policies or in moments of crisis. Barack Obama, considered the "social media president," spoke to the nation on the state of American security while standing in the Oval Office—not on his Twitter feed. In contrast, President Trump tweets about every major moment. After almost a year in office, Trump has tweeted about health care, immigration, tax reform, North Korea, Russian meddling in the 2016 election, and the National Anthem controversy. How do Trump's tweets compare to his traditional communicative actions? According to the C-SPAN Video Library, President Trump has delivered an inauguration speech, an address to a joint session of Congress, a speech on the Iran nuclear agreement, a statement on the Las Vegas mass shootings, weekly presidential addresses, and more. How does presidential discourse differ in the Twittersphere versus the traditional media? How does this dialogue impact the public? Do Trump's tweets stick more in citizens' minds than Trump's speeches?

It is well known that the media landscape is ever-changing—just as Buozis, Rooney, and Creech suggest in Chapter 10. Today's journalism consists of user-generated news, real-time reporting, and self-selected information from Yahoo! News. But how did we get here? The authors have neatly laid the groundwork for examining the changing discourse among professional news organizations using the C-SPAN Video Library. They note research opportunities and offer several research questions. Drawing on an analysis of C-SPAN videos of professional news organizations' panels, speeches, and talks, they ask: How have journalist norms and boundaries changed? How has news media transitioned to the digital era? How has the definition of a professional journalist been altered? Has the definition of "soft news" shifted from "talk show" to "blog" among professional news organizations? Other possibilities include examining how these news organizations in C-SPAN footage framed the rise of the Internet, blogs, and social media platforms. Did news organizations in the 1990s frame their discourse as an "opportunity" or a "risk"? These frames, if used, may help explain the professional guidelines used today in the journalism industry (see Lee, 2016).

Humor has been highly studied in politics, indicating that laughing matters (e.g., Baumgartner & Morris, 2007; Stewart, 2012). Eubanks, Stewart, and Dye's conclusion that Trump was funnier than Clinton in the 2016 presidential debates ties nicely into prior research on political humor and comedy. The C-SPAN Archives offers presidential and vice-presidential debate footage from 1960 to 2016, which would allow a historical analysis of audible audience responses. Did previous presidential candidates elicit similar amounts of boos, applause, and laughing during debates? Does the funnier candidate have an advantage on the road to the White House? Obama was funny. George W. Bush was more humorous than Al Gore. Reagan entertained millions with amusing tales and anecdotes. A systematic look at audible audience responses during presidential debates as well as State of the Union addresses and official presidential speeches (available in the C-SPAN Video Library) may reveal interesting patterns. It would also be worthwhile to examine how audience response, measured by traditional polls or Twitter sentiment, is correlated with the audible response on television. Do public opinion polls reflect the audience's boos, applause, and laughter? Does the Twittersphere react to debates that trend with televised audible responses? Or consider linking reactions to a smartphone application, such as HillaryDonald,[1] which gives users the ability to shake their cell phone to register remote applause or boos. Is dial-testing dead?

Previous studies employing C-SPAN videos in the college classroom have examined how videos can help explain communication theories and American government concepts as well as create interactive learning beyond the lecture hall (see Browning, 2014). Hlozkova makes clear that video selection is critical. Her criteria are useful to any instructor employing C-SPAN videos in a learning environment. Once the best video is selected and then viewed in class, however, it remains unknown how watching and discussing C-SPAN videos contributes to measurable learning (i.e., grades). As Hlozkova discusses, students can digest video content at their own pace and explore content more deeply. Do students better recall information in video format? Does video facilitate thinking and problem-solving? Pedagogical research suggests that video can inspire and engage students when linked to assignments (Willmot, Bramhall, & Radley, 2012). An experiment could compare student grades in a class utilizing C-SPAN videos as a learning tool to student grades in a class without C-SPAN videos, controlling for content, instructor, and academic assessments. Would academic achievement be higher in the C-SPAN classroom?

NOTE

1. http://hillarydonald.com/#mobile-apps.

REFERENCES

Baumgartner, J., & Morris, J. (2007). *Laughing matters.* New York, NY: Routledge.

Boydstun, A., Glazier, R., Pietryka, M., & Resnik, P. (2014). Real-time reactions to a 2012 presidential debate. *Public Opinion Quarterly, 78,* 330–343.

Browning, R. (2014). Part IV: Teaching case studies. In R. Browning (Ed.), *The C-SPAN Archives* (pp. 123–152). West Lafayette, IN: Purdue University Press.

Gainous, J., & Wagner, K. (2013). *Tweeting to power.* New York, NY: Oxford University Press.

Lee, J. (2016). Opportunity or risk? How news organizations frame social media in their guidelines for journalists. *Communication Review, 19*(2), 106–127.

Parmelee, J., & Bichard, S. (2012). *Politics and the Twitter revolution.* Lanham, MD: Lexington Books.

Stewart, P. A. (2012). *Debatable humor.* Lanham, MD: Lexington Books.

Towner, T. L. (2016). The influence of Twitter posts on candidate perceptions: The 2014 Michigan midterms. In J. A. Hendricks & D. Schill (Eds.), *Communication and mid-term elections* (pp. 145–167). New York, NY: Palgrave.

Willmot, P., Bramhall, M., & Radley, K. (2012). *Using digital video reporting to inspire and engage students.* Retrieved from http://www.raeng.org.uk/publications/other/using-digital-video-reporting

CHAPTER **14**

"LOOK AT THE TAPE, MR. CHAIRMAN": REFLECTIONS ON CONGRESS AND TELEVISION

Keynote Remarks of Dr. Ray Smock

Dr. Ray Smock, former historian of the U.S. House of Representatives and director of the Robert C. Byrd Center, gave the keynote address at the fourth annual conference of the C-SPAN Archives on May 15, 2017. He reflected on the coverage of Congress on television and the 30 years of archiving of that coverage by the C-SPAN Archives.

I want to thank Robert Browning for inviting me to this conference. I jumped at the opportunity to come see the home of the C-SPAN Video Library, one of the most exciting and unique digital archives in the nation. I extend my hearty congratulations to everyone at C-SPAN for the creation of this fantastic archive. And special thanks to Robert Browning for his three decades of demanding work and creativity in building this national treasure for research on Congress, on national policy, on virtually any topic under the sun and the moon that comes before the legislative branch of government. With the later expansion of C-SPAN networks into broader subjects, this Video Library contains rich veins of history and culture that can be used for all kinds of studies and for classroom use at virtually every level of education.

To all of you who are attending this conference and exploring the many ways to use this wonderful new resource, I wish you good hunting that will lead to important insights.

Of the approximately 230,000 hours of recordings in this archive, I think I may take up about 30 hours of it. Naturally when the archive came online I searched my own name first. The oldest tape was of an appearance I made with the Senate historian, Richard Baker, on January 5, 1987, more than 30 years ago. I feel preserved in history. I will be glad to be around, even if only in a digital format, for many years to come.

When Robert called to ask me to speak at this conference, he said he thought a congressional historian who started work at the House not long after the House began to televise its coverage might offer a perspective on what this has meant to our understanding of Congress and the federal government since the advent of C-SPAN in 1979.

At the very moment that Robert called me on the phone, I was watching a video clip of an exchange between Senator Al Franken and Senate Judiciary Committee chairman Chuck Grassley. Senator Grassley was mildly rebuking Senator Franken for trying to set up Neil Gorsuch with some unfair questioning during his testimony before the committee on his Supreme Court nomination.

In his reply to Chairman Grassley, Senator Franken denied trying to set up Judge Gorsuch, and said, "Look at the tape, Mr. Chairman." Al Franken had given me the title for my remarks.

Senator Franken was pointing to evidence from a video clip from the day before to prove that he was right. The video clip was evidence of what actually transpired, not the way Senator Grassley preferred to remember it. It was a simple but powerful statement that a video told the truth and all you had to do was look at it and see that truth.

More recent televised events have raised the bar of the use of videotapes to seek truth far beyond the innocent little exchange between Senators Franken and Grassley. Since the president of the United States fired the director of the FBI last week, a constitutional crisis has erupted and right now the battle is being played out with a series of competing but completely contradictory video clips and tweets.

The White House Press Corps reported the reasons for the president's firing of Director Comey and then President Trump sat down with Lester

Holt of NBC and contradicted his own press people as well as the vice president. Whatever investigations are going on behind closed doors and out of the public eye, what we are seeing on television and in social media is a confusing jumble of contradictory video evidence, where the truth is almost impossible to determine.

Such is the power of the medium of television to shape our actions and our politics. From the mildest forms of entertainment to the highest levels of information and news about the conduct of government and world affairs, it all comes to us via television and more recently by newer forms of social media, which also rely heavily on video imagery.

When I was appointed as the first official historian of the U.S. House of Representatives in 1983, my understanding and appreciation of television took on a new dimension. The House had been televising its floor proceedings for four years before I arrived on the scene. The Senate was still trying to figure out if they should televise their proceedings. They finally began an experiment with TV on June 2, 1986, and while they thought it was an experiment, it became permanent very quickly. There was no turning back.

With the House getting a seven-year head start on the Senate, many senators found they were less well known back home than some House members. Senate leaders who had been leery of TV in their chamber, like Senator Robert Byrd of West Virginia, slowly came around to the necessity of it. Republican leader Howard Baker, whom Senator Byrd worked with closely, was the leading advocate of TV in the Senate. He saw the power of television to expand to a vast audience the rather cloistered proceedings of the Senate.

Just about every office on the House side, even in those early days, had TVs, somewhere. It was always on even if you hardly paid attention to it.

One of my mentors on the Hill was the House parliamentarian, William Holmes Brown. His office was just off the House floor in the Speaker's Lobby. I would visit Bill in his high-ceilinged, ornate office, filled with bookcases and shelves with volumes of the House precedents, which his office compiled. Bill always had one eye on the TV watching the floor, just steps away. On several occasions during my visits in his office, he would suddenly interrupt our conversation and say, "Sorry, Ray, I've got to go to the floor right now. Wait here, I'll be back." I would watch him exit his office, then I would turn to the TV and I would watch him enter the chamber on television. This man who had been a real live person one minute ago was now on TV. He would go to the rostrum, whisper something to the speaker, and then I would watch him leave the chamber on TV, and then the door of his office would open and he would step in, and we would continue our conversation.

I had two senses of different realities that the parliamentarian could go back and forth between a TV image and a real person so quickly. Both seemed quite real. The House floor was a TV studio, albeit a tightly controlled one in those days with fixed cameras with limited angles of view.

The founders of the United States talked a lot about the fact that government should be transparent and that for our representative democracy to work, the public needed useful information about what government was doing. They certainly had no conception of television but in the 20th century it seemed to be a perfectly appropriate tool to accomplish the mission of informing the public.

It also kept the members and the staff informed, instantly, of what was happening on the floor at any given time. It changed the way the entire institution, House and Senate, communicated through video imagery.

I learned that the daily broadcasts were controlled by the House. The TV feed that was controlled by the House was passed on to C-SPAN, this new creature of the cable industry that brought public affairs to the American people who had cable TV. Each day the video of the floor proceedings was recorded on tape and stored.

Being a historian, I asked the folks in the Recording Studio an innocent historical question: Do you keep a permanent archive of the tapes? I recall a look of curiosity on the faces of those in the room at the time. An archive? What for? The notion of a permanent archive had never crossed their minds. The video was kept for anywhere from 60 to 90 days, and then the tapes were used over to record subsequent floor coverage.

The tapes were temporary documents of temporary use for news organizations who needed a clip for the nightly news. I was flabbergasted that there was no conception of the video as a valuable historical resource of enduring value.

This is the situation and the question I posed to the Recording Studio people and that I used to help convince the Speaker and others that the tapes should be permanently saved. Imagine we had television in the House in 1848. A freshman member of Congress from Illinois by the name of Abraham Lincoln rises on the floor of the Old House Chamber to give a rousing speech in opposition to our war with Mexico. Don't you think that a videotape of that occasion would become a priceless piece of American history worthy of being saved for generations yet unborn?

I had been hired to plan for the 200th anniversary of Congress and to be a promoter of the rich history of the House of Representatives. I saw the recordings of the House sessions as history, not as something for a few news cycles.

Part of the reluctance of the House to consider the tapes as a permanent record was that it was the *Congressional Record* that was the official record of what occurred on the floor of the House. The *Congressional Record* could be revised, extended, and speeches entered into the record that never occurred on the floor. If a member misspoke during debate, the record could be changed later. But a videotape could not be easily edited or changed without destroying its authenticity. So, the House legal minds had to make sure that the printed *Record* remained the official version while the video was added as supplemental to the printed *Record*.

Then the issue became who was responsible for keeping this video archive that would grow like Topsy into thousands and thousands of hours of recordings. The Library of Congress wanted them. The National Archives, the official depository of the committee records of Congress, thought they should have them.

Rather than cut the baby in half, the House declared they had twins, so both the Library of Congress and the National Archives received appropriations to keep copies of the video recordings. I recall about this time that the Senate historian, Richard Baker, and I also had discussions with Brian Lamb about what kind of archive C-SPAN should create and maintain for its powerful educational value. Brian, Robert Browning, and others at C-SPAN figured this out on their own, but we may have helped by planting a seed. I'd like to think so.

I was often asked if I think televising the House and Senate have changed the way we perceive Congress and the public understanding of it. My answer always begins positively because I see it positively. It gives the citizens of this country the opportunity to sit in the gallery of the legislature and judge for themselves the conduct of the proceedings, the debates, the speeches, the special events such as the State of the Union addresses. It is a window on Congress that can enhance citizenship and understanding of government. Al Gore Jr. was the first to speak on television on opening day of House televised coverage. He said: "The marriage of this medium and of our open debate have the potential, Mr. Speaker, to revitalize representative democracy." I believe what Congressman Gore said that day.

C-SPAN was a godsend to the House and Senate historians. Dick Baker and I were trying to expand our audience of Americans who wanted to know more about the history of Congress. We could not cut it with quaint newsletters that reached a few hundred people. C-SPAN gave us a national audience like nothing else could. It is not that we were on camera that much, it was what we were doing behind the scenes that was broadcast. Our special events, the Joint Session of Congress on the 200th anniversary of Congress, Senator Byrd's speeches on the history of the Senate, a special session of Congress held in Philadelphia in Independence Hall, it was all there on C-SPAN and now it is all here in this Archives. Thank you, C-SPAN, for carrying our work to a larger audience and preserving it for future generations.

Having said this, however, there are serious critical aspects to televised government. Back in the 1960s the TV critic Marshall McLuhan, trying to understand the impact of television on American culture, coined the phrase "the medium is the message." What he meant by that was that television by its very nature is such a leap forward in our ability to be eyewitnesses to all kinds of things, that the medium itself becomes how we perceive things. We believe what our eyes see. We believe we are witnessing something real.

When President Trump, who by all accounts is a person who responds viscerally and often immediately to what he sees on television, witnessed video of Syrian children suffering death throes from a gas attack, he spoke emotionally about what he had seen on TV. He launched 56 missiles at an airbase in Syria in retaliation. Would the president have had the same visceral reaction had the information about the gas attack come to him in a printed intelligence brief? Was the medium of television the real messenger that determined his response?

We know that television can deceive, that it can be the most powerful tool of the propagandist or the political campaigner. Video can deceive, by accident or on purpose.

Newt Gingrich, the Georgia Republican who came to Congress in the early days of House TV coverage, cleverly used House rules and television to create a national name for himself and a handful of fellow conservatives.

They did this right under the nose of the Democratic leaders who had no idea of the power the medium of television had to impact people.

Using the time called special orders, where members could speak up to an hour on any subject after regular House business was over, Newt and other members began holding forth on their conservative agenda, giving speeches, pretending to debate, when they were really talking to an empty chamber. The cameras were fixed on the member who was speaking. It appeared as if they were talking to the full House. This appearance could be exaggerated with a little acting on the part of the House members who would gesture as if they were talking to someone across the aisle.

Newt would go unchallenged when he said controversial things to an empty chamber. It appeared as if his arguments were so strong that his opponents were dumbfounded and confined to silence. He was in control of the medium. He knew how to use it to his advantage.

Eventually this practice went too far. Gingrich, always pushing the envelope, challenged Democrats not in the room and questioned their patriotism. Speaker Tip O'Neill had enough. He ordered the cameras to pan the room to show that it was empty. In doing so, the Speaker violated the rules that called for cameras to be fixed on the person speaking. Later O'Neill stormed into the chamber, mad at Newt, and from the floor chastised Gingrich for his unseemly behavior. The Speaker said it was the lowest thing he had heard in 30 years in Congress. In challenging Gingrich when he was angry, the Speaker went too far in impugning Gingrich, and members of Gingrich's group immediately asked that the Speaker's words be taken down. This parliamentary maneuver meant that if the presiding officer and the parliamentarian agreed that the Speaker was out of line, he had to stop talking. A back-bench member from Georgia had beaten the Speaker of the House on television. It was a victory that many say was the launching point of Newt's rise to power, and the eventual Republican control of the House in the election of 1994, and Newt's ascendency to the Speakership.

I suspect, but do not have evidence, that TV coverage has contributed significantly to the polarization of American politics. I am not talking about C-SPAN coverage of the House and Senate, but television news, the rise of cable news, CNN as the first 24-hour cable news station. All this happened in the late 1970s and early 1980s with the rise of a new militancy and more focused ideology that Newt Gingrich used to rise to power and take control of the House. Later the Internet, the new social media, the rise of the use of Twitter in the last presidential campaign suggest that we have all learned how to use mass media to reach specific targeted audiences who engage in echo chambers of their own choosing.

The impeachment of Bill Clinton became a television spectacle where the medium delivered a lot of mixed messages, leaving those trying to understand the process in a state of confusion. This had less to do with the actual medium of television than to what had become of how television news was reported.

Talking heads and pundits, many of whom were lawyers, tried to weave a story of Bill Clinton's guilt or innocence based on their understanding of law conducted by a judge and jury in petty courtrooms across America. The pundits/lawyers failed to grasp the fact that an impeachment was a constitutional and political process, not a simple courtroom drama.

The House managers of the Clinton impeachment made their case with partisan vigor in the House, but when they marched into the Senate chamber they were frustrated and hamstrung by Senate rules. The House managers wanted Monica Lewinsky to sit in the Senate and be deposed in front of the nation on TV for maximum impact. Senator Robert C. Byrd told the entire Senate, in a rare closed-door meeting with Republicans and Democrats in attendance, that "Bill Clinton had sullied the White House, but that the Senate would not be sullied with the spectacle of Miss Lewinsky appearing in that body." Her deposition was taken elsewhere in a hotel in DC. She never appeared in the Senate. Senator Byrd wanted the decorum of the Senate maintained throughout the trial. He didn't want the House managers grilling Ms. Lewinsky and turning the Senate chamber into a televised soap opera about sex in high places.

We remain in a complex dance with our politics and mass media, especially television. In the age of the 24/7 news cycle the news industry needs hours and hours of video clips. Constantly breaking news is a beast with a voracious appetite for video.

How we use television, and how you are all able to research American politics, history, and government using the C-SPAN Video Archives and other resources, still requires the same kind of integrity about the use of documentary sources, be they old handwritten documents on parchment, or a series of video clips of a political debate; both kinds of documentary sources require that they be used carefully, authentically, and as closely to their original context and meaning as possible. Each video resource has a specific time and place and context. When it is used in a different context, merely as an illustration, for example, it begins to lose its authenticity. Television news producers move videos around as if they are random illustrations. In doing so they create a different reality than what the camera originally recorded at a specific time and place. It would be like a textbook chapter on a battle in World War II in Europe, where the accompanying illustration was of a wounded soldier in the Pacific. When we are this casual with our images, we create false realities and move away from truth and authenticity.

We do research to seek a better understanding of things. We are looking for a true picture of what happened and how it happened. When Al Franken told Senator Grassley to "Look at the tape, Mr. Chairman," he understood that the tape would tell the truth. When we use these video resources for this purpose and do it carefully, we can indeed find truth.

CONCLUSION

The chapters in this volume cover broad themes. What unites them is their use of C-SPAN videos to make their arguments and points. But the topics covered, the issues raised, and the conclusions reached vary widely. Looking back, it might be useful to review the conclusions of each chapter.

There is no consistent use of scandal and crisis in Congress, we learn from Wildrick and Novak. Scandals and crises are used strategically to advance an argument or point of view. They "serve to modify the intensity and severity of a problem." Their use ranges across issues from abortion to the War on Terror.

Discourse about law enforcement was the topic of the second chapter by Wilson and Scacco in this volume. This discourse was shaped by external forces including that on social media. The language of law enforcement has changed because of external events such as police violence. The image of law enforcement is no longer that of protection. In turn, the congressional communication that reflects public discourse can result in laws and legislation.

Understanding how former Federal Reserve chairman Alan Greenspan communicated uncertainty about the economy was the topic of Hearit and Buzzanell's chapter. Because of the way that the markets could react to his testimony on Fed behavior, a great deal of attention was paid to Greenspan's testimony. Greenspan effectively added uncertainty to his testimony. The authors link their analysis to organizational communication, something that has not been done before.

Nancy Brown, a historian contributing to this volume, examines the Human Rights Campaign Fund and the AIDS Action Council's messages and strategies using videos from the C-SPAN Archives' online Video Library. She finds strategies of fundraising and efforts to put gay issues at the center of mainstream debate. At the end of her chapter, she also reflects on the value of the C-SPAN Video Library for historians. This is a valuable piece because of the importance of the C-SPAN Video Library for historical research.

In Wulbrecht's study of the framing of mental health, she found that there was sympathy for the situation of veterans and adolescents involved in violence. They were deserving of treatment. Mentally ill adults were not seen as deserving of treatment as these other two groups. There was support for treatment as a tool to reduce violence. How members of Congress talk about mental illness and violence was the focus of this study.

Another textual study is that of Lam and Ganchoudhuri, who look at how health policy was portrayed during the 2016 election. Politics and parties matter, they find, influencing how health was talked about during the campaign. Sometimes health policy was talked about just to generate broader public support, especially by Donald Trump. Hillary Clinton talked about health care much more than Trump did and emphasized children and families. Trump, not surprisingly, was critical of the Affordable Care Act in many of his speeches.

As Trump became president, he continued his active tweeting that was the hallmark of the campaign. Harness and Scacco examine the differences between Trump's tweets in the first 30 days and his speeches during that same period. This is one of the first important studies of a major element of the Trump presidency. The authors find that tweets provide a direct communication, inoculate Trump from opposition, and provide a "pseudo-interactivity" with the media. In contrast to Obama, Trump is much more reserved in using his family in speeches. Not surprisingly, there is a nationalistic element to his speeches in the way that he presents Americanism. This continues a theme from the campaign into the presidency.

Buozis, Rooney, and Creech present a thoughtful chapter on journalistic organizations featured in the C-SPAN Video Library to study the evolving journalism of today. Because the videos span 30 years, they provide a base from which to study these organizations. Each organization provides a different type of journalism, thus opening a new avenue for research. The C-SPAN Video Library contains many journalistic reflections, panels, and interviews, so this is an important study that urges scholars to exploit this genre of programs.

With each volume in this series, scholars have examined nonverbal communication in debates. In this volume, Eubanks, Stewart, and Dye look at audience reactions during the Clinton and Trump presidential debates. Trump had twice the number of speaking turns as did Clinton, reflecting his interruptions and outsider stature. However, there was almost four times the amount of laughter during Trump's speeches as there was during Clinton's. The authors argue that this further demonstrates the "enthusiasm gap" referenced by other observers.

Pavla Hlozkova explores how C-SPAN videos can be used in teaching a graduate business class. This chapter fits in a long tradition of studies that address teaching. What is different here is that the course is a business and graduate MBA course. The author reflects on what should go into selecting clips and provides insights for anyone who is thinking about incorporating C-SPAN videos in the classroom.

In these chapters it is not just the conclusions that matter, but the methods and approaches to the studies. These methods range from textual analysis, network analysis, content analysis, nonverbal communication analysis, to sentiment analysis. All these authors analyzed videos in some way to reach their conclusions. Since the chapters in this volume were written primarily by graduate students, the variety of methods employed is not surprising. They collectively show the promise of innovative research methods using videos.

CONTRIBUTORS

Nancy E. Brown is a doctoral candidate of history at Purdue University. Her research explores the relationships between civil rights movements in the 1970s and 1980s. Her dissertation in progress considers advocacy during the early years of the AIDS crisis and the connections between disability rights and gay and lesbian rights organizations, objectives, and strategies. She is also intrigued by digital approaches to history. She is a Project Advisor for the Ryan White Letters Project, funded by the Institute for Museum and Library Services.

Michael Buozis is a doctoral student at Klein College of Media and Communication at Temple University. His research, which has been published in *Journalism Studies, Communication and Critical/Cultural Studies,* and *Convergence,* examines the cultural and epistemological dimensions of journalism and other nonfiction forms.

Patrice M. Buzzanell is Chair and Professor of the Department of Communication at the University of South Florida. A Fellow of the International Communication Association (ICA), she has served as President of ICA, the Council of Communication Associations (CCA), and the Organization for the Study of Communication, Language and Gender (OSCLG). Most recently, she was awarded ICA's B. Aubrey Fisher Mentorship Award, was recognized as a Distinguished Scholar by the National Communication Association (NCA), and earned the Provost Outstanding Mentor Award at Purdue University, where she was University Distinguished Professor and Endowed Chair and Director of the Susan Bulkeley Butler Center for Leadership Excellence.

Brian Creech is Assistant Professor of Journalism at Temple University in Philadelphia. His research uses critical and cultural theory to interrogate journalism's modes of representation, new media technologies, and international media forms. Recent articles have appeared in *Journalism; Communication, Culture, and Critique;* and the *Communication Review,* among other journals.

Reagan G. Dye (BA, University of Georgia) is an MA student in the Department of Political Science at the University of Arkansas, Fayetteville. Her research interests include political communication and psychology.

Austin D. Eubanks is an experimental psychology PhD student in the Department of Psychological Science at the University of Arkansas under the mentorship of Dr. Scott Eidelman. Broadly, he studies social psychology, but specifically his research focuses on political psychology and the formations and understandings of political ideology and political value systems. However, his interest and expertise in research methodology and data analysis have led to his involvement in a wide variety of research projects across psychology, political science, and communication.

Somrita Ganchoudhuri is a doctoral candidate at the Department of Communications and New Media (CNM). She received her master's degree in Communication Studies from the University of Hyderabad, India. Her primary research interests are in the field of health communication, media content analysis, and the culture-centered methodologies to develop community-driven communication solutions to various issues. Currently her thesis is concerned with examining the role of nongovernmental organizations in the health sector and the communication processes and strategies and tactics they use in the realm of HIV/AIDS in Nagaland, while also asking critical questions about health disparities, culture, and health to identify the extent to which health issues have been addressed. Previously she worked at Thomson Reuters as a publishing specialist.

Delaney Harness (MA, Purdue University) is a doctoral student in the Department of Communication Studies at the University of Texas at Austin. Her research focuses on political organizations as change agents in international contexts, including how nongovernmental organizations (NGOs) communicatively negotiate identity within the international system.

Lauren Berkshire Hearit completed her doctoral work in Organizational Communication at Purdue University and is an assistant professor in the Department of Communication at Hope College. Her research interests lie at the intersection of communication, finance, and economics.

Pavla Hlozkova hails from the Czech Republic and is an MBA graduate from the New York Institute of Technology in Vancouver. She has years of experience working in international team ventures, which included working for a Canadian university as well as working with the leading tech agency of the European Union for global positioning technologies, where she developed her skills in international diplomacy and commerce. She cooperated on the project Creative Collaborative Learning, which has been used as a learning method at the MBA classes at NYIT and published in several educational journals. She is multilingual and offers knowledge and experience from living and working in Europe and North America.

Chervin Lam is a doctoral student in the Department of Communications and New Media (CNM), National University of Singapore (NUS), and recipient of the President's Graduate Fellowship. His research interest is in health communication, particularly in advocacy and campaigns that may help alleviate health issues or disparities. He received his master of science in health communication, with a minor in mixed methods, from Purdue University. During his time at Purdue, he coauthored a book, *Health Advocacy: A Communication Approach,* which explores communication strategies and processes in championing changes in health policies. His research also has been published in *Review of Communication* and achieved top paper awards at the Central States Communication Association (CSCA) 2015 conference.

Janet M. Martin is Professor of Government and Legal Studies at Bowdoin College. Her research and teaching interests center on the U.S. presidency and Congress. She is a former APSA Congressional Fellow and worked for Senator Herb Kohl (D-WI) and Majority Leader George Mitchell (D-ME). She is the author of *Lessons from the Hill: The Legislative Journey of an Education*

Program, and *The Presidency and Women: Promise, Performance, and Illusion* (winner of the 2004 Richard Neustadt Prize). She has coedited two books with MaryAnne Borrelli, *The Other Elites: Women, Politics and Power in the Executive Branch* (1997) and *The Gendered Executive: A Comparative Analysis of Presidents, Prime Ministers, and Chief Executives* (2016).

Alison N. Novak is Assistant Professor of Public Relations and Advertising at Rowan University. She is a graduate of Drexel University's doctoral program in Communication, Culture and Media. Her work explores political discourses and citizen engagement in civic issues. She is the author of *Media, Millennials and Politics: The Coming of Age of the Next Political Generation* and the editor of *Defining Identity and the Changing Scope of Culture in the Digital Age.* Her work was featured in *Wired Magazine, Redbook,* and NBC News.

Zoe M. Oxley (PhD, Ohio State University) is Professor of Political Science at Union College. Her research interests include the effects of the media on public opinion, gender and public opinion, women in electoral politics, and political psychology. She is the coauthor of *Public Opinion: Democratic Ideals, Democratic Practice* (CQ Press), and she has published articles in several journals, including the *American Political Science Review, Journal of Politics, Political Research Quarterly,* and *Politics & Gender.*

Shannon Rooney is a doctoral student in media and communication at the Klein College of Media and Communication at Temple University in Philadelphia. Her research areas of interest include journalism and representation as well as social memory and gender.

Joshua M. Scacco (PhD, University of Texas at Austin) is Assistant Professor in the Brian Lamb School of Communication and courtesy faculty in the Department of Political Science at Purdue University. He also serves as a Faculty Research Associate with the Center for Media Engagement at UT–Austin. Professor Scacco's research focuses on how emerging communication technologies influence established agents in American political life, including news organizations and the presidency. His work has been published in the *Journal of Computer-Mediated Communication, International Journal* of *Communication*, *International Journal of Press/Politics*, and *New Media & Society*.

Ray Smock is Director of the Robert C. Byrd Center for Congressional History and Education at Shepherd University. He served as Historian of the U.S. House of Representatives from 1983 to 1995. He holds a PhD in American History from the University of Maryland, College Park. He is coeditor of the 14-volume series, *The Booker T. Washington Papers*, and is the author of *Booker T. Washington: Black Leadership in the Age of Jim Crow* (2009). He is coeditor of the 2-volume *Congress Investigates: A Critical History with Documents* (2011). He is past president of the Association for Documentary Editing, the Society for History in the Federal Government, and the Association of Centers for the Study of Congress.

Patrick A. Stewart (PhD, Northern Illinois University) is Associate Professor of Political Science at the University of Arkansas, Fayetteville. In addition to his book *Debatable Humor: Laughing Matters on the 2008 Presidential Primary Campaign* (2012), he has published research concerning emotion and nonverbal communication in the journals *American Behavioral Scientist*, *PLOS ONE*, *Political Psychology*, *Motivation and Emotion*, *International Journal of Humor Research*, *PS: Political Science & Politics*, *Presidential Studies Quarterly*, and *Politics and the Life Sciences*. His work on nonverbal communication by political leaders has been published in the *New York Times* and the *Washington Post* and reported on by such popular outlets as *Forbes*, *U.S. News and World Report*, *Wired*, *Vocativ*, *Vox*, *National Review*, *New Republic*, and *Huffington Post*, among others. He is a certified Facial Action Coding System (FACS) coder whose current research concentrates on the emotional response of followers to leaders and those wishing to become leaders. He is researching audience applause, laughter, and booing in response to comments by candidates during presidential debates and how individuals respond to different types of facial displays and other types of nonverbal behavior by politicians.

Terri L. Towner is Associate Professor of Political Science at Oakland University in Michigan. Her research focuses mainly on the role of social media in campaigns and elections, with a particular focus on Facebook, Twitter, and Instagram. She recently coedited the book *The Internet and the 2016 Presidential Campaign* (2017). Her research has also been published in several book chapters, most recently in *The Presidency and Social Media: Discourse, Disruption, and Digital Democracy in the 2016 Presidential Election* and *Communication and Mid-Term Elections: Media, Message, and Mobilization*. She has also published in numerous journals including *Social Science Computer Review*, *Journal of Political Marketing*, *Journal of Women, Politics & Policy*, *New Media & Society*, and *Journal of Political Science Education*.

Alyssa A. Wildrick graduated in 2016 with a dual degree in public relations and advertising. After graduating with her BA degree in three years, she pursued a master of arts in public relations, which she completed in 2017. Throughout her graduate studies, she obtained a Certificate of Graduate Study in both School Public Relations, and Integrated Marketing Communications and New Media. Her research interests include crisis communication, sports marketing, and consumer culture.

Cody Blake Wilson is a graduate student in the Brian Lamb School of Communication at Purdue University. He received his BA in Sociology from Purdue University in 2014 and his MAT from Marian University in 2016. His areas of study include issue and crisis management, police-community relationships, as well as computational research methods. He is particularly interested in the role reconciliation plays in organizational relationships. Before joining the Brian Lamb School, he taught kindergarten and first grade at KIPP Indy Unite Elementary School in Indianapolis, Indiana, in partnership with Teach For America.

Elizabeth Wulbrecht is a native of Lafayette, Indiana. She received her bachelor's degree in Political Science and Anthropology from Purdue University in 2015 and her master's degree in Political Science from Purdue in 2017, majoring in American Politics and Public Policy.

INDEX

Page numbers in italics refer to figures.

A

ABC, 208
Abe, Shinzo, 154, 161
Abraham, Ralph, 38
Accessibility in presidential discourse, 147–149, 153
Acheson, Dean, 184
Affordable Care Act, 132, 134–137, 142, 248
AIDS Action Council, 76, 79–86, 247
AIDS Project Los Angeles, 79
Altman, R., 23
American Society of Newspaper Editors, 175, 179, 180–182, 230
Anderson, John, 206
Andreaseen, T., 3
Ansolabehere, S., 6
Arrington, M. I., 125–126
Audience reactions during presidential debates. *See* Presidential debates, 2016
AutoMap, 152

B

Baker, Dick. *See* Baker, Richard
Baker, Howard, 239
Baker, Richard, 238, 241, 242
Barry, C., 111, 124, 127
Bay of Pigs invasion, 181
Bazell, Robert, 83
Berger, C. R., 48–49
Bernhardt, J. M., 125
Betweenness centrality, 153
Beullens, K., 124, 126
Bishop, Rob, 8–9, 15
Black Lives Matter, 22, 29
Blair, N. A., 125
Bleakley, A., 125
Blue Lives Matter, 29
Boffey, Philip, 84, 87
Booker, Cory, 34–35
Bourdieu, Pierre, 177
Brown, Michael, 22, 23, 29, 33
Brown, Nancy, 142–143, 247–248
Brown, William Holmes, 239

Browning, Robert, 237–238, 241
Brüggemann, M., 188
Bull, P., 206
Buozis, Michael, 230, 233, 248
Bush, George H. W., 7–8
Bush, George W., 25, 68, 161, 233
Buzzanell, Patrice M., 65, 68–69, 247
Byrd, Robert, 239, 242, 244

C

Calabrese, R. J., 48–49
Callaghan, K., 96
Campaign Zero, 29
Carlson, Matt, 174, 175
Carter, Jimmy, 206
Cartwright, Matt, 109
Castro, Julian, 11–12
Children's Health Insurance Program, 132
Cleeren, A. J., 2
Clinton, Bill, 150, 161, 244
Clinton, Hillary, 10, 127–129, 150, 199–201, 248
  discussion of findings on health portrayal by, 134–137
  health portrayal findings and results, 130–134
  health portrayal study method and, 130
  presidential debates, 2016 (*See* Presidential debates, 2016)
CNN, 204, 206, 208
Coe, K., 148, 149–150

Cohen's kappa, 105–106
Coherence in narrative rationality, 24
Comey, James, 238
Communicators, The, 15
Conditional voice, 175
Congress
  Alan Greenspan's communications with, 45–61, 68–69
  crisis and scandal language used by, 1–16, 66–67, 69–70
  discourse on mental health and violence, 93–114
  framing by, 95–97
  law enforcement narrative and, 21–41, 67–68
  reactionary policy by, 1, 9, 15
  reflections on the C-SPAN Video Library and the study of, 65–70
  television and, 237–245
Congressional Black Caucus (CBC), 28, 34–37
Congressional Record, 88, 96, 241
Connolly, Gerald, 10–11
Conscious discourse, 12
Continuous response measures (CRM), 200, 213
Cooper, Anderson, 208
Cornia, A., 188
Cornyn, John, 110
Cranston, Alan, 73
Creative Collaborative Learning (CCL), 219–227, 231–232
  challenges and difficulties related to clip selection for, 225

INDEX   259

C-SPAN clips selection, evaluation, and examples, 222–224
   instructor's intervention, 225–226
Creech, Brian, 230, 233, 248
Crisis and scandal, congressional language regarding, 1–2, 66–67, 69–70
   academic research on, 4–5
   building support for or opposition to legislation, 6–10
   conclusions on, 16
   C-SPAN data set and methodological approach to, 5–6
   definitions and terminology, 2–4
   discussion of strategy of, 14–16
   enacting relationships within and outside the congressional community using, 10–12
   findings on, 6–14
   fostering media and public attention, 12–14
   speeches and governance in response to, 5
Critical Core, 126
C-SPAN (Cable Satellite Public Affairs Network) Video Library
   ability to access discourse of elected officials through, 21
   analysis of first 30 days of Trump's presidency using, 151–167
   analyzing tone of political discourse related to law enforcement and, 30, 67–68
   in changing spaces of political communications, 229–234
   content analysis of the 2016 presidential debates analyzed using, 207–214
   of crisis and scandal language, 5–14, 66–67, 69–70
   discourse on mental illness and violence, 93–114
   Federal Reserve and Alan Greenspan archives, 48, 51–61, 68–69
   historians and, 86–90
   journalism and, 173–190
   political discourse of HIV/AIDS, 1985-1987, 71–90
   portrayal of health its narratives, 123–138
   portrayal of public policy discourse, 141–143
   reflections on study of Congress and the, 65–70
   research questions and future directions for teaching with, 232–234
   video clip selection for creative collaborative learning, 219–227, 231–232

D

Danger framing, 102–104
   analysis of, 106–109
Dannemeyer, William, 75, 81–82, 87

Davis, Garret, 31
DeGette, Diana, 110
Degree centrality, 152–153
Democratic party
　crime policies and, 28
　LGBT organizations and, 76
　storytelling tone used by, 34–35
　transcendent tone used by, 38–39
"Designing Creative Collaborative
　　Learning (CCL) for Economics:
　　Using Professionals and Video
　　Clips in MBA Classroom," 223
Deuze, M., 176
DICTION software, 29–31
Disclosure in presidential
　communication, 160–161
Dodd-Frank Amendment, 11
Dominance of attention in the
　presidential debates, 201–202
Donoghue, Marguerite, 76
Dougherty, D. S., 49
Dye, R., 248–249

E

Eboh, I., 124, 127
Economic policy communication
　(EPC), 48
Edelman, M., 25
Eigenvector centrality, 153
Eisenbeis, R. A., 3
Elison-Bowers, P., 126
Ellison, Keith, 36–37, 68
Endean, S., 74
Engelman, Robert, 84

Eshbaugh-Soha, M., 148
Esser, F., 188
Eubanks, A., 248–249

F

Facebook, 126
"Fake news," 148, 155, 157
Fattah, Chaka, 38–39
Federal Open Market Committee
　(FOMC), 46
Federal Reserve System, 45–48, 68–
　69, 223, 247
　coding improvement regarding, 55
　coding stability regarding, 56–57
　coding uncertainty regarding,
　　55–56
　content analysis method, 51–57
　development of codebook
　　regarding, 53–55
　limitations and future directions in
　　study of, 60–61
　previous research on, 48–51
　study results, 57–58
　uncertainty management and,
　　50–51
Federation of AIDS Related
　Organizations (FARO), 72
Fidelity in narrative rationality, 24
Financial crisis and recession, 2008,
　9, 11
Fink, S., 3
"First responders," 25
Fisher, W. R., 23
Fontes, Eric, 31

Foucault, Michel, 178
Fox & Friends, 145
Fox News, 204, 206, 208
Framing, 95–97, 141–142
    danger, 102–104, 106–109
    of mental illness and gun violence, 97–98
    treatment, 103–104, 106–109
Franken, Al, 104, 238, 245
Freedom Forum, 175, 179, 186–188, 190, 230

G

Gabbard, Tulsi, 31–32
Ganchoudhuri, Somrita, 142, 248
Gannett Company, 186
Garner, Eric, 22, 29
Garrett, Laurie, 83
Gay Men's Health Crisis, 76, 79
Gay Rights National Lobby (GRNL), 76
Gee, J. P., 6, 8, 10, 12
Gingrich, Newt, 78, 89, 242–244
Gollust, S. E., 124, 127
Goodier, B. C., 125–126
Gore, Al, 233, 241–242
Gorsuch, Neil, 238
Graham, Lindsey, 11
Grand gestures, 41
Grassley, Chuck, 238, 245
Great Depression, 147
Greenberg, David, 86
Greenspan, Alan, 45–48, 50, 51, 65, 247

coding improvement regarding, 55
coding stability regarding, 56–57
coding uncertainty regarding, 55–56
content analysis on, 51–57
development of codebook regarding, 53–55
limitations and future directions on study of, 60–61
study results, 57–58
Groesz, L. M., 126
Gruber, Brian, 76
Gun control, 112–113. *See also* Mental illness

H

Hager, Mary, 75, 84
Hansen, P. H., 2
Hardy, R. P., 148, 149
Harness, Delaney, 230, 248
Hart, R. P., 30, 52, 147
Hatfield, E., 202
Hathi Trust Digital Library, 87
Health portrayal, 123–124, 142–143, 248
    conclusion, 137–138
    discussion of findings on, 134–137
    findings and results, 130–134
    by media, 124–125
    in political media, 126–129
    on social media, 126
    study method, 129–130
    traditional approach to studying media, 125–126

Hearit, Lauren Berkshire, 65, 68–69, 247
Heitkamp, Heidi, 109–110
Helping Families in Mental Health Crisis Act of 2013, 101, *102*
Heroism narrative, 26, 36, 41
Historians and C-SPAN, 86–90
HIV/AIDS, 71–72, 142–143
    AIDS Action Council and the public health crisis of, 76, 79–86
    Human Rights Campaign and political power, 73–79, 85–86
Hlozkova, Pavla, 231, 234, 249
Holt, Lester, 238–239
Hudson, Rock, 74, 83
Human Rights Campaign Fund (HRCF), 72, *73*, 85–86, 247
    political power and, 73–79
Humans as storytellers, 23
Humprecht, E., 188
Hurricane Sandy, 34–35

I

Ingram, H., 98–99, 142
In-group messaging, 162–163
Interactivity in presidential discourse, 153–155
International Monetary Fund (IMF), 223
Israel-Palestine conflict, 13
Iyengar, S., 97

J

Jackson Lee, Sheila, 7–8, 33
Jamieson, P. E., 125, 126
Jensen, L., 99
John Q., 126
Jones, P. E., 6
Journalism, 173–175, 230–231
    American Society of Newspaper Editors and, 175, 179, 180–182, 230
    conclusion, 188–190
    Freedom Forum and, 175, 179, 186–188, 190, 230
    meta-journalistic discourse, 174, 175–178
    National Press Club and, 175, 179, 184–186, 189, 190, 230
    public authority of, 175–178
    Society of Professional Journalists and, 175, 179, 182–184, 230
    videos related to, in the C-SPAN Video Library, 179–188
Joy, M. W., 27

K

Kaine, Tim, 9
Kalb Report, The, 184–185, 186
Keith, Tamara, 145
Kennedy, John F., 181, 188
Kennedy, Ted, 78
Kerner Report, 182
Kerry, John, 10, 13, 66

Kildee, Dan, 13
Kinder, D., 99
King, Angus, 112–113
King, Rodney, 22
Koop, C. Everett, 89
Korean War, 184
Kramer, M. W., 49, 59
Krippendorff, K., 52
Kunst, Robert, 89

L

Lagarde, Christine, 223
Lam, Chervin, 142, 248
Lamb, Brian, 75
Law enforcement narrative, 21–22, 67–68
    analyzing tone in political discourse and, 29–31
    conclusion on, 40–41
    congressional communication and, 27–29
    differences by individual factors, 34–37
    differences by structural factors, 37–38
    differences by year, 38–39
    findings and discussion, 31–34
    grand gestures and, 41
    narrative perspective and, 22–24
    political discourse and, 24–27
    previous research on Congress' navigation of, 22–31
    storytelling tone in, 23, 30, 31–32
    tradition tone in, 31, 33–34
    transcendence tone in, 30, 32–33, 40
Legislation, crisis language building support for or opposition to, 6–10
Levi, Jeffrey, 76–77, 85
Levine, M. P., 126
Lew, Jack, 11
Lewinsky, Monica, 244
Library of Congress, 241
Life magazine, 74
Lincoln, Abraham, 240–241
Link frequency, 152
Lorne, Frank, 224
Lysiak, Matthew, 93

M

MacDonald, Gary, 79–80
Makropoulos, M., 2, 15
March for Gay and Lesbian Rights, 1987, 85
May, Theresa, 224
McCain, John, 46–47
McCarthy, Kevin, 13
McGinty, E., 97, 111, 112
McGuire, Jean, 80
McHugh, M., 106
McLuhan, Marshall, 242
McSween, J., 99
Meaning-making, 8
Media and public attention, crisis and scandal fostering, 12–14

Media portrayal of health, 124–125
    traditional approach to studying, 125–126
Mental illness, 93–94, 142
    analyses of discourse on, 105–109
    archives search terms and inter-rater reliability test, 120–121
    concept of framing and, 95–97
    conclusion, 114
    C-SPAN research methodology, 101–102
    dependent variable in studying discourse of, 102–104
    framing of gun violence and, 97–98
    independent variables in studying discourse of, 104–105
    limitations of analysis of discourse on violence and, 113–114
    social construction of, 98–100
Merriam, Jim, 82–83
Meta-journalistic discourse, 174, 175–178
Meta-narratives, 30
Miskinis, K., 206
Mondale Fritz, 73–74
Moreno, M. A., 126
Morgan, E. M., 126
Morimoto, Chad, 31
Morris, J. S., 27
Motivation, crisis as, 7–8
Muir, David, 157
Murnen, S. K., 126
Murphy, Chris, 112
Murphy, Tim, 101, *102*
MySpace, 126

N

Nadler, A., 177
Narrative force, 30
Narrative perspective, 22–23
Narrative rationality, 23–24
National Archives, 241
National Gay Task Force (NGTF), 76, 79
National Press Club, 175, 179, 184–186, 189, 190, 230
National Public Radio, 83
National Review, 78
National Sheriffs' Association, 159
Navarro, V., 126–127
NBC, 83
Nelson, T., 99
Neuharth, Al, 186
Newseum, 186–188
Newsweek, 75, 93
New York Institute of Technology (NYIT), 223–224
New York Times, 148
Nielsen, R. K., 188
NodeXL, 152
Novak, Alison N., 65, 66, 247
NYPD Blue, 126

O

Obama, Barack, 10, 150, 160, 161, 186, 206, 232, 233, 248
O'Muircheartaigh, C., 114
O'Neill, Tip, 243
Osborn, June, 81–82

Osbournes, The, 125
Out-group messaging, 164–165

P

Pelosi, Nancy, 12, 66
Pendo, E., 126
Person, B., 124–125
Personality in presidential discourse, 149–150, 158–161
Peters, Gary, 12
Pierce, T. A., 49
Pluralism, 150–151, 161–165
Political media, health portrayal in, 126–129
Popham, Paul, 76
Presidential debates, 2016, 199–201, 231
  analysis method, 209
  analysis results, 209–212
  applause and cheering during, 203–204
  audience response to political figures and, 202–206
  content analysis on C-SPAN, 207–214
  discussion, 212–214
  dominance of attention in, 201–202
  heckling and booing during, 205–206
  laughter during, 204–205
Presidential discourse, 145–146, 230. *See also* Trump, Donald
  accessibility and, 147–149, 153
  personality and, 149–150, 158–161
  pluralism and, 150–151, 161–165
  presidential ubiquity in, 146–147
Presidential ubiquity, 146–147
Public authority of journalism, 175–178
Public policy discourse, 141–143
Puerto Rico debt crisis, 9, 15

Q

Quaglia, L., 4

R

Raddatz, Martha, 208
Radio-Television News Directors Association, 82
Rainmaker, The, 126
Rasinski, K., 114
Rationality, narrative, 23–24
Ravenscroft, S., 3–4
Raymond, L., 95
Reactionary policy, 1, 9, 15
Reagan, Ronald, 78, 206, 233
Rehnquist, William, 76–78
Relationships within and outside the congressional community, crisis and scandal for enacting, 10–12
Republican Party
  crime policies and, 28

Republican Party *(continued)*
    Senate majority loss, 1986, 78
    transcendent and traditional language used by, 34, 38
Research Possibilities of the C-SPAN Archives, The, 65
Rhetorical presidency, 146–147
Richard, Anne, 10
Romano, R., 4
Romer, D., 125, 126
Romney, Mitt, 206
Rooney, Shannon, 230, 233, 248
Roosevelt, Franklin, 147
Roth, Nancy, 76
RStudio, 151
Russian poverty as humanitarian crisis, 7–8
Rwanda, 11
Ryan, Paul, 1, 8, 32–33
Ryfe, D., 175, 177

S

Scacco, Joshua M., 50, 65, 67–68, 148, 149–150, 230, 247, 248
Scandal, 13
Schepers, A., 124, 126
Schneider, A., 98–99, 142
Schnell, F., 96
Schriner, K., 100, 113
Schudson, Michael, 174, 176
Sclafani, Jennifer, 158
Scott, Walter, 22
Scowcroft, Brent, 7–8
Scripps Howard News Service, 84
Seale, C., 125
Second National AIDS Forum, 72
Semantic networks, 151, 152–153
September 11, 2001, terrorist attacks, 25
Serious mental illness (SMI), 94, 97
Shank, J., 2
Singh, R., 125
Smith, R., 124, 125, 126
Smock, Ray, 237
Snelson, C., 126
Sobran, Joseph, 78
Social construction of mental illness, 98–100
Social media, 126, 145–146, 148, 247. *See also* Trump, Donald
    as personal, 149
Society of Professional Journalists, 175, 179, 182–184, 230
Speier, Jackie, 111
State of the Union addresses, 241–242
Stewart, P., 248–249
Storytelling, 23, 30, 31–32, 34–35
Syrian war, 10–11, 242

T

Television, 237–245
    contribution to polarization of American politics, 243–244
    deception via, 242–243
    impeachment of Bill Clinton and, 244
    State of the Union addresses on, 241–242

Terrorism, 15, 25, 32–33, 247
Testimony, court, 24
Thompson, J. R., 5
Thurmond, Strom, 77
Tradition tone, 31, 33–34
Transcendence, 30, 32–33, 38–39, 40
Trans-Pacific Partnership (TPP), 224
Treatment framing, 103–104
  analysis of, 106–109
Trump, Donald, 10, 127–129,
    166–167, 199–201, 248. *See
    also* Presidential discourse
  accessibility of, 153
  analysis methodology, 151–153
  antipluralism and, 150–151,
    161–165
  audience laughter evoked by, 205
  communication across multiple
    types of platforms, 155–158
  data collection on tweets and
    speeches of, 151–152
  disclosure by, 160–161
  discussion of findings on health
    portrayal by, 134–137
  findings and discussion on,
    153–165
  health portrayal findings and
    results, 130–134
  health portrayal study method
    and, 130
  informality in communication by,
    157–160
  in-group messaging, 162–163
  interactivity in communication by,
    153–155
  interview with Lester Holt, 238–239
  out-group messaging, 164–165
  personality of, 157–161
  preprocessing data on, 152
  presidential debates, 2016 (*See*
    Presidential debates, 2016)
  rhetorical presidency and, 146–147
  semantic networks and, 152–153
  use of Twitter, 145–146, 148, 230
Trump, Ivanka, 160–161
Trump, Melania, 161
Twitter, 145–146, 148, 230. *See also*
    Trump, Donald
  interactivity with, 154–155
  as personal, 149–150

U

Uncertainty management
  in organizational contexts, 49–51
  theories in, 48–49, 52
Uncertainty management theory
    (UMT), 48–51
Uncertainty reduction theory (URT),
    48–51, 52
United Press International, 82
USA Today, 185–186

V

Vernick, J., 111
Veterans Affairs, 7
Veterans Mental Health Accessibility
    Act, 109
Viechnicki, P., 114

Vietnam War, 188
Vocalizations, audience. *See* Presidential debates, 2016

W

Wahl, O., 98
Wallace, Chris, 208
Wallerstein, N., 126
Warning, crisis as, 8–10
War on Terror, 15, 247
Washington, Kerry, 13
Watergate scandal, 188
Waxman, Henry, 73, 78, 81–82, 87
Webster, D., 111
Weekend at Bernie's, 47
Weicker, Lowell, 73, 81
Weiss, Ted, 73, 77, 81
West, D. M., 203, 205–206
West Wing, The, 125
Wildrick, Alyssa A., 65, 66, 247
Williams, P. F., 3–4
Wilson, Cody Blake, 65, 67–68, 247
World Trade Center attacks, 25
Worrell, T., 125
Wulbreht, Elizabeth, 141–142

Y

Yahoo! News, 233
Yellen, Janet, 223
Young Americans for Freedom, 78
YouTube, 126, 145
Yue, S. K., 125

Z

Zelizer, B., 176
Zoller, H. M., 125